CHUCK and GAIL'S
FAVORITE BIKE RIDES

by Chuck & Gail Helfer

75 Great Rides in the Mid-Atlantic
from the Chesapeake Bay to the Shenandoah Valley

Cover photo – Utica Covered Bridge in Frederick County, Md.

All photographs by Chuck Helfer except as noted: pg. 14 by G. Helfer; pg. 48 by N. Sandler; rear cover by K. Heising

Cover design by F. Yvette Benjamin

Published by Cycleways Publications
P.O. Box 5328
Takoma Park, Maryland 20913

Library of Congress Catalog Card Number 92-71424

ISBN 0-9614137-8-6

Manufactured in the United States of America

PREFACE

The Mid-Atlantic states are home to some of the finest bicycling rides found anywhere. We began writing bicycle guidebooks in 1984 to help fellow cyclists learn about this great area, and to share our route knowledge with them. Nine publications later, we are still discovering new places to pedal.

This book began when we were continually asked by other cyclists to name our favorite rides. A favorite ride can offer fine scenery, little or no traffic, go to a point of interest, have historical significance, provide relaxation or any and all of these. Most of all, a favorite ride is one to which we want to return. What you have in your hand is a compilation of our favorite 75 rides.

These rides lie along the shores of the Chesapeake Bay, around Washington, D.C., in Virginia's horse country, in Maryland's heartland, in southern Pennsylvania, in the Great Valley of Maryland and in Virginia's Shenandoah Valley.

We lay out our rides the only way we know how — we pedal each and every one with a tape recorder, maps and notebooks in our jersey pockets. This book gave us the opportunity once again to ride new roads and trails as well as rediscover old friends. Several hundred rides and several thousand variations later, we arrived at these 75. We hope you enjoy them as much as we do.

CONTENTS

❖ indicates unpaved riding surface

INTRODUCTION

City
Favorites

The
Heartland

Horse
Country

The Big Valley

Chesapeake
Treasures

CREAGERSTOWN
GROCERY

Only a handful of places in the world combine the scenic beauty of the seashore, mountains, bucolic horse country and farmlands with excellent traffic-free bicycling roads and paths, history, culture and climate.

The region covered by this book, from the shores of the Chesapeake Bay in Maryland, to the parks of Washington, D.C., to the orchards of southern Pennsylvania, to the farm and estate country of rural Virginia, presents bicyclists with some of the finest bike rides in the country.

As life-long bicycle enthusiasts, we never tire of riding through the countryside of the Mid-Atlantic States. In our backyard lies a dazzling variety of bicycle rides. Bike trails lead from the cities to a maze of country roads. Fine vineyards with mountain vistas sit near villages from earlier centuries. Narrow lanes meander through pastoral landscapes to wildlife refuges and beautiful marshes.

Local cyclists ride past monuments to the country's heroes, to the War of 1812 and Civil War sites and enjoy the beauty of our nation's capital. They know famous places that shaped our history: Chancellorsville, Harpers Ferry, Gettysburg, C&O Canal. When riding in the region, you can enjoy brunch on the Potomac River, lunch on the Chesapeake Bay and dinner in the Shenandoah Valley, although not in one day.

We selected the 75 rides in this book from the several thousand we have ridden over the years. They capture the essence of the region and represent the diversity of scenery, history and terrain found here.

In the last few years the Mid-Atlantic cycling community has enjoyed tremendous growth and become one of largest bicycle markets in the country. Each year more cyclists come to the region for a cycling vacation. Go to one of the region's well-loved bike trails on a warm spring afternoon and you see a steady stream of cyclists of all ages on all types of bikes: city, hybrid, mountain, racing, triathlon and an occasional tandem.

You almost always see other cyclists on the country roads in popular areas such as Middleburg, Virginia and Frederick County, Maryland. On Maryland's Eastern Shore you will see throngs of cyclists disembarking the Oxford Ferry, riding to and from St. Michaels.

We love the sense of freedom bicycling gives us. On a bicycle, the sun shines on your face and no walls confine you. Cycling helps put the daily stresses behind and lets you feel you can ride as far as you want. So pump up your tires and let us show you some of our favorite rides. See you on the road.

The Rides

What qualifies a ride to be included in a "favorite" collection? First, a ride has to have light or no auto traffic. It must be open to cyclists and travel through areas where personal safety is not a major concern. Nice scenery, a pleasant destination or a point of interest is valued. Finally, we want to come back to cycle it again.

Opposite page photos, clockwise from top right: View of the Lincoln Memorial from the Mount Vernon Trail; A Chesapeake Bay lighthouse; Riding north from Waterford, Va. on Route 665; On tour in Virginia's Shenandoah Valley; A refreshment stop at Creagerstown in Frederick County, Md.

Most of the rides are on public roads that have little auto traffic. Twelve use mostly bike trails or roads closed to cars at certain times of the day or week; three use forest roads completely closed to cars. Sixteen rides use unpaved trails or roads; the rest are paved.

The rides vary in length and difficulty to meet the needs of virtually any cyclist. Loop rides are from five to 60 miles long; bike trails five to 185 miles. The terrain ranges from flat to easy hills to difficult climbs. The rides are found throughout the region and reflect the wide variety of scenery the Mid-Atlantic offers.

This book includes only trails, roads, bridges and forest roads open to cyclists. Unpaved roads through parks and forests are used if there is a written policy on bikes or if the forest manager has stated they are open. Hiking trails are not included.

The growth spurt of the 1980s gobbled up some previously good cycling areas, making it difficult to stay ahead of the developers. Fortunately, the development was uneven, claiming some areas and leaving others almost untouched. You will find most of the rides in this guide clustered in the undeveloped areas. Rides in danger of becoming built up in the next few years were excluded.

Each ride offers the following information:

- General description
- Rating of difficulty
- Road or trail surface
- Start place
- Directions to the start place
- Detailed map
- Cue sheets with turn-by-turn directions

The Cue Sheets and Maps

The heart of this guide is its cue sheets and maps. These are your primary means to navigate each ride. Some cyclists prefer cue sheets, others maps. Although the cue sheets and the maps are designed to be independent, we recommend you use both.

On most rides you have a main route and optional variations. This allows us to show you more "good" roads than if there were only one route per ride. It also enables you to choose the distance you feel like riding.

The cue sheets take you from the parking lot, around the route and back to your start. They are full-sized and have lots of white space, for easy reading. Generally, there are no cue sheets for the marked bike paths since none are needed.

Maryland, Virginia and the District of Columbia take care to keep their roads well marked. Maryland and the District of Columbia generally use road names, Virginia road numbers. Loudoun County in Virginia added road names to the numbers in the last two years, and has been changing names ever since. When you ride in Loudoun County, use both the road number as well as the name, and don't be too surprised if the road name is different from that listed. West Virginia and Pennsylvania have many more unmarked roads than Maryland or Virginia. When a road or intersection is unmarked, the cue sheet describes some other landmark.

Each ride has its own map. The maps show the main ride and variations as well as other roads and trails. This allows you to use the maps to modify the rides as you wish. The maps distinguish paved roads from unpaved roads and trails, and primary roads from secondary roads. In the rural areas the maps show all roads. In urban areas and towns

Having fun on *Passage Thru Mudhole Gap*

the maps show only the ride and the main roads. Both the maps and cues indicate the locations of stores and restaurants.

We have bicycled each ride and checked each cue sheet and map for accuracy. We have made this guide as accurate as possible at the time of publication. Please note that conditions change – road signs disappear or become turned, counties rename or remove roads, road conditions improve or deteriorate, or new roads and developments appear.

Please drop us a note if a change comes to your attention. Comments from our readers have made our guidebooks more useful over the years.

Weather

The region covered by this book clearly has four distinct seasons, with a wide range of weather conditions. The area has two prevailing weather patterns: from the northwest and from the southwest. The northwest wind generally brings cooler and drier air; the southwest wind generally brings warmer and moister air. The northwest wind is somewhat more common although either pattern can prevail at any time of year. Near the Chesapeake Bay and the Atlantic Ocean the winds are more uncertain and more variable, often blowing from the water onto the land.

With nearly 40 inches of precipitation annually, you might get rain at any time. October and November are the driest months with less than three inches of rain each month. July and August are the two wettest months with thunderstorms bringing over four inches each month. During the summer rain storms often blow quickly through the area. When it rains, you can frequently wait a short time and the sun will soon reappear.

AVERAGE TEMPERATURES (°F)

Time of Year	Average High	Average Low
Dec, Jan, Feb	44	28
Mar, Apr, May	64	44
Jun, Jul, Aug	85	66
Sep, Oct, Nov	67	48

Local cyclists are able to ride most of the year, with spring and fall the favorite cycling seasons. During these two seasons the temperatures are often in the 60s and 70s, and the air is crisper and clearer.

The area is notorious for its hot, humid summers, where temperatures frequently climb into the 90s and have matching humidity. The weather is so variable that you can find nice cycling weather even during the summer. On the hottest days, begin your rides early in the day and finish before the mercury climbs too high.

During the winter local cyclists ride on all but the coldest weeks. Temperatures often climb into the 40s and 50s by late morning, offering bearable riding if you dress warmly.

Safety

Bicycling is an inherently dangerous sport. We always wear helmets and strongly recommend you do too. We don't want to belabor the point, but we have been whacked in the head by oak limbs while mountain biking and have landed head first on the pavement after a moment of carelessness.

The beginning cyclist generally heads to the nearest bike path and doesn't want to ride on the roads with cars. On the bike paths a cyclist's greatest danger is from other people using the path. The region's bike trails are most crowded when the weather is nicest.

Some cyclists take to the unpaved roads or forest roads to find new territory or avoid cars. Unfortunately, there are relatively few rides of this type in our region. Loudoun and Fauquier Counties in Virginia are the only local counties with extensive networks of unpaved roads. Many of the unpaved trails in parks and forests are closed to cyclists. George Washington National Forest is one of the few places where most trails are open.

On forest trails the greatest danger comes during the fall hunting seasons. It is a good idea to check the local papers for the hunting season dates before venturing into the woods.

After making use of the region's many trails, cyclists usually begin to venture onto the road system. Here automobile traffic presents the greatest danger. Cyclists must remember that the roads were not designed, nor do drivers drive, with the cyclist's safety as a primary concern.

Virginia, Maryland and the District of Columbia define the bicycle as a vehicle and expect that cyclists obey all laws pertaining to vehicles. Legally, cyclists have the right to ride on public roads. It is *your* responsibility as a cyclist to learn the laws pertaining to bicycles and follow them. Breaking the rules of the road only invites danger, fines and the scorn of the drivers and cyclists who do obey the law.

Railroad track crossings always present the possibility of trapping a front tire and causing a fall, especially if they cross diagonally. To cross railroad tracks, ride slowly and carefully, at a right angle to the tracks.

This guide makes great use of the less-travelled roads. When a ride does use a busier road (usually to connect two quieter roads or to exit a town), the cue sheet will warn you. The rides use the roads with the fewest cars whenever there is a choice.

The user of this book assumes full responsibility when cycling these rides. We make no guarantee about the relative "safety" of cycling or the rides. And always ride defensively.

Riding Surface

When it comes to riding surfaces, cyclists hate surprises. A long paved downhill that turns unpaved without warning can just ruin your day. Each ride has a description of the surfaces you will encounter – paved roads, unpaved roads, rough forest roads, paved or unpaved bike trails or any combination of these. The maps show which roads and bike trails are paved and which are unpaved.

The mix of surfaces in this guide reflects that found in the region. The area has more paved country lanes than unpaved roads and forest roads suitable for mountain biking. Thus, the book includes more paved than unpaved rides. The region has both paved and unpaved bike paths; the best of both are shown. We have tried to avoid mixing riding surfaces – rides are either completely paved or at least half unpaved.

County road departments often repave rural roads by putting layers of gravel and tar over the old surface and letting the cars pack the new gravel into the roadbed. This usually happens in June and July. If you are unlucky enough to encounter a recently graveled road, ride it carefully and then return in a month to enjoy the new surface.

Bikes on Metro

Thanks to the efforts of local cyclists in the 1980s, the Metro subway system in Washington, D.C. allows cyclists to take their bicycles into the last car of each train. Metro allows bicycles on the trains, space permitting, on weekday evenings after 7 p.m. and weekends if the bicyclists has a "Bikes-on-Metro" permit. To get a five year permit, Metro requires you to pay a $15 fee and take a short examination. You can obtain permit information from Metro at (202) 962-1116 or (202) 962-1327.

Some of the rides are near Metro stations. These stations are marked on the maps. By using the Shady Grove Metro Station, you could ride the entire length of the Rock Creek Park trail system from downtown Washington, D.C. and not backtrack. The W&OD Trail in Virginia passes near the East Falls Church and the Dunn Loring Stations. The Mount Vernon Trail is near the Rosslyn, Arlington Cemetery and National Airport Stations.

Ride Classification

Ride difficulty is rated on a five-point classificaion system. This rating system is based on the "average" hills and difficulty found in the region. A "I" rating indicates an "easy" ride, "III" an "average" ride of moderate difficulty, and "V" a "very hard" and challenging ride.

I   Mostly flat; few if any hills; an "easy" ride

II   Mostly rolling hills; less challenging than the average number and length of hills found in the area; somewhat easier than average difficulty

III   Moderately hilly; the average number and length of hills found in the area; average difficulty

IV   Hilly; more challenging than the average number and length of hills found in the area; more difficult than average

V   Very hilly and challenging; many long steep hills; very difficult

One person's "rolling" will be another's "hilly". The rides are rated on whether they are more or less difficult than the "average" hills found in the region. A "III" rating means the ride has "average" difficulty and hills. When one rating will not describe an entire ride, we use different ratings on the different variations.

Generally, the easier rides are on the bike trails and to the east. The more difficult rides are to the west and north. The easiest rides are on the Eastern Shore and along the rivers. The most difficult rides are in the Blue Ridge Mountains.

Tandems on a flat "I" ride on the Eastern Shore, east of
Blackwater Wildlife Refuge

EXPLANATION OF CUE SHEET SYMBOLS

The cue sheets use the following symbols.

L	Left	R/L	Right, then Left	Y	"Y" Intersection
R	Right	S	Straight	Food	Restaurant
BL	Bear Left	SS	Stop Sign	Store	Groceries
BR	Bear Right	TL	Traffic Light	☹	Auto Traffic
L/R	Left, then Right	T	"T" Intersection		
☞*	The optional ride marked with * leaves the main ride here, before the next turn.	*☞	The optional ride marked with * joins the main ride here, before the next turn.		

EXPLANATION OF MAP SYMBOLS

The maps use the following symbols.

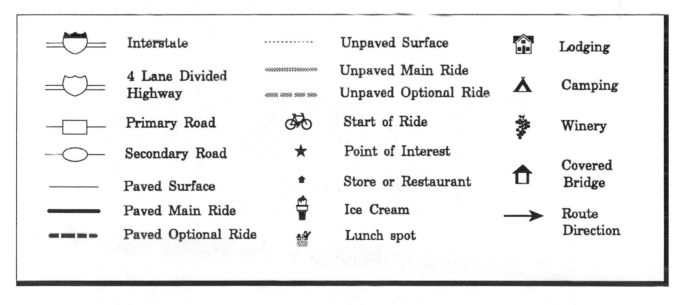

Interstate	Unpaved Surface	Lodging
4 Lane Divided Highway	Unpaved Main Ride / Unpaved Optional Ride	Camping
Primary Road	Start of Ride	Winery
Secondary Road	Point of Interest	Covered Bridge
Paved Surface	Store or Restaurant	Route Direction
Paved Main Ride	Ice Cream	
Paved Optional Ride	Lunch spot	

CITY FAVORITES

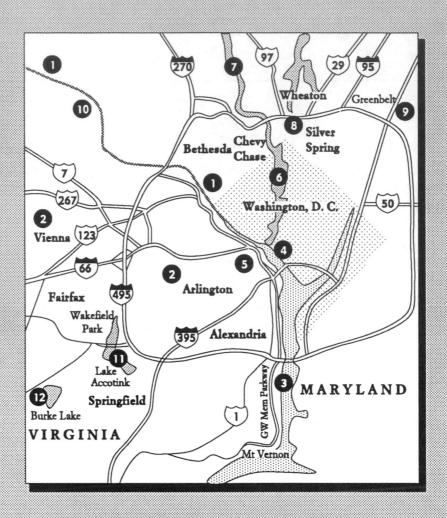

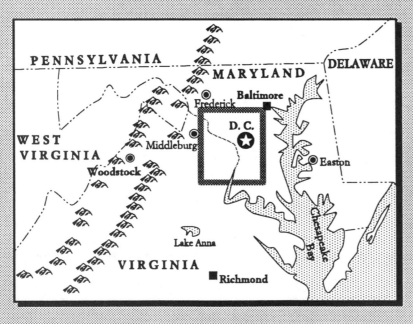

Whenever friends and relatives visit Washington, they invariably want to visit the standard attractions: the Capitol, White House, and the Smithsonian. They have rarely heard about the C&O Canal, Great Falls, Rock Creek Park or the view from the Mount Vernon Trail. It is as if there is a conspiracy to herd the tourists together, keeping the nicest places secret. These lesser known spots are the places Washington cyclists know and savor.

Washington area cyclists enjoy many parks, bike trails and quiet places off the beaten path. These offer the best cycling in the sprawling metropolis. Most of the rides in this chapter are on bike trails. Here cyclists enjoy traffic-free riding of almost any distance they want. Some of the bike trails lead you from the city to the countryside. Other rides use roads with light traffic and sections closed to cars on weekends and holidays. One-third of the rides in this chapter use unpaved trails perfect for hybrid and mountain bikes.

Bicycling in Washington would be tougher if cyclists had to rely solely on city streets. More experienced cyclists have learned how to manage, but less skilled cyclists find the roads and traffic daunting. Fortunately, Washington offers a reasonably good network of bike trails.

Thanks to the efforts of local cyclists and clubs, this network is expanding and becoming better all the time. Several trails, notably the Mount Vernon and Rock Creek Trails, are heavily used and could use widening and updating.

In the last several years new trails have resulted from the rails-to-trails movement. The W&OD Trail in Virginia and the B&A Trail near Annapolis are good examples. The W&OD Trail provides the best exit from Washington into the Virginia countryside.

New trails are in the works and may become available in the next several years. The Capitol Crescent Trail will link the C&O Canal with the Rock Creek Trail. The lower part of this trail parallels the C&O Canal and is scheduled to be paved. The land for the Maryland section is available, but cyclists are still working out the details with the local governments. Other trails to look for are the Metropolitan Branch Trail and the WB&A Trail.

We didn't include all bike trails in this section. Our criteria included a length of least five miles, good scenery, good trail conditions and safety.

We have included in this section several areas frequently used by stronger cyclists for training loops. The first is the 3.3 mile loop around Hains Point found on the longer ride of *Washington's Waterfront*. The second is Beach Drive in Rock Creek Park on the *Saturday-Sunday Special* and *Urban Wilderness*. The third is the Beltsville Agricultural Research Center in *The Last Open Space*.

1. The Quiet Treasure (up to 185 miles one way; I)

Unpaved canal towpath; starts at parking lots along the canal. Suggested starts are Old Angler's Inn off MacArthur Boulevard, Seneca Creek Aqueduct (see directions in Ride #14), Edwards Ferry (Ride #13, Monocacy Aqueduct (Ride #18, Point of Rocks Train Station (Ride #19) and C&O Canal Headquarters (Ride #66).

Whenever we want a quick escape from the city, we cruise the unpaved Chesapeake & Ohio (C&O) Canal towpath on mountain bikes. On one side, the Potomac River crashes over its rocky bed. On the other side, the canal waters languish between massive stone lift locks. Overhead a canopy of trees blocks out the sunlight. We easily imagine the mules pulling 90-foot canal boats at a slow four miles per hour, taking five days to travel the canal's length.

A remnant from a bygone era, the canal stretches from Washington to Cumberland along the north bank of the Potomac River. The canal was such a grand undertaking that President John Quincy Adams dedicated its ground-breaking on the Fourth of July, 1828. The lower 23 miles began operating in 1831 and the canal was completed to Cumberland in 1850, 22 years after it had begun and much over budget. The Baltimore and Ohio Railroad, which also had broken ground on the same day, beat the canal to Cumberland by eight years.

The canal never did reach Ohio. It ceased operating in 1924 and in 1971 became a much loved national historic park. It is ironic that the modern canal as a park has succeeded where the original canal never did as a commercial venture.

We find mountain and hybrid bikes best for cycling the towpath. The upright riding style lends itself to slower riding and sightseeing. The wider tires handle the packed dirt and tree roots better than a touring bike. A touring bike with inch and a quarter tires will do, but not in wet weather. After heavy or extended rain, expect miles of gooey, grabbing clay and many puddles. At most other times the towpath is in good shape.

The towpath has two rough sections where some carrying is necessary – Widewater between miles 13 and 14 and at Big Slackwater between miles 84 and 89. An alternate at Widewater is the unpaved Berma Road on the east side Widewater. Access is at mile 12.7 just below Widewater and at mile 13.7 at the stop gate. An alternate at Big Slackwater is Dam 4 Road to Dellinger Road, to Charles Mill Road to Charles Mill.

Most people pick a section of the canal and cycle it as a day ride, riding as far as they like and returning to their start. The first 14 miles from Georgetown to Great Falls is the most scenic and the most crowded. The section from Seneca to Whites Ferry offers fewer people and a tranquil part of the river. From Point of Rocks to Harpers Ferry the river travels through several beautiful ridges. Above Harpers Ferry the canal travels far away from crowds and most towns.

Hiker-biker campgrounds, on a first-come basis, sit about five miles apart between miles 26 and 180. To ride the canal's length, most cyclists box their bikes and take the bus to Cumberland. Then they ride back, camping as they go.

The best guide to the canal is the *Towpath Guide to the C&O Canal* by Thomas F. Hahn, fifth edition 1987, American Canal and Transportation Center. Another good guide (with less detail but easier to carry) is *184 miles to Adventure* by the Mason-Dixon Council, Boy Scouts of America, 1970.

Expect to slow down when you ride the towpath. The old canal wasn't built for speed and trying to ride it fast will only frustrate you. There are too many pictures to take, too many places to stop and simply too much to see. Shift into a lower gear, look about you, and enjoy one of our great national treasures.

2. The Great Escape (Up to 45 miles one way; I)

Paved bike trail with numerous road crossings; starts at parking lots along the trail. Suggested starts are Barcroft Park on Four Mile Run Drive in Arlington, Vienna Community Center on Park Street in Vienna, Herndon Community Center on Ferndale Avenue in Herndon, Douglas Community Center on Sycolin Road in Leesburg and Loudoun Valley High School in Purcellville (see Ride #39).

At the turn of the century, Washingtonians boarded the trains of the Washington &Old Dominion (W&OD) Railroad to escape the city. Now they board their bicycles and ride the paved W&OD Trail to accomplish the same purpose. Like an arrow, the W&OD Trail points 44.5 miles through the Virginia suburbs, straight to the quiet countryside around Leesburg and Purcellville.

This is a well-loved (some will say over-loved) trail. Racers and accomplished cyclists use it as an exit route to the countryside. Children use it to learn to ride. New cyclists use it because, apart from its many street crossings, it is traffic free. The trail becomes rather crowded on warm weekend days.

You find the prettiest parts of the trail between Route 28 and Leesburg, and between Leesburg and Purcellville. The section west of Leesburg is as pretty a trail as you will find anywhere. You will find many services along the trail, especially in Leesburg and near its end in Purcellville.

3. To George's House (Up to 18 miles one way; I)

Paved bike path with signed city streets in Alexandria; starts at Roosevelt Island in Rosslyn, Va.: From I-395 take exit 11B, the George Washington Memorial Parkway North. In 0.7 miles bear right at 66/Dulles Airport sign to remain on the parkway. The Roosevelt Island parking lot is on the right in 1.4 miles. Also starts at parking lots along the George Washington Memorial Parkway, including Gravelly Point north of National Airport, the Sailing Marina south of National Airport, Belle Haven Picnic Area south of Alexandria, Fort Hunt Park south of Belle Haven, Riverside Park just east of Mount Vernon, and Mount Vernon.

On the Mount Vernon Trail along the Potomac River

A good trail provides good scenery as well as a good destination. Judging by the use, views and destination, the Mount Vernon Trail rates as a very good trail. Mount Vernon, George Washington's plantation, lies at the southern end of this scenic bike trail. Many consider the view from the main house the most magnificent on the Potomac River. You can lock your bike in the bike racks if you wish to visit the estate (admission fee $5.00 for adults, $4.00 senior citizens and $2.00 children under 12).

This heavily used trail is one of Washington's most popular bike paths. Commuting bicyclists use it during the week. Recreational cyclists ride it during the weekends and evenings. Runners and walkers use it all the time. The trail has good views of the Potomac River and the monuments of Washington, D.C.. Several sections run through woods and on wooden bridges over swampy areas. The trail south of Alexandria is quieter than the northern section and has several short hills.

The trail begins at Theodore Roosevelt Island and runs south on the west bank of the Potomac River to Mount Vernon. The trail passes National Airport and goes through Alexandria, an 18th century port with many Georgian buildings. The section of trail through Alexandria uses marked public roads. The rest of the trail travels on paved bike path. Many sections of the trail are narrow, requiring you to ride carefully.

The trail is well marked, although the sections along National Airport and at both ends of Alexandria can be somewhat confusing. Several road crossings near National Airport have heavy cross traffic. At the north end of Alexandria the path splits in two and joins together again. The section that stays closer to the river is the newer and more scenic section.

4. Washington's Waterfront (6 or 10 miles; I)

Paved bike path and park roads; starts at Roosevelt Island in Rosslyn, Va.: see directions in Ride #3.

You find some of Washington's best views along the Potomac River. These are classic views of monumental Washington, the Washington of the picture books. This ride combines bike paths, quiet roads through East and West Potomac Park and the sidewalks of the Memorial and Fourteenth Street Bridges. You start at the entrance to the Theodore Roosevelt Memorial and pass the Lincoln and Jefferson Memorials.

At the southern end of the ride you cycle around Hains Point. This is one of Washington's most popular bike training areas. The 3.3 mile loop around Hains Point sees countless cyclists on a summer evening. On warm weekend afternoons many people come to Hains Point and the car traffic increases. Use the wide sidewalks along the waterfront if the traffic bothers you.

5. Loop D'Arlington (17 miles; I/II)

Paved bike paths and a short section of road or sidewalk; starts at Roosevelt Island in Rosslyn, Va.: see directions in Ride #3.

If you like bicycle trails with little automobile traffic, explore Arlington, a city with a good trail network. This ride connects four trails into a single 17 mile loop. Beginning at Theodore Roosevelt Island on the Potomac River, you cycle west on the Custis Bikeway. The Custis Bikeway runs along I-66 and offers several hills to challenge you. Commuting cyclists frequently use this trail during the work week.

You join the W&OD Trail and ride it through pleasant Bluemont Park. At the beginning of the W&OD, you ride through Shirlington on either sidewalks or roads to the

Wayne F. Anderson Bikeway. This bike trail takes you back to the Potomac River where you connect with the Mount Vernon Trail. You then ride this trail north to your start.

6. Saturday-Sunday Special (Up to 21 miles roundtrip; I)

Paved bike path and roads; starts at Candy Cane City in Chevy Chase, Md.: From I-495, Washington Beltway, take Connecticut Avenue, Route 193 south. In 1.0 mile turn left on Route 410, East-West Highway. In 1.0 mile turn right on Beach Drive. In 0.3 miles park on the left at the blinking light. Also starts at Pierce Mill off Beach Drive or Lincoln Memorial in D.C..

For years, Rock Creek Park has provided a haven for cyclists. Its bike path and roads run along a scenic creek through a heavily wooded canyon. You cycle through the middle of Washington, yet the park itself looks and feels like the wild mountains to the west.

Rock Creek is very popular with cyclists. A bike path runs from the Lincoln Memorial past the National Zoo to Pierce Mill, a restored grist mill. Pierce Mill is open for visitors on the weekends. The ride uses Beach Drive north of Pierce Mill.

Most of the 4.5 miles on Beach Drive between Pierce Mill and the District line is closed to cars on Saturdays, Sundays and holidays. You share the roadway with cars on two sections, from Joyce Road to Sherrill Drive and from Wise Road to West Beach Drive. You also share Beach Drive with cars between the District Line and Candy Cane City. Many cyclists, runners and walkers use the bike path and the closed sections during weekends.

You find water and restrooms at Pierce Mill, the Park Police Station just south of Joyce Road and Candy Cane City. The unpaved horse paths and hiking trails in the park are closed to cyclists. The ride becomes dangerous during the week as drivers use Beach Drive as a major commuting artery to and from downtown Washington. During the weekends, however, Beach Drive belongs to the cyclists, runners, walkers and roller bladers who travel under their own power.

7. Urban Wilderness (Up to 27 miles roundtrip; I/II)

Paved bike path and some roadway; starts at Candy Cane City in Chevy Chase, Md.: see directions in Ride #6.

You find the most rustic and quietest parts of the Rock Creek Trail north of the District. Several sections of this trail feel very far from the city suburbs even though they are all around you. In the upper sections the woods thicken and Rock Creek becomes narrower. The ride provides good shade and is popular during the summer heat.

You cycle north from Candy Cane City on the bike path and follow it to Lake Needwood. In the lower and middle sections, the trail isn't well marked. There are many side trails that take you out of the park and into neighborhoods. Going north, follow the signs to Rockville and Lake Needwood. If you end up in a neighborhood, just backtrack to the main trail.

In two short sections you ride on little-travelled roads. These are between Candy Cane City and East-West Highway at the southern end and just north of Viers Mill Road in the middle section. The rest of the ride uses paved bike path.

In the lower section, many cyclists use parallel Beach Drive and Jones Mill Road instead of the bike path. Beach Drive becomes a popular training ride for stronger cyclists during the weekends.

The bike path ends in a parking lot at Lake Needwood. If you ride through the parking lot and go left toward the lake, you will come to a concession stand. Here you can buy food in season and enjoy a picnic lunch on the shore.

8. Shady Sligo (Up to 10 miles roundtrip; I)

Paved bike path, some roadway and a short unpaved section; starts at Montgomery Blair High School in Silver Spring, Md.: From I-495, take Colesville Road south. Turn left onto Sligo Creek Parkway at the bottom of the hill. In 0.8 miles turn right on Wayne Avenue. In 0.1 miles turn right into the school, by the track. The Sligo Creek Trail starts at Sligo Cabin by the parking lot.

On long summer evenings, we like to ride up Sligo Creek to Wheaton Regional Park. There we park our bikes in the bike rack and walk into Brookside Gardens. Brookside Gardens is one of the best public gardens in the Washington area. We then spend the next hour enjoying well-tended flower gardens and conservatories. Returning to our bikes, we contentedly ride back down the Sligo Creek Bike Path before darkness falls.

The Sligo Creek Bike Trail lies next to sylvan Sligo Creek. You follow the trail north, following the bike trail signs. Many cyclists use the parallel Sligo Creek Parkway between Wayne Avenue and University Boulevard. The trail crosses University Boulevard at the traffic light on the east side of Sligo Creek Parkway.

Above University Boulevard you continue north on the bike trail, following the signs to the Wheaton Regional Park Ice Rink. The signed route brings you onto a short section through suburban streets. After crossing Arcola Avenue, you enter the park. Ride north past the Ice Rink and onto the dirt road down the hill. Just past Pine Lake turn right and you will see a bike rack at the entrance to Brookside Gardens. Bikes are not allowed on the garden grounds. This might sound complicated, but it's not. If you have time explore the park on the paved bike trails.

9. The Last Open Space (5 or 10 miles; II)

Paved roads through the Agricultural Research Center; starts at Crider Memorial Garden in Beltsville, Md.: From I-95, Washington Beltway take the Baltimore-Washington Parkway north. In 3.5 miles exit onto Powder Mill Road east, turning right at the end of the ramp. In 0.1 miles turn right on Soil Conservation Road. In 1.2 miles turn left on Beaver Dam Road. The parking lot is on your right.

At first glance, you swear you are somewhere in the middle of farm country, far removed from the city. A narrow lane meanders between well tended crops, livestock and dense woods. You will occasionally catch a glimpse of deer grazing in the fields. Yet you are never more than a few miles away from Washington's Beltway. This is the Beltsville Agricultural Research Center, a cyclist's oasis in the middle of the urban sprawl.

The roads through the research center rate as one of Washington's major cycling areas. On summer evenings and weekends you will see all types of cyclists, some several times as they use these roads for their training loops. Local cycling clubs offer numerous rides on these roads.

Powder Mill and Edmonston Roads carry commuter traffic during rush hour. There is a good shoulder on Edmonston Road and a passable shoulder with some broken sections on Powder Mill Road. Powder Mill Road has an acceptable amount of traffic before and after the rush hours.

10. Great Great Falls (5 or 6 miles; III)

Unpaved park fire roads and a short section of paved road; starts at Great Falls Park in Great Falls, Va.: From I-495, Washington Beltway, take Route 193, Georgetown Pike toward Great Falls. Follow for 4.2 miles and turn right into the park at the traffic light. Turn right into the first parking lot, just after the entrance booth.

When you ride in Great Falls National Park, you feel far away from the city and in the wilderness. The powerful river surges over a massive waterfall and rushes through a narrow, cliff-lined gorge. Overlooking Mather Gorge on the Potomac River, would you believe you are only minutes from the beltway and 14 miles from the White House? You are in one of the more popular national parks in the United States.

Great Falls National Park

Mountain biking in Great Falls National Park on the Virginia side of the Potomac River ($3 admission fee) is delightful and legal. The National Park Service, which administers this nearby wilderness, allows cyclists on about five miles of unpaved park fire roads. With its proximity to the city, the park is popular with cyclists, rock climbers, hikers, kayakers, runners, sunbathers and many others.

You enjoy good river views at Sandy Landing and Difficult Run. Along Difficult Run you enjoy views of a very pretty stream. The rest of the ride is through dense woods. During the winter you get good river views from the Ridge Trail. The visitor center has water, restrooms and a snack bar.

The park rangers welcome cyclists as long as they stay on the trails open to cycling. These are the Old Carriage Road, the road to and from Sandy Landing, the Ridge Trail, Difficult Run Trail and the Equestrian Trail north of the visitor's center. Other trails are rough, narrow hiking trails closed to cycling. The closed trails are signed and marked as closed.

If we ride safely and are courteous to the many others who use the park trails, cyclists will continue to be welcome. Don't ride fast and always give runners, hikers and equestrians the right of way. After the ride walk over to the water's edge and view Great Falls. This is one of the area's most spectacular sites and a superb spot for a picnic.

11. A Lakeside Jaunt (5 or 9 miles roundtrip; II)

Unpaved crushed gravel bike path with a short paved section; starts at Wakefield Park in Annandale, Va.: From I-495, Washington Beltway, take Braddock Road west. At the first traffic light after the interchange turn right at Queensberry Avenue into the park. In 0.2 mile turn left into the first parking lot.

Here is a pleasant trail for those who want a quick spin after work or a short "get back early" ride on the weekends. This trail, with its smooth crushed gravel surface, is the perfect place for riding a hybrid bike.

The trail begins in Wakefield Park next to the Washington Beltway. From the park you ride south along wooded Accotink Creek. Soon the stream widens to become Lake Accotink. The trail twists and turns and follows the shoreline of the lake. When you reach the southern end of the lake, you arrive at a marina. Here you either turn around or continue to the west side of the lake. The trail crosses the outlet of the lake, which can be difficult to cross in high water. After a steep but short hill, the trail flattens out to a pleasant trail through the woods. When you get to the end of the path, turn around and ride in reverse to your start.

12. By the Lakeside (5 miles; I)

Unpaved crushed gravel bike path; starts at Burke Lake Marina in Burke, Va.: From I-495, Washington Beltway, take Braddock Road west. Follow for two miles and turn left onto Burke Lake Road, Route 645. Follow for 4.8 and turn left onto Ox Road, Route 123. In 0.5 miles turn left into Burke Lake after the golf course. Turn left in 0.5 miles at sign toward the lake. The parking lot is 0.2 miles ahead.

For those who like "zen cycling" we offer the hiker-biker trail in Burke Lake Park. This mostly flat five mile trail takes you far away from the stresses and cares of modern life. You glide quietly on the smooth, crushed gravel path as it meanders around the lake. There are many places along the trail to stop and contemplate the water and the lake's natural beauty. At the end of the ride, the ducks and geese near the marina concession stand provide entertainment as they beg for food.

There is an admission fee to the park for non-Fairfax County residents on weekends and holidays. The snack bar at the marina is open during the summer.

The trail is wide enough to accommodate the many runners, walkers and cyclists who use it. Riding in the park makes you feel quite serene and far removed from the city, the perfect zen ride.

1. The Quiet Treasure

Distance:	Up to **185** miles one way
Rating:	I; Unpaved canal towpath
Start:	Parking lots along canal in Md. or D.C. (see ride description)

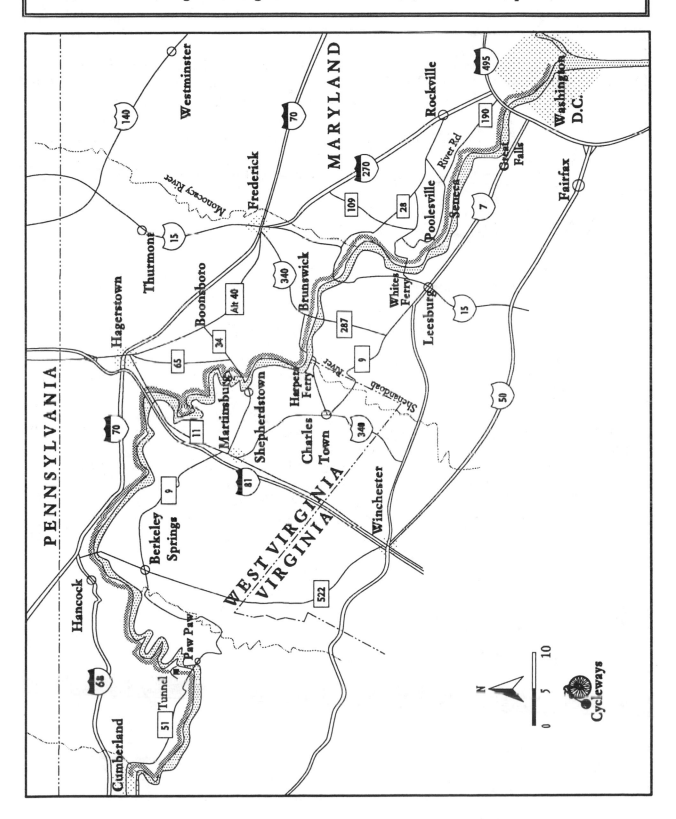

2. The Great Escape

Distance:	Up to **45** miles one way
Rating:	I; Paved bike trail with numerous road crossings
Start:	Parking lots along trail in Va. (see ride description)

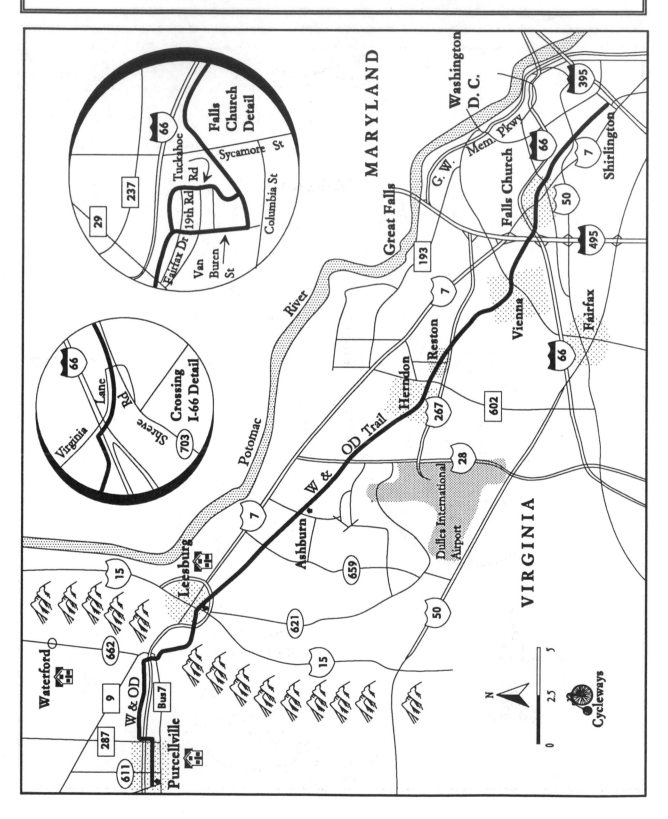

3. To George's House

Distance:	Up to **18** miles one way
Rating:	I; Paved bike path with signed city streets in Alexandria
Start:	Roosevelt Island in Rosslyn, Va. or along the George Washington Memorial Parkway in Va.

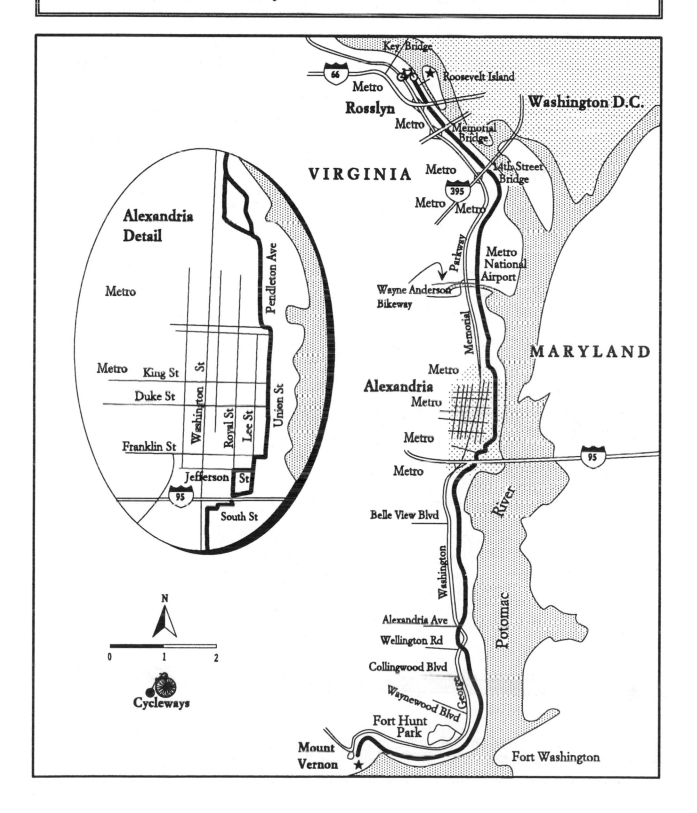

4. Washington's Waterfront

Distance:	6 or **10** miles
Rating:	I; Paved bike path and park roads
Start:	Roosevelt Island in Rosslyn, Va.

10 Mile Ride

0.0	L	Mt Vernon Trail South from parking lot with river at your back
0.1	BL	onto boardwalk to stay on Mt Vernon Trail
1.1	R	onto bike path crossing northbound George Washington Pkwy after crossing under 2nd bridge; ride onto and over Memorial Bridge, crossing the Potomac River
1.9	R	onto 2nd road at SS after coming off Memorial Bridge; Lincoln Memorial to your left
1.9	S	Ohio Drive at TL at Independence Ave; follow around circle entering West Potomac Park
2.6 ☛*	BR	toward Jefferson Memorial and Hains Point
2.7	R	unmarked road at T, toward East Potomac Park
3.2	L	Buckeye Dr (unmarked) at SS following signs to Hains Point at Do Not Enter sign
3.5	R	Ohio Dr at T
6.4	S	at SS toward West Potomac Park
6.9 *☞	S	toward Jefferson Memorial at 1909 Bridge
7.0	R	onto bike path to go onto George Mason Memorial (I-395) Bridge over the Potomac River at Do Not Enter sign; Jefferson Memorial to your left
7.7	L	onto Mt Vernon trail (unmarked) at end of bridge
8.6	S	Mt Vernon trail toward Roosevelt Island, staying close to the river
9.7		Arrive at parking lot

* 6 Mile Ride

2.7	L	unmarked road at T, toward Jefferson Memorial (Pick up cues in 0.1 miles at mile 7.0 on the 10 mile ride – *☞)

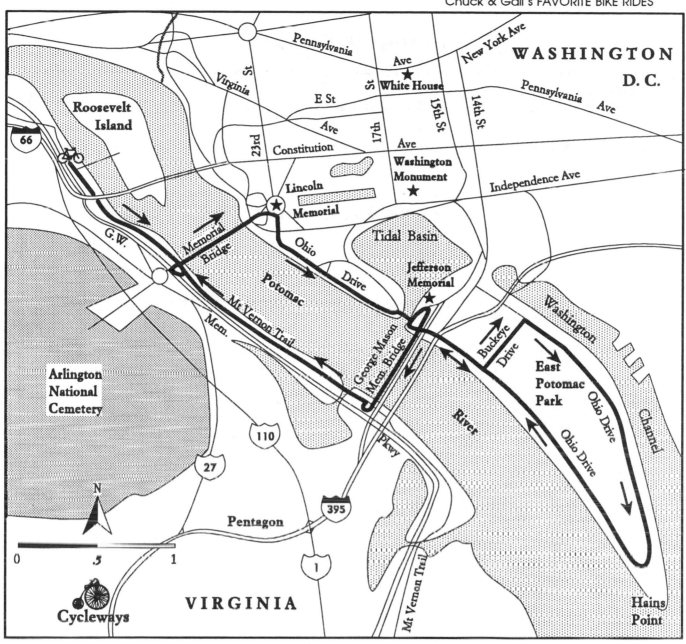

5. Loop D'Arlington

Distance:	17 miles
Rating:	I/II; Paved bike paths and a short section of road or sidewalk
Start:	Roosevelt Island in Rosslyn, Va.

17 Mile Ride

0.0	R	onto bikepath (north) thru parking lot with the river at your back
0.3	S	onto sidewalk/bikepath at N Lynn St at TL following signs toward Custis trail; follow bikepath as it crosses over I-66
4.8	L	W&OD trail at T after crossing to southside of I-66 (Water); follow signs for W&OD trail
8.8	R	at Shirlington Hwy to cross Four Mile Run at end of W&OD; follow sign to I-395 pedestrian overpass and Wayne Anderson bike path
8.9	R	Arlington Mill Rd following bike trail sign on sidewalk
9.0	L	Quincy St
9.1	L	28th St continuing to follow the bike trail signs
9.1	L	onto pedestrian overpass over I-395
9.3	L	Martha Custis Rd from end of overpass; use either sidewalk or road
9.7	S	Valley Drive
9.9	L	W Glebe Rd at T ⊗
10.1	R	Wayne F. Anderson Bikeway at South Glebe Rd
10.8	S	Follow signs to the Mt Vernon Trail at Arlington Ridge Rd staying on north side of stream. Or you can cross to the south side of the stream and follow the Wayne F. Anderson Bikeway.
11.8	S	Mt Vernon Trail (unmarked) after underpasses at the south end of the National Airport parking lots
15.5	S	Mt Vernon trail toward Roosevelt Island staying close to the river
16.6		Arrive at parking lot

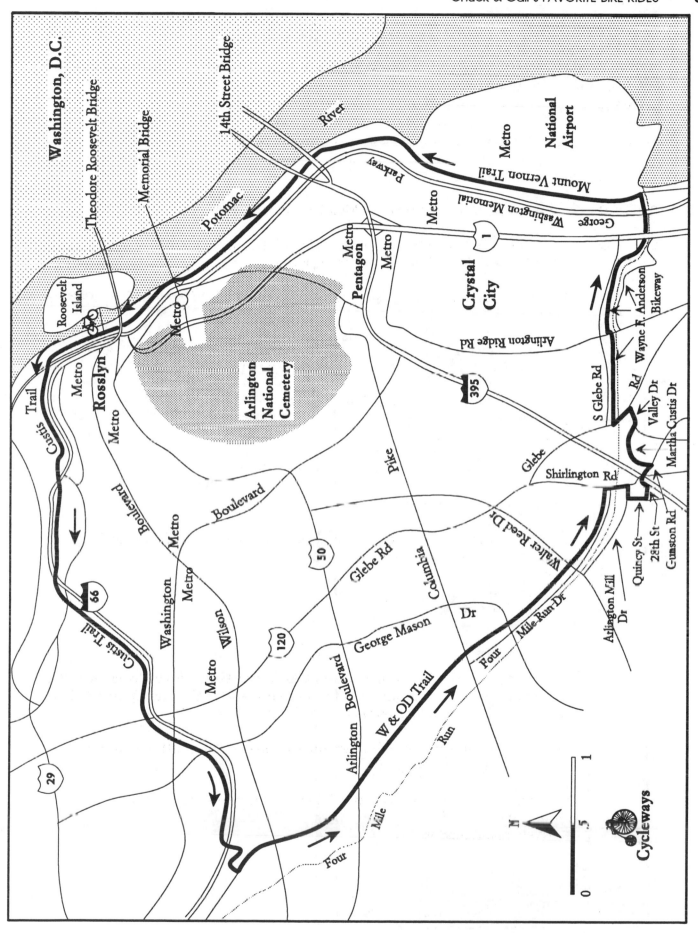

6. Saturday-Sunday Special

Distance:	Up to **21** miles roundtrip
Rating:	I; Paved bike path and roads
Start:	Candy Cane City in Md.; Pierce Mill or Lincoln Memorial in D.C.

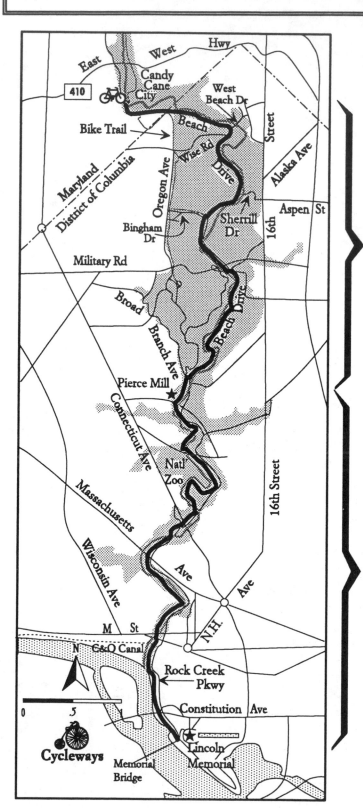

This section of the Rock Creek Trail, from Broad Branch Ave. to Candy Cane City in Maryland, follows Beach Drive. The following sections of Beach Drive are closed on holidays and weekends: Broad Branch Ave. to Joyce Rd., just above Sherrill Dr. to Wise Rd. and W. Beach Dr. to the D.C. line. A short section of paved bike trail runs from Joyce Rd. to Bingham Dr.

This section of the Rock Creek trail, from the Lincoln Memorial to Broad Branch Ave., is on paved bike trail paralleling the Rock Creek Parkway and Beach Drive.

7. Urban Wilderness

Distance:	Up to **27** miles roundtrip
Rating:	I/II; Paved bike path and some roadway
Start:	Candy Cane City in Chevy Chase, Md.

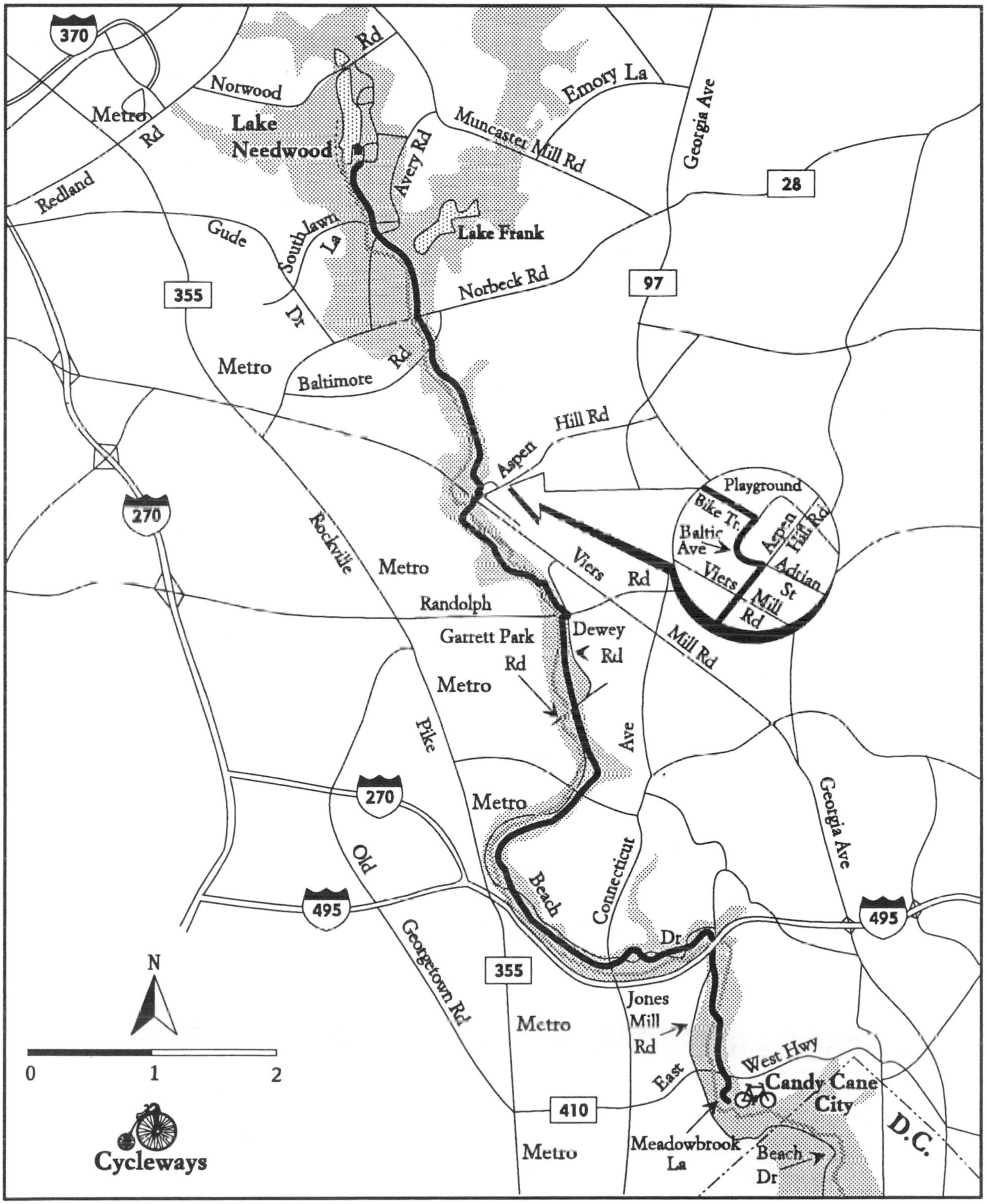

370

Norwood Rd

Metro

Rd

Lake
Needwood

Redland

Avery Rd

Muncaster Mill Rd

Emory La

Georgia Ave

28

Gude

Southlawn La

Lake Frank

355

Dr

Norbeck Rd

97

Metro

Baltimore Rd

Hill Rd

270

Aspen

Playground

Bike Tr.

Aspen Hill Rd

Baltic
Ave

Rockville

Metro

Viers   Rd

Viers

Adrian
St

Randolph

Dewey
Rd

Mill
Rd

Mill Rd

Garrett Park
Rd

Metro

Pike

Ave

270

Metro

Old

Beach

Connecticut

Georgia Ave

495

495

N

Dr

355

Jones
Mill
Rd

West Hwy

0   1   2

Metro

East

Candy Cane
City

D.C.

410

Metro

Meadowbrook
La

Beach
Dr

Cycleways

8. Shady Sligo

Distance:	Up to **10** miles roundtrip
Rating:	I; Paved bike path, some roadway and a short unpaved section
Start:	Montgomery Blair High School in Silver Spring, Md.

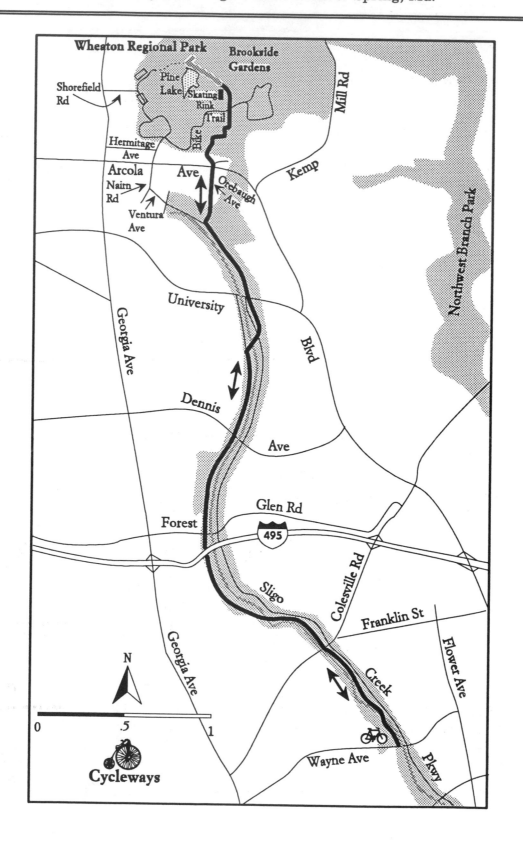

9. The Last Open Space

Distance:	5 or **10** miles
Rating:	II; Paved roads through the Beltsville Agricultural Research Center
Start:	Crider Memorial Garden in Beltsville, Md.

10 Mile Ride

0.0	L	Beaver Dam Rd from parking lot
3.2	R	Edmonston Rd ⊗; shoulder
3.5	R	Powder Mill Rd at TL; shoulder
6.8	R	Springfield Rd
8.7	R	Beaver Dam Rd
10.3	L	into parking lot

5 Mile Ride

0.0	L	Beaver Dam Rd from parking lot
0.1	R	Soil Conservation Rd at SS
1.2	R	Powder Mill Rd at Y
1.6	R	Springfield Rd
3.4	R	Beaver Dam Rd
5.0	L	into parking lot

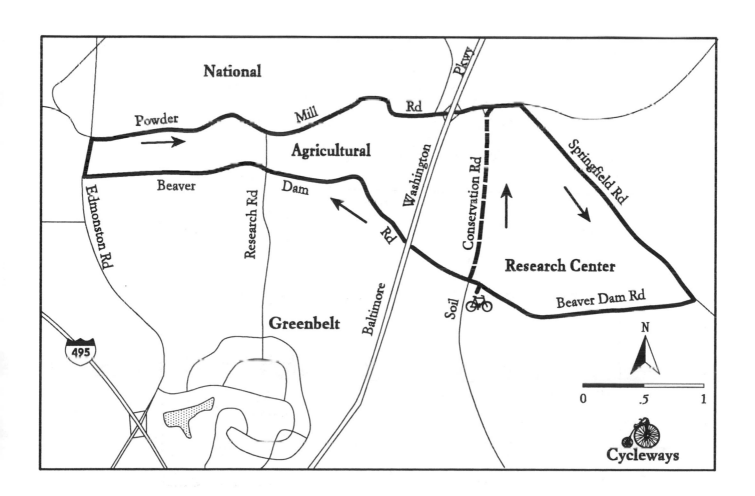

10. Great Great Falls

Distance:	**5** or 6 miles
Rating:	III; Unpaved park fire roads and a short section of paved road
Start:	Great Falls Park in Great Falls, Va.

5 Mile Ride

0.0	S	onto dirt road from end of parking lot at "Do not enter" sign
0.1	BR	onto Old Carriage Rd at restrooms; go past gate
0.7	L	onto gravel road at first intersection to the left after the Swamp Trail
0.9		Arrive at a nice overlook before descending to the river; turn around and return to the Old Carriage Rd
1.1	L	Old Carriage Rd (unmarked) at T
1.4	L	Ridge Trail near top of the hill; follow signs; blind corners on this trail
2.2	R	at Trail Junction to Difficult Run, after picnic tables; steep descent
2.3	L	Difficult Run Trail at T to Potomac River; steep descent near the end
2.5		Arrive at the Potomac River at the mouth of Difficult Run; Turn Around
3.2	R	unmarked Georgetown Pike after gate ⊗; ride on dirt next to pavement
3.4	R	onto first dirt road (unmarked Old Carriage Road); go past gate

> * For the **6 mile ride**, turn left onto Ridge Trail (some rough steep sections) at mile 3.6 at the top of the hill. Ride 0.6 miles to the paved entrance road, turn around and return to the Old Carriage Road.

4.6	L	to stay on Old Carriage Rd at restrooms, after gate, and immediately
4.6	BL	toward parking lot
4.7		Arrive at parking lot

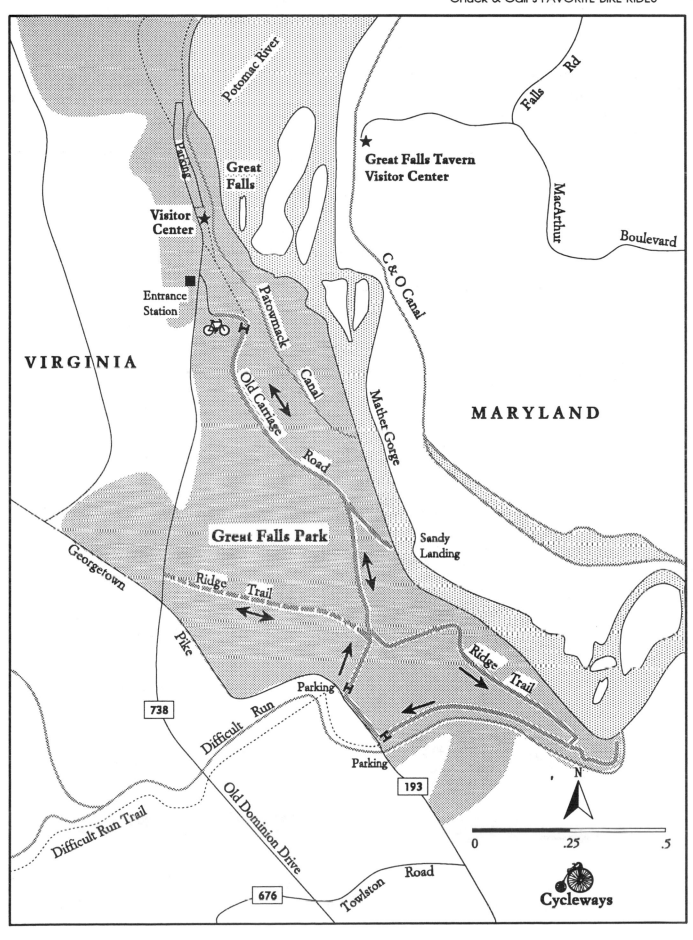

Potomac River

Falls Rd

Great Falls Tavern
Visitor Center

Falls

MacArthur

Boulevard

Great
Falls

Parking

Visitor
Center

C & O Canal

Entrance
Station

Patowmack Canal

VIRGINIA

Old Carriage

Mather Gorge

MARYLAND

Road

Great Falls Park

Sandy
Landing

Georgetown

Ridge   Trail

Ridge   Trail

Pike

738

Difficult   Run

Parking

Difficult Run Trail

Old Dominion Drive

Parking

193

N

Towlston   Road

676

0   .25   .5

Cycleways

11. A Lakeside Jaunt

Distance:	5 or **9** miles roundtrip
Rating:	II; Unpaved crushed gravel bike path with a short paved section
Start:	Wakefield Park in Annandale, Va.

0.0	L	Wakefield-Accotink Trail from south end of parking lot; follow Accotink Trail signs
2.5	R	thru parking lot onto paved road at Lake Accotink Marina
		* Turn around for the 5 mile ride
2.6	BR	onto paved path crossing stream below dam, before railroad bridge; becomes dirt
4.0	S	at Lake Accotink Park Trail sign to the right
4.4		arrive at gate; turn around and reverse route

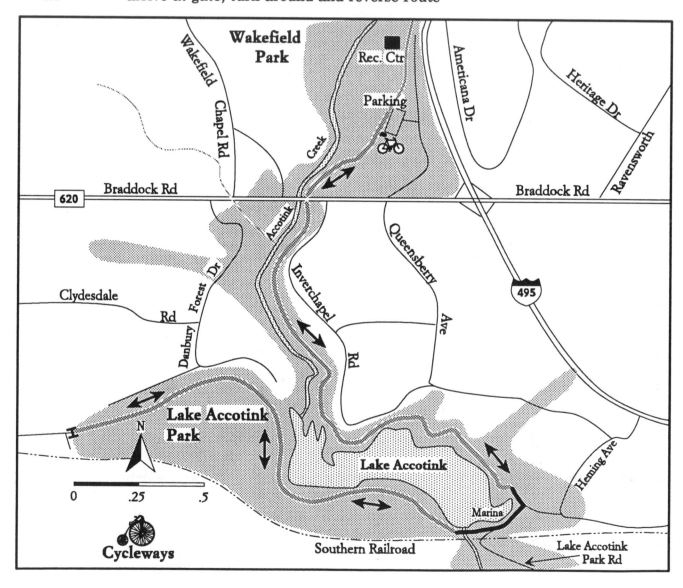

12. By the Lakeside

Distance:	**5** miles
Rating:	I; Unpaved crushed gravel bike path
Start:	Burke Lake Marina in Burke, Va.

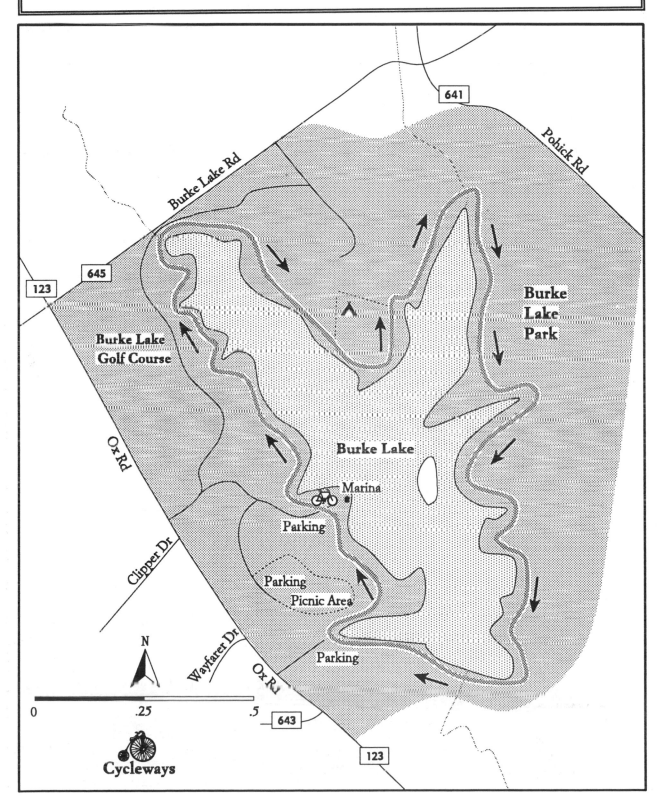

THE HEARTLAND

The name heartland brings images of rural countryside, of scenic roads, of simpler times. The clip-clop of horse's hooves on stone and covered bridges interrupts the silence. Mules strain as they pull loaded canal boats and wagons to market. Weary armies in blue and gray march down dusty roads. Quiet forests give refuge to deer and wildlife.

For years the area northwest of Washington and Baltimore has given cyclists an easy escape from the cities. It offers the closest rural riding to these cities and was one of the first areas mapped by cyclists. When we began cycling in the region, our first rural ventures were into this area. We first learned about the region's great rural cycling roads in these nearby Maryland counties.

Most of the rides in this chapter lie within Montgomery and Frederick Counties, extending north into southern Pennsylvania. Others are in western Howard, Carroll, Baltimore and Anne Arundel Counties.

Western Montgomery County, west of Seneca Creek, remains an attractive area to bicycle. Strict zoning laws have protected it from the growth that has eaten large tracts east of I-270. The area begins at Seneca Creek Aqueduct on the Potomac River in the south and stretches north to Sugarloaf Mountain. Between are miles of little-travelled country lanes that pass bucolic farms and babbling brooks. You will find some roads that are only one lane wide. The center of this area lies in the town of Poolesville.

To the north is Frederick County, home of another popular cycling area. Most of the cycling here lies in the Frederick Valley which stretches from the Potomac River north to the Pennsylvania Border. The Catoctin Mountains present a barrier to the west, and hilly Carroll County lies to the east. Within this area are many dairy farms and pretty views of the mountains. The center of the valley is the city of Frederick.

Two covered bridges remain in Frederick County. There were three until recently, but vandals burnt the third bridge in 1991. LeGore Bridge, a magnificent five-arch stone bridge, crosses the Monocacy River east of the covered bridges. You can wander through the restored remains of Catoctin Furnace south of Thurmont.

The valley extends north into Pennsylvania, across the Mason Dixon Line. North of Gettysburg you find pleasant countryside dotted with fruit orchards and rural roads. South of town the Gettysburg Battlefield, a monument to one of the greatest battles of the Civil War, extends peacefully into the countryside.

Tough climbs await as you head west from the Frederick Valley over the Catoctin ridge and into the hilly Middletown Valley. Cycling in this area rewards you with good vistas and long downhill runs. Of course, you have to do a little work before you enjoy the rewards.

East of the Poolesville area and Frederick Valley the terrain becomes choppy and hilly, but with distinct charms. The suburban growth in Howard, Carroll, Baltimore and Montgomery Counties has sharply reduced the number of back roads available to cyclists. Much of these counties' rural flavor disappeared in the last decade.

In Carroll County you ride through quaint small towns, each with a different personality. In eastern Montgomery County you visit Brookeville, the town President Madison fled to during the War of 1812. Baltimore County offers one of the best rails-trails in the region. The Northern Central Railroad Trail avoids the hills by running along shady streams in narrow, wooded valleys.

13. The Two Ferry Loop (10 miles; I)

Unpaved roads and unpaved C&O Canal towpath; starts at Edwards Ferry, Md.: Take I-270 north to exit 6B, Route 28 West. Follow Route 28 west for 11.5 miles. Turn left on Route 107, Whites Ferry Road, and continue for 6.6 miles, past Poolesville. Turn left on Edwards Ferry Road and go 1.6 miles. Bear right on Edwards Ferry Road at Westerly Road. In 2.1 miles bear left at the bottom of the hill toward the river and the parking lot.

This loop offers an easy ride for newer cyclists. It is a good ride if you like riding on dirt, flat terrain and avoiding traffic.

Both Edwards and Whites Ferries connected roads between Poolesville, Md. and Leesburg, Va., beginning in the late 18th century. Edwards Ferry operated until 1936. Whites Ferry is the last operating ferry on the Potomac River and the only crossing for the 40 miles between the Washington Beltway and Point of Rocks, Md. Confederate General Jubal A. Early, for whom the present ferry boat is named, used both ferries during his retreat from his attack on Washington in July 1864.

You begin the ride on the Potomac River at Edwards Ferry. The dirt roads in the first half of the ride have minimal traffic. When you arrive at Whites Ferry, take a lunch stop under the tall shade trees along the river. High water during floods will prohibit the ferry from operating. Note the high water mark from the 1972 flood on the second story of the store. You then ride back to your start on the flat C&O Canal towpath.

14. Back by Noon (25 or 38 miles; III)

Paved roads; starts at Seneca Creek Aqueduct on the C&O Canal, Seneca, Md.: From I-495, Washington Beltway, take exit 40, River Road, Route 190 West. Follow for 11 miles and turn left at T to remain on River Road. In 0.5 miles turn left onto Rileys Lock Road and follow it to the end. Turn left into the parking lot.

During Washington's legendary summers, the asphalt softens and grabs your tires. The heat and humidity press down on you like a fist. On these 4H days (high heat, haze and humidity) the only solution is to be on the bike early and be back by noon.

In contrast, we laid out our first Cycleways ride, a variant of this ride, on a cold February day in 1984. At each intersection we would stop, remove heavy wool mittens and write down the cue and mileage.

This area remains a favorite for us in hot or cold weather. Close to Washington, it offers a good selection of rural roads. We stumbled upon this particular combination of roads and liked it. Montgomery County recently paved some of these roads and opened them up for skinny-tired cyclists. On hot days you are likely to find us on these roads early, getting in miles and trying to beat the worst of the heat.

15. Shades of the Past (12 or 22 miles; II or III)

Paved roads; starts at Poolesville High School in Poolesville, Md.: Take I-270 north to Exit 6B, Route 28 West. Follow Route 28 west for 11.5 miles. Turn left on Route 107, Whites Ferry Road, and continue for five miles into Poolesville. Turn left onto West Willard Road. In 0.2 miles turn left into the parking lot at the rear of the school.

Countless new cyclists have fallen in love with the sport on the country roads of western Montgomery County. Protected by anti-growth zoning, the area west of Seneca Creek retains its rural charm. These quiet country lanes offer the closest rural cycling to the city of Washington. On any weekend day you will probably meet other cyclists, especially at Poolesville or Seneca Creek.

West Willard Road at the start of the ride and River Road are the only roads with yellow lines. The rest are narrow country lanes, one only one lane wide. Seneca Creek Aqueduct, the destination for the longer ride, sits on the Potomac River. The aqueduct once carried the canal boats over Seneca Creek; now it carries walkers, runners and cyclists. The aqueduct parking lot provides a good alternative start.

16. All Sides of Sugarloaf (24 or 35 miles; III or IV)

Paved roads; starts at Poolesville High School in Poolesville, Md.: see directions in Ride #15.

Sugarloaf Mountain from Barnesville, Md.

Sugarloaf is Washington's local *mountain*, a large hill that sits apart from the main ridges to the west. With a good choice of country roads, you can cycle to its base, around it, or up it. We laid out our first bicycle ride here in 1977. We recently cycled it and found it was still good, an unexpected pleasure given the recent growth.

We find the ride easier in the counter-clockwise direction we have described. If you attack the long downhill just south of Flint Hill on Park Mills Road, you can approach 50 mph.

The shorter ride passes the entrance to Sugarloaf Mountain. Here you have the choice of cycling an optional 1.5 mile climb up the mountain. From the top you enjoy good vistas of the surrounding area. On the descent you pass the Strong mansion. Gordon Strong once owned the mountain and formed the Stronghold Corporation that manages the land. When the peaches ripen in August, be sure to stop at the fruit stand at Peach Tree Road and Route 28.

17. No Loafin' (12 or 15 miles; IV)

Unpaved and paved roads; starts at Sugarloaf Mountain, Md.: Take I-270 north to Route 109, Old Hundred Road, south toward Barnesville. In 2.8 miles turn right on Comus Road in Comus. Follow for 2.4 miles to the intersection with Mount Ephraim Road, at the entrance to Sugarloaf Mountain. Park in the marked spaces.

Nestled close to Sugarloaf Mountain are beautiful unpaved roads never seen by cyclists who don't venture off the pavement. These roads travel through hilly terrain, close to the mountain, through dense woods and along several creeks. Bennett Creek offers several places that beckon for a long break, especially on a hot day.

The steep climb to Flint Hill from Bennett Creek presents a challenge. Once on top you enjoy a long downhill on paved Park Mills Road. Just don't enjoy the downhill so much that you miss your left turn onto Mount Ephraim Road before the bottom. Mount Ephraim Road passes through dense woods where you feel closer to West Virginia than the nation's capital.

The longer ride offers a hillier challenge and reduces the distance ridden on pavement. It visits the Urbana Fishing Lake, another quiet place for a break.

18. Half & Half (26 miles; IV)

Unpaved C&O Canal towpath, unpaved and paved roads; starts at Monocacy Aqueduct on the C&O Canal near Dickerson, Md.:   Take I-270 north to exit 6B, Route 28 West. Follow Route 28 west for 20 miles. Just past Dickerson turn left on Mouth of Monocacy Road. Follow for 1.2 miles and turn left toward the aqueduct at the Y. Arrive at the canal in 0.1 miles.

This ride truly is half and half. It is half in Virginia, half in Maryland. It is half flat and half hilly. It is half unpaved towpath and half roads. Half the roads are dirt and half paved. You explore a quiet section of the C&O Canal towpath in Maryland and rural roads in Loudoun County, Virginia.

The Monocacy Aqueduct, the largest aqueduct on the C&O Canal, is your start. The section of the canal between Whites Ferry and Point of Rocks sees fewer people than the section below Seneca Creek. After you cross the Potomac River on Whites Ferry, the terrain changes. In Virginia, the ride becomes hillier and you ride on unpaved and paved public roads.

A steep grade takes you over the Catoctin Ridge and down a breathtaking downhill run. You then climb on a windy dirt road in order to plunge down to the Potomac River. You make a second crossing of the Potomac River at Point of Rocks, Md. Then pedal back to your start on the flat canal towpath.

19. A Bit of Everything (23 or 30 miles; II or IV)

Paved roads; starts at Point of Rocks Train Station in Point of Rocks, Md.: Take I-270 north to exit 6B, Route 28 West. Follow 28 west for 27.8 miles to Point of Rocks. As you enter the town, the railroad station is on your left.

A ride in the southern Frederick Valley allows you to sample a little bit of everything rural Maryland has to offer. Starting at the Victorian train station at Point of Rocks, you cycle north through the west side of the valley. Just before you meet Frederick's growth, you turn south and head through the valley's center.

Cap Stine Road offers good vistas of the Catoctin Ridge as it winds its way through open fields. Nearly flat and open, New Design Road becomes fun when a strong north wind pushes you southward down the valley. The shorter ride visits Adamstown where you can eat lunch in an old bank.

The longer ride changes in terrain and scenery. It becomes more wooded and you cross the Monocacy River twice. You climb the flank of Sugarloaf Mountain and pass through Flint Hill. From Flint Hill you descend the long hill that local cyclists call *the wall*. Throughout the ride you get good views of the valley and the Catoctin Ridge to the west.

20. Hill Climber's Delight (30 or 40 miles; V)

Paved roads with several climbs; starts at Point of Rocks Train Station in Point of Rocks, Md.: see directions in Ride #19.

The name says it all. We include this ride as a gift to the tough guys and gals who love one hill after another. If you hate hills, skip immediately to another ride.

From the Potomac River you climb to Lovettsville, Virginia. You then descend to the railroad town of Brunswick, Maryland. Route 287 carries some traffic so be alert. The Middletown Valley north of Brunswick features frequent, long hills.

The longer ride climbs South Mountain at Crampton Gap. The Union Army captured the Gap from Confederate forces in the Battle of South Mountain. In the gap at Gathland State Park stands the War Correspondent's Arch, a one of a kind nominee for the strange monument award. You then descend and visit Middletown. Like moths to a light, cyclists are drawn to Main's Ice Cream on the main street through town. You then ride south to picturesque Jefferson and climb Mar-Lu Ridge over the Catoctins.

If you do not feel like climbing South Mountain, shorten the ride by turning toward Jefferson and Mar-Lu Ridge. This significantly reduces the number of hills. It shortens the long climbs from two to one.

21. Catoctin Climber (47 or 48 miles; V)

Paved roads; starts at Waverly Elementary School in Frederick, Md.: Take I-270 North to Route 15 North in Frederick. From Route 15, take exit 6 West onto Route 40 West, Patrick Street. Go 1.3 miles and turn right onto Waverly Drive. In 0.6 miles turn left into the school.

What is a hard ride if it doesn't have a tough start? With little warm up you climb west over Catoctin Ridge into the Middletown Valley. The ride features long climbs, breathtaking views and exciting downhill runs.

If the first climb was not hard enough, you can choose to climb Harp Hill on Harp Hill Road. This 400 foot, 15 percent grade was used for King of the Mountain points on two professional stage races, the Tour de Trump and the Tour du Pont. We wisely avoid it, instead pointing out the shaded virtues of Route 17 as it runs along a pleasant stream.

The longer ride offers a seven mile downhill run as you descend into Thurmont from Catoctin Mountain Park. On the shorter ride you stay in the park and add two more climbs. The shorter ride features long climbs and descents on Park Central Road and Catoctin Hollow Road. Both rides return to Frederick on quiet rural roads in the Frederick Valley.

22. Up the Creek (13 or 15 miles; IV)

Mostly unpaved roads; starts at Bethel Lutheran Evangelical Church in Bethel, Md.: Take I-270 to Route 15 North in Frederick. Follow Route 15 north for 8 miles and turn left on Sundays Lane. Go 2.3 miles and turn right on Opossumtown Pike. In 1 mile turn right into the parking lot at Bethel Road.

This ride reminds us of higher and more distant mountains. You enter the mountains through a cleft in the ridge, passing summer cottages and hemlocks more reminiscent of New York's Adirondacks than Maryland. The creek we ride along and the mountain laurel bring back memories of West Virginia. Mid-May is a good time to cycle this ride since many wild flowers and the mountain laurel are in bloom. Migrating birds fill the forest in spring and fall.

You begin on paved roads that head toward the ridge. The road turns to dirt in the Frederick watershed. From here you ascend a picturesque fork of Fishing Creek on well-maintained gravel roads. You then leave the creek and continue to climb to the top of the ridge where you ride through heavy woods and logged areas.

The shorter ride offers a gentle descent along a creek. The longer ride has a steeper, more adventurous descent that ends in a ford of Fishing Creek. You then continue to descend along the creek and eventually return to paved roads and your start.

There are many old logging roads that go off from the maintained gravel roads. If you feel adventurous and have a sturdy mountain bike, you might try one of these unmarked roads. As long as you stay between the gravel roads, you can't get too lost!

The ride begins in a church parking lot. Please do not use this start on Sunday mornings when the church holds services. Alternative starts are found in the watershed, on pullouts along the unpaved roads. Starting in the watershed shortens the ride and eliminates most of the paved roads.

23. Bridges to the Past (19 or 30 miles; III or IV)

Paved roads; starts at Thurmont Community Park in Thurmont, Md.: Take I-270 north to Route 15 North in Frederick. Take Route 15 north for 16.3 miles to the Thurmont exit, Route 806. At the end of the exit ramp turn right then left at the traffic light onto Route 806. In 0.5 miles turn left into the park.

Lets face it, there is something very bucolic and restful about cycling through a covered bridge. It makes you slow down a little and takes you back to a simpler era. A lime kiln ruins, a restored furnace and an impressive stone bridge stand as tributes to earlier centuries. Stone farmhouses and dairy farms dot the surrounding Frederick County countryside. The Catoctin Mountains lie to the west of you, a reminder that the real hills begin there.

The covered bridges that sit astride streams in the Frederick Valley remain popular, drawing large numbers of cyclists from Washington and Baltimore. The original rides began in Frederick and were longer than most beginning or casual cyclists wanted to tackle. We have moved the start to Thurmont to make the bridges accessible to riders not hardened to 50 miles through hills. It also avoids the growth near Frederick. And the best reason for starting in Thurmont is just down the road from the start – the Cozy Inn. It has all-you-can-eat meals with all-you-can-eat desserts, a cyclist's delight if there ever was one.

The 19 mile ride takes you through one covered bridge and Creagerstown, a pleasant rural town with a good general store. On the 30 mile ride you pass through both remaining covered bridges and the town of Lewistown. This ride also takes you over LeGore Bridge, a splendid stone bridge over the Monocacy River. On the longer ride you visit the recently restored Catoctin Furnace which made cannonballs for the Revolution and operated into the 1920s.

24. Leisurely Pursuits (36 miles; III)

Paved roads; starts at Thurmont Community Park in Thurmont, Md.: see directions in Ride #23.

When most cyclists come to the northern Frederick Valley, they don't venture further north than the covered bridges. Consequently, they miss the serene beauty that awaits them just a few miles north on Maryland's border with Pennsylvania.

Frederick County has helped by kindly paving several previously dirt roads for us to ride. You ride northeast over one of the few remaining metal truss bridges, through pleasant terrain and into Pennsylvania. You can ride 0.4 miles off the ride to the Mason Dixon Dairy on Mason Dixon Road in Pennsylvania. The dairy is open weekdays and Saturdays before noon and features "real" ice cream. You cycle north a few more miles into Pennsylvania then turn south and ride next to a quiet stream. Liberty ski area comes into view among the hills on your return to Maryland.

The town of Emmitsburg, with its closely spaced buildings on Main Street, is worth a stop. The restaurants in the center of town have warmed many a cyclist's stomach. You return to Thurmont by cutting through Mount Saint Mary's College and cycling through Roddy Covered Bridge. Don't forget the Cozy Inn for lunch, just down the road from the community park.

If you want more miles, combine this ride with the High Water Mark for a 47 mile ride. If you want fewer miles, continue straight on Harney Road at mile 15.5 and turn right on Route 140. Follow Route 140 into Emmitsburg and rejoin the ride at mile 26.3. This shortens the ride to 29 miles.

25. The High Water Mark (8 or 20 miles; III)

Paved roads; starts at the Cyclorama Center in Gettysburg, Pa.: Take I-270 to Route 15 North in Frederick. Follow Route 15 north for 33 miles into Pennsylvania. Take the exit for Route 134, Taneytown Road. Turn left at the end of the exit onto Route 134 toward Gettysburg. Follow for 2.9 miles and turn left into the Cyclorama parking lot.

No other Civil War battlefield feels quite like Gettysburg. The scope of what happened here on three hot days in July 1863 still awes us. Once on a ride with 15 cyclists, all of us became silent when we entered the battlefield. Hardly anyone spoke until well after we left. It was here, this place, that the most famous battle of the Civil War was fought. Here, a determined Union Army pushed back the Confederate tide.

Following his decisive victory at Chancellorsville, Virginia, General Robert E. Lee invaded Pennsylvania. He clashed with the Union Army, under the command of General George Meade, for three days in the fields around the hamlet of Gettysburg. When the fighting ended on July 3, 1863 both armies had lost 50,000 men. Lee withdrew into Virginia, never to threaten Pennsylvania again.

A stop at the visitor center before your ride gives an excellent overview of the battle. At any time of year you will meet many park visitors. We like to cycle this ride in the spring or late fall, preferably early in the day.

Take some time at the Virginia Memorial, the statue of Lee astride his horse on West Confederate Avenue. Here, on the third and final day of the battle, 12,000 Confederate soldiers marched across the mile of open field toward the Federal troops. The attack was as spectacular as it was doomed. Notice the cannon and trees on the far ridge. Later in the ride you will stand there and look back onto what became known as Pickett's charge.

Fall cycling in Gettysburg National Battlefield Park

The longer ride leaves the battlefield and visits the countryside to the west and south. You pass a covered bridge that sits to your left at the bottom of the long hill on Pumping Station Road. You pass the Mason Dixon Dairy, open on weekdays and from 9 a.m. to noon on Saturdays. Here you can indulge and enjoy good ice cream. Then you cycle north and return to the battlefield.

Another stop of note on the battlefield is Little Round Top with its commanding view. This area was the scene of some of the fiercest fighting on the second day of the battle. As you descend Little Round Top, the battlefield opens up before you and presents a sweeping view of the site of Pickett's Charge.

Take a final break at the High Water Mark, the place where the Union forces repulsed the Confederate attack. Over 7,500 of the 12,000 Confederates who started across the field did not return. Only 800 of Pickett's 5,000 men reported to duty the next day. On that day the Union troops celebrated their best Fourth of July since the war began and Lee began his long retreat to Virginia.

26. The Orchard Tour (29 or 37 miles; III)

Paved roads; starts at the Cyclorama Center in Gettysburg, Pa.: see directions in Ride #25.

Most people who visit Gettysburg never get far beyond the battlefield. To the west and north of town lie miles of fruit orchards. When the trees are in bloom, they delight the nose as well as the eyes. You cycle west to the base of the mountains and then north through the orchards to Orrtanna, Cashtown and Arendtsville.

If you are feeling strong at the first of the ride, continue straight over the steep hill to Orrtanna Road instead of turning right onto Railroad Lane. As you cycle through Cashtown, you turn at the historic Cashtown Inn which is said to be haunted by the ghost of a Civil War soldier. On Cashtown Road at mile 14.8 you pass a rare round barn on your right.

The shorter ride takes a more direct route back to Gettysburg while the longer ride visits more orchards and throws in a few more hills. The shorter finish travels almost two miles along a pleasant creek before turning south to Gettysburg and provides a direct finish.

27. Small Towns Tour (30, 37 or 42 miles; IV)

Paved roads; Westminster Elementary School in Westminster, Md.: Take I-270 north to Route 27 North. Stay on Route 27 for 31 miles to Westminster. Turn left on Main Street. In 0.5 miles turn left onto Uniontown Road just before Western Maryland College. Go 1.2 miles and turn left into the school.

When you are looking for a little travelled, out of the way place, consider western Carroll County. Tucked into the hills and valleys are pleasant small towns frozen in time. Country roads with little traffic link the towns and provide scenic bicycle rides.

Each town offers a different view on Maryland's rural past. The various rides visit Pleasant Valley, Taneytown, Middleburg, Union Bridge, Detour and Uniontown.

The rides go north through hilly terrain before the hills moderate. All three rides visit Pleasant Valley and Taneytown. Taneytown, the oldest town in Carroll County, dates from the 1740s. The longest ride visits Detour, a sleepy town next to the railroad tracks. The original name, Double Pipe Creek was too long for the railroad and was changed to the present name. Nobody remembers what the detour was.

The two longer rides visit Middleburg and Union Bridge, first called Buttersburg for its dairy industry. The railroad museum in Union Bridge is open Sunday afternoons between May and October. The short ride runs straight from Taneytown to rustic Uniontown, where it meets the two longer rides. Uniontown has been described as "one perfect street of homes and churches."

28. When Rail Was King (Up to 40 miles round trip; I)

Unpaved rail-trail; starts at the trail's southern end in Cockeysville, Md.: From I-695, Baltimore Beltway go north on I-83 N. In 5.8 miles take exit 20A, Shawan Road. Follow for 1.0 mile and turn right onto York Road, Route 45. In 0.3 miles, turn left onto Ashland Road. Go 0.5 mile and turn right to remain on Ashland Road at Paper Mill Road. Proceed through the subdivision to the start of the trail.

Phooey on shadeless rides during the summer months! On hot steamy days, give us the roads and trails lined by tall trees. Even better is a ride that travels along streams, giving you a place to refresh your hot feet.

The Northern Central Railroad Trail north of Baltimore offers the perfect place to ride on a hot August day. While not as well known as the C&O Canal, it is quickly being discovered for the treasure it is. The trail starts in Cockeysville north of Baltimore and follows the bed of the abandoned railroad for 20 miles, almost to the Pennsylvania border.

If we were to conjure up the perfect bike trail, it would look a lot like this one. The trail runs through beautiful, secluded valleys and along scenic streams. The trail passes through small sleepy hamlets left over from an earlier, quieter era. It is removed from reminders of the urban sprawl. In short, it offers a welcome respite from the hurley burley pace of modern life.

The railroad operated for 134 years, from 1838 to 1972, and connected Baltimore with York, Pennsylvania. It connected the rural villages along the route with Baltimore and transported their goods to Baltimore's market. During the Civil War, Abraham Lincoln rode this way to Gettysburg to deliver his Gettysburg Address. In 1865 after his assassination, the same rails transported his body to Harrisburg.

At mile seven take a break at Monkton where you find a restored train station and a small museum. Here you visit the only place with food on the trail. Throw in an extra sandwich and a candy bar if you cycle much further than Monkton. You can find water and restrooms at several places along the trail.

The trail has a well-packed, crushed stone surface that is suitable for any bike with inch and a quarter or wider tires. It is not the sort of trail where you want to push hard. Instead, the tranquility makes you want to slow down and enjoy the ride.

Be warned: the trail is being discovered. Parking lots along the lower part of the trail fill up quickly. Our advice: start early and be back by noon. That way you beat the heat as well as the crowds.

29. Rails No More (up to 27 miles roundtrip; I)

Paved rail-trail; starts along the trail or at the Park & Ride lot near the south end of the trail in Arnold, Md.: Take I-50 east over the Severn River. Take Exit 26, Route 2 North/450 South. Bear right onto 450 south toward the Naval Academy. In 0.3 miles turn right into the Park & Ride lot (easy to miss) just before Manresa Road/Boulters Way. Follow signs to the start of the B&A Trail, 0.6 mile north on Boulters Way.

The builders of rail-trails on abandoned railroad beds are learning how to do it right. The lower half of the Baltimore & Annapolis Trail is wide and travels through a wooded suburban area. The many stores and restaurants next to the trail offer much temptation to eat and shop rather than pedal.

You begin on the east side of the Severn River, east of Annapolis, and ride north through Severna Park to Glen Burnie. The southern half is the more pleasant and scenic part. The northern part of the trail travels past shopping malls and through a commercial area. This part is older and narrower than the southern section and not nearly as attractive.

30. Capital for a Day (15 or 29 miles; IV)

Paved roads; starts at Sherwood Elementary School in Sandy Spring, Md.: From I-495, Washington Beltway, take New Hampshire Ave. North, Route 650. Continue north for 10.2 miles and turn left onto Route 108, Ashton Road in Ashton. In 1.1 miles turn right into the school.

Stop for a moment and imagine the scene. Washington is in a panic. The invasion force is marching on the city, having defeated the American defenders. This could never happen, right? Well, it did, in August 1814 during the War of 1812. The British set fire to Washington, and the government fled.

President Madison escaped north along Georgia Avenue into the Maryland countryside to Brookeville, where he spent the night. Ever since, the town has been known as "Capital for a Day." Brookeville retains its 19th century charm although suburban growth has reached it.

You begin the ride in Sandy Spring, a community settled by Quakers. The short ride passes over Brighton Dam with its large azalea garden and view of Triadelphia Reservoir. The long ride circles around the reservoir into Howard County. You will find many hills on the way, especially east of the Patuxent River and near the dam. Local cyclists consider this an excellent place to work on their hill climbing techniques.

13. The Two Ferry Loop

Distance:	**10** miles
Rating:	I; Unpaved roads and unpaved C&O Canal towpath
Start:	Edwards Ferry, Md.

10 Mile Ride

0.0	L	Edwards Ferry Rd from parking lot
0.1	L	unpaved River Rd at Y; do **not** go up hill
1.5	L	River Rd at Elmer School Rd at T
5.2	L	at paved road and sign towards Whites Ferry
5.2	L	onto unpaved C&O towpath after crossing canal (Store at ferry)
10.0	R	into parking lot just after milepost 31 at Edwards Ferry

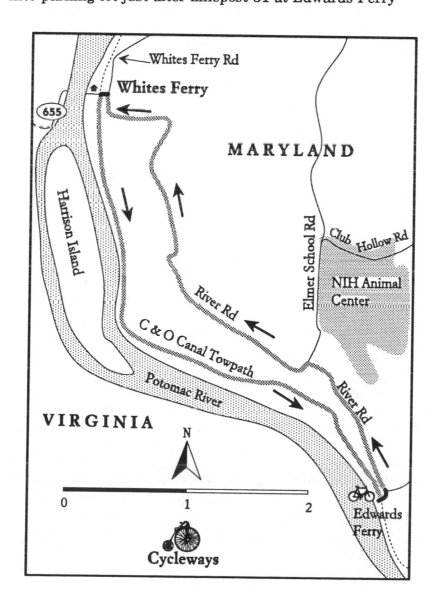

14. Back By Noon

Distance:	25 or **38** miles
Rating:	III; Paved roads
Start:	Seneca Creek Aqueduct on the C&O Canal, Seneca, Md.

38 Mile Ride

0.0	R	Rileys Lock Rd from parking lot
0.7	L	River Rd at T
0.8	R	Old River Rd (Store)
1.0	R	Montevideo Rd at T
3.2	R	Sugarland Rd at Y
4.8	L	Rte 28, Darnestown Rd at T
4.9	R	121, White Grounds Rd
6.6	BL	White Grounds Rd at Schaeffer Rd
7.5	L	Old Bucklodge La (unmarked)
9.5	L	Bucklodge Rd at T
10.1 ☞*	R	Whites Store Rd
11.9	R	Peach Tree Rd at T
12.4	L	Selman Rd at SS
13.0	L	Beallsville Rd, 109 at T

14.5	R	Big Woods Rd (Picnic lunch spot at Dickerson Park at mile 16.7)
17.0	L	Dickerson Rd, Rte 28 at T (Store)
18.2	BR	Martinsburg Rd
19.4	BR	Martinsburg Rd at Wasche Rd at Y
22.9	R	Whites Ferry Rd at T
23.1	L	Elmer School Rd
25.2	L	Club Hollow Rd
27.2	R	Edwards Ferry Rd at T
27.3	BR	Edwards Ferry Rd at Westerly Rd
28.7	L	West Offutt Rd
29.5	S	Mt Nebo Rd; becomes River Rd
37.0	R	Rileys Lock Rd
37.7	L	into parking lot

* 25 Mile Ride

11.9	L	Peach Tree Rd at T
14.5	L	Rte 28, Darnestown Rd at T (Fruit stand in season)
14.8	R	Cattail Rd
16.7	L	Cattail Rd (unmarked) at SS
16.8	L	Fisher Ave at T in **Poolesville** (Store to right)
16.9	R	Wootton Ave

17.1	L	Hughes Rd
20.1	L	Sugarland Rd; stay on Sugarland Rd
22.0	R	Partnership Rd
23.7	L	River Rd at T
24.5	R	Rileys Lock Rd
25.2	L	into parking lot

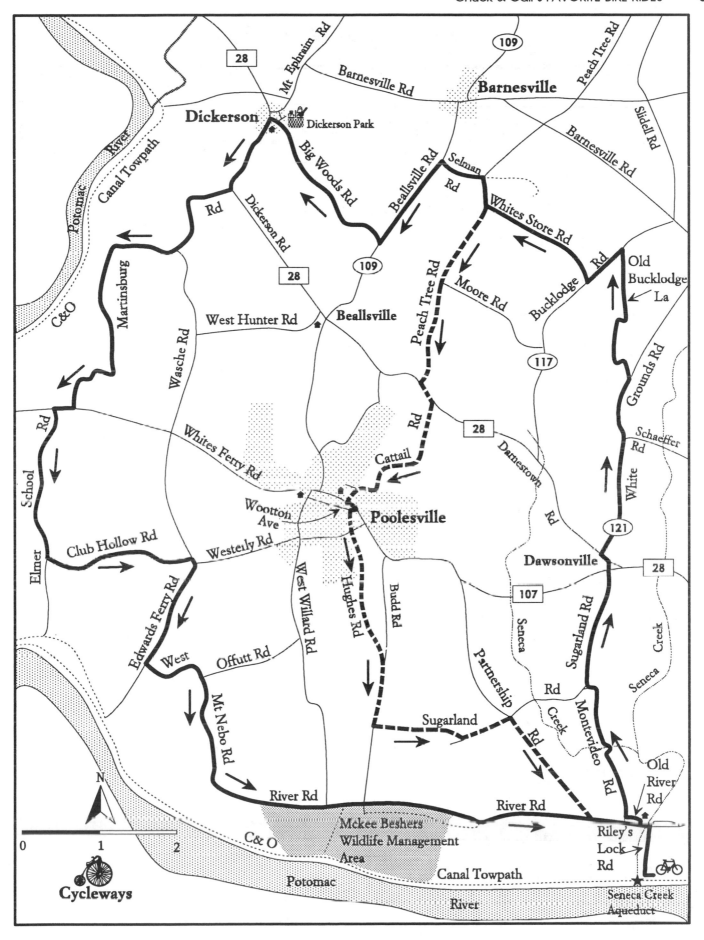

15. Shades of the Past

Distance:	12 or **22** miles
Rating:	II or III; Paved roads
Start:	Poolesville High School in Poolesville, Md.

22 Mile Ride (III)

0.0	L	West Willard Rd from parking lot behind school
0.3	R	Westerly Rd
1.7	L	Edwards Ferry Rd at T
3.1	L	West Offut Rd
3.9	S	Mt Nebo Rd; becomes River Rd
11.5	R	Riley's Lock Rd at bottom of hill
12.2		Arrive C&O Canal Park at Seneca Aqueduct (Water at lock house); Turn Around
12.9	L	River Rd at T
12.9	R	Old River Rd (Store - closed Sunday)
13.2	R	Montevideo Rd at T
15.4	L	Sugarland Rd at Y; stay on Sugarland Rd
18.5	R	Hughes Rd at T
21.5	L	Wootton Ave at T
21.9	L	West Willard Rd at T
22.1	L	into parking lot

* 12 Mile Ride (II)

7.6	L	Hughes Rd
11.8	L	Wootton Ave at T
12.2	L	West Willard Rd at T
12.4	L	into parking lot

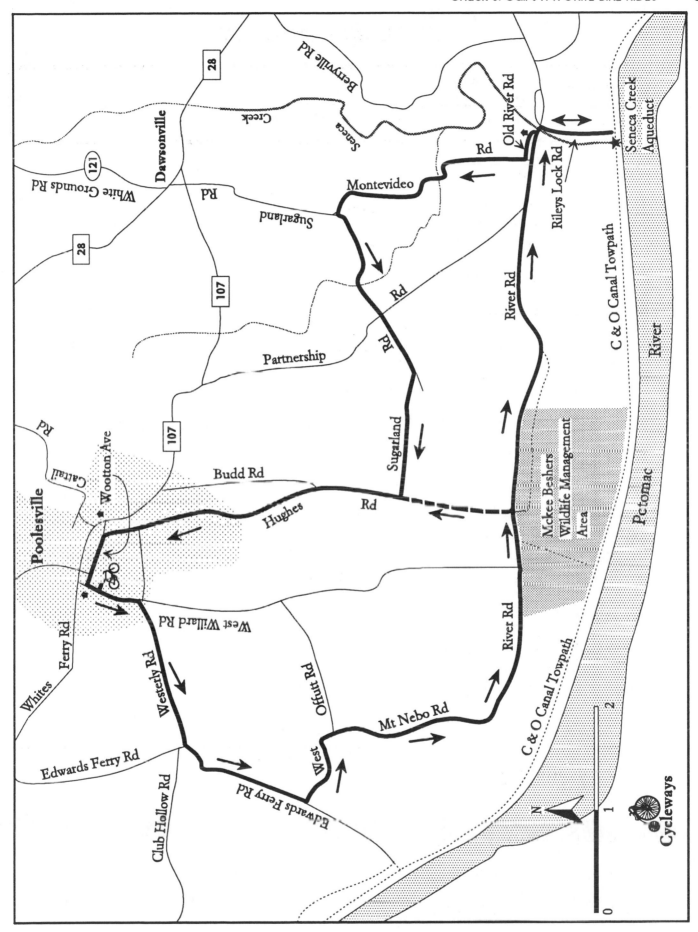

16. All Sides of Sugarloaf

Distance:	24 or **35** miles
Rating:	III or IV; Paved roads
Start:	Poolesville High School in Poolesville, Md.

35 Mile Ride (IV)

0.0	R	West Willard Rd from parking lot behind school	12.4	L	Thurston Rd, on downhill
0.1	R	Wootton Ave	17.5	L	Fingerboard Rd at Y
0.7	L	Rte 107, Fisher Ave	18.8	L	Park Mills Rd (Store in **Flint Hill**)
0.8	R	Cattail Rd	25.5	L	Dickerson Rd, Rte 28 at T (Store in **Dickerson**)
0.9	R	Cattail Rd at T	*☞		
2.8	L	Rte 28, Darnestown Rd at T	28.9	R	Martinsburg Rd
3.1	R	Peach Tree Rd	30.2	L	Wasche Rd at Y
6.2	R	Peach Tree Rd at Selman Rd crossing over RR	32.9	L	Whites Ferry Rd; becomes Fisher Ave in **Poolesville**
9.9 ☞*	L	Comus Rd	35.0	R	West Willard Rd
11.2	R	Old Hundred Rd, 109 (Store, Food)	35.2	L	into school parking lot

* 24 Mile Ride (III)

11.2	S	Comus Rd at Old Hundred Rd (Store, Food)
13.7	BL	Mt Ephraim Rd at entrance to **Sugarloaf** (optional climb up Sugarloaf adds an extra 2.5 miles)
16.5	L	Dickerson Rd, Rte 28 at T (Store) (Pick up cues in 1.2 miles at mile 28.9 on the 35 mile ride — *☞)

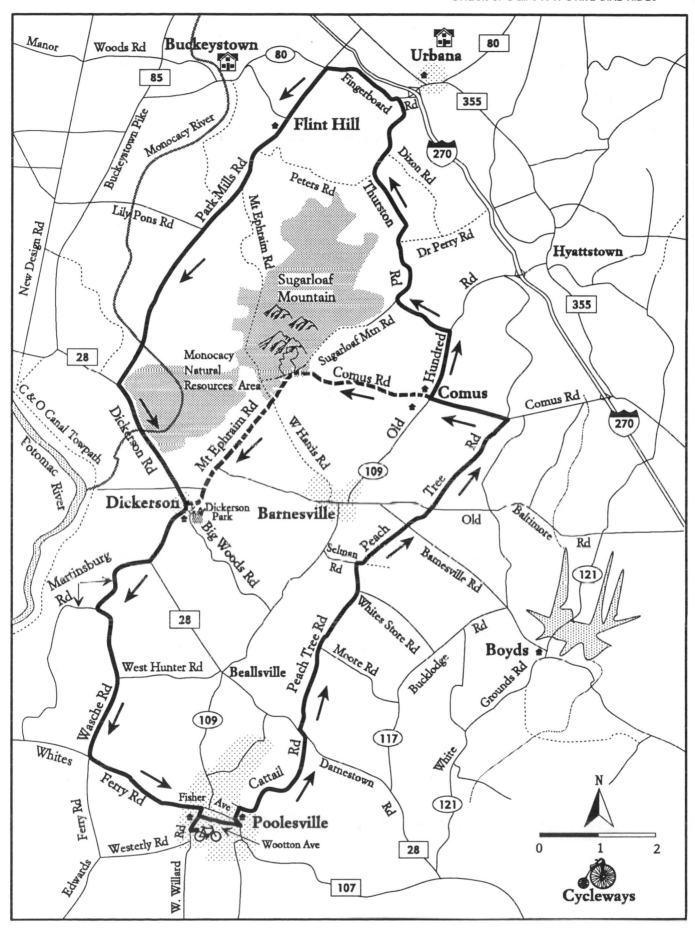

17. No Loafin'

Distance:	**12** or 15 miles
Rating:	IV; Unpaved and paved roads
Start:	Sugarloaf Mountain, Md.

12 Mile Ride

0.0	L	Sugarloaf Mtn Rd (uphill), with the entrance to Sugarloaf Mtn at your back; becomes unpaved then paved again
2.5 ☞*	L	Thurston Rd at SS
4.8	L	Peters Rd; becomes unpaved
7.0	L	Park Mills Rd at T (paved) (Store 0.3 miles to R in **Flint Hill**)
7.7	L	Mt Ephraim Rd, on the long downhill; becomes unpaved
11.5	L	Comus Rd
11.9		Arrive at parking lot

* 15 Mile Ride

3.3	R	Dr Perry Rd (unpaved)
4.0	L	Dixon Rd
4.5	R	toward Urbana Fishing Lake
5.1		Arrive at parking lot; Turn Around. Lake is 0.1 mile ahead down trail
5.7	R	Dixon Rd (unmarked) at T; becomes paved
7.1	L	Thurston Rd at T
7.4	BR	Peters Rd; becomes unpaved
9.7	L	Park Mills Rd (paved) (Store 0.3 miles to R in **Flint Hill**)
10.4	L	Mt Ephraim Rd on the long downhill; becomes unpaved
14.2	L	Comus Rd
14.6		Arrive at parking lot

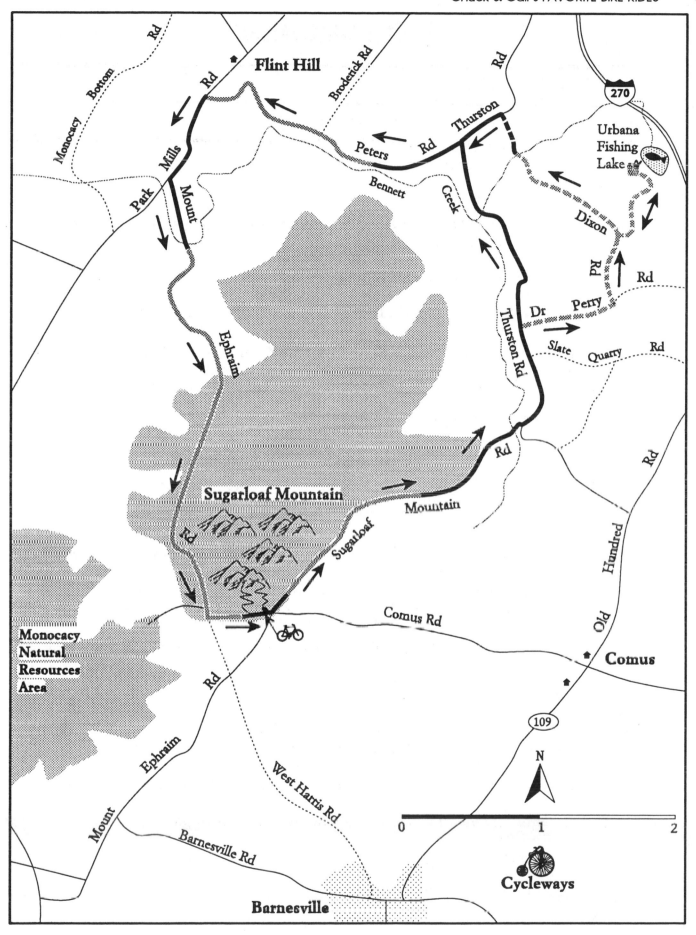

Flint Hill

Monocacy Bottom Rd

Broderick Rd

270

Thurston Rd

Urbana Fishing Lake

Peters Rd

Park Mills Rd

Mount

Bennett

Creek

Dixon Rd

Perry Rd

Dr

Slate Quarry Rd

Ephraim

Thurston Rd

Sugarloaf Mountain

Rd

Mountain Rd

Sugarloaf

Monocacy Natural Resources Area

Comus Rd

Old Hundred Rd

Comus

109

Ephraim Rd

Mount

West Harris Rd

N

0   1   2

Barnesville Rd

Cycleways

Barnesville

18. Half & Half

Distance:	**26** miles
Rating:	IV; Unpaved C&O Canal towpath, unpaved and paved roads
Start:	Monocacy Aqueduct on the C&O Canal near Dickerson, Md.

26 Mile Ride

0.0   L   unpaved C&O Canal towpath, past barrier at end of parking lot

6.3   R   Whites Ferry Rd, first paved road (store); cross river on the ferry (50¢) and continue onto paved road (unmarked 665)

7.7   R   Rte 15, James Monroe Hwy at T (⊗, use unpaved shoulder)

9.2   L   unpaved 661, Montresor Rd; stay on 661

12.3   R   paved 662, Stumptown Rd at T

12.9   L   paved 663, New Valley Church Rd

13.5   BR   paved 663, Taylorstown Rd at 673, Bald Hill Rd

14.7   BL   unpaved 663, Taylorstown Rd at 664, Wilt Store Rd; steep hill; becomes paved on downhill

16.5   R   unpaved 665, Furnace Mountain Rd (Store in **Taylorstown** 0.2 mile ahead on 663)

18.8   R   paved 672, Lovettsville Rd at SS

18.8   L   Rte 15, James Monroe Hwy at T (⊗, use sidewalk across bridge)

19.2   R   Rte 28 in **Point of Rocks**

19.3   R   Commerce St (Stores); follow paved road across RR tracks

19.4   L   Around gate onto C&O Canal, just past bridge

25.6   L   into parking lot after crossing Monocacy Aqueduct

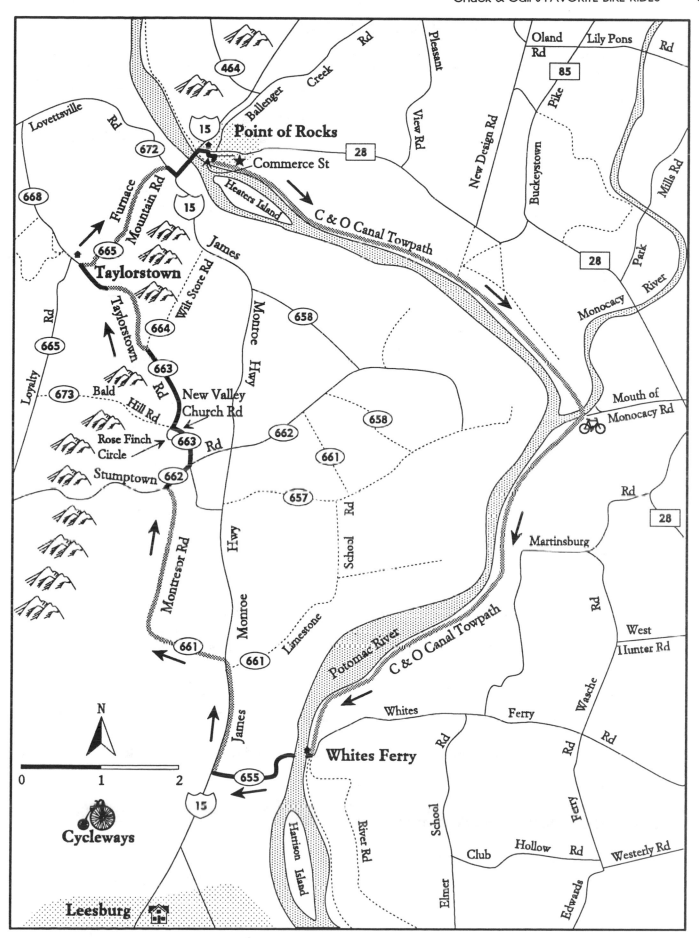

19. A Bit of Everything

Distance:	**23** or **30** miles
Rating:	II or IV; Paved roads
Start:	Point of Rocks Train Station in Point of Rocks, Md.

23 Mile Ride (II)

0.0	L	Rte 28 from train station
0.2	R	Ballenger Creek Rd (Water on corner)
5.4	L	Cap Stine Rd
9.7	R	Elmer Derr Rd at Rte 340
12.2	R	New Design Rd (unmarked) at T
☎*		
15.6	R	Adamstown Rd
16.4	L	Mountville Rd at T in **Adamstown** (Food/Store)
17.6	R	New Design Rd
20.1	R	Rte 28 (unmarked) at SS
23.3	L	into train station parking lot

---

* 30 Mile Ride (IV)

14.4	L	Manor Woods Rd (unmarked) at SS, 1st crossroads
15.5	S	Michaels Mill Rd (unmarked) at Rte 85 in **Buckeystown** (Store)
16.7	L	80, Fingerboard Rd at T
18.7	R	Park Mills Rd at top of hill (Store at mile 21.1 in **Flint Hill**)
22.1	R	Lily Pons Rd (unmarked) after long downhill; becomes Oland Rd
24.6	L	New Design Rd (unmarked) at T
27.1	R	Rte 28 (unmarked) at SS
30.3	L	into train station parking lot

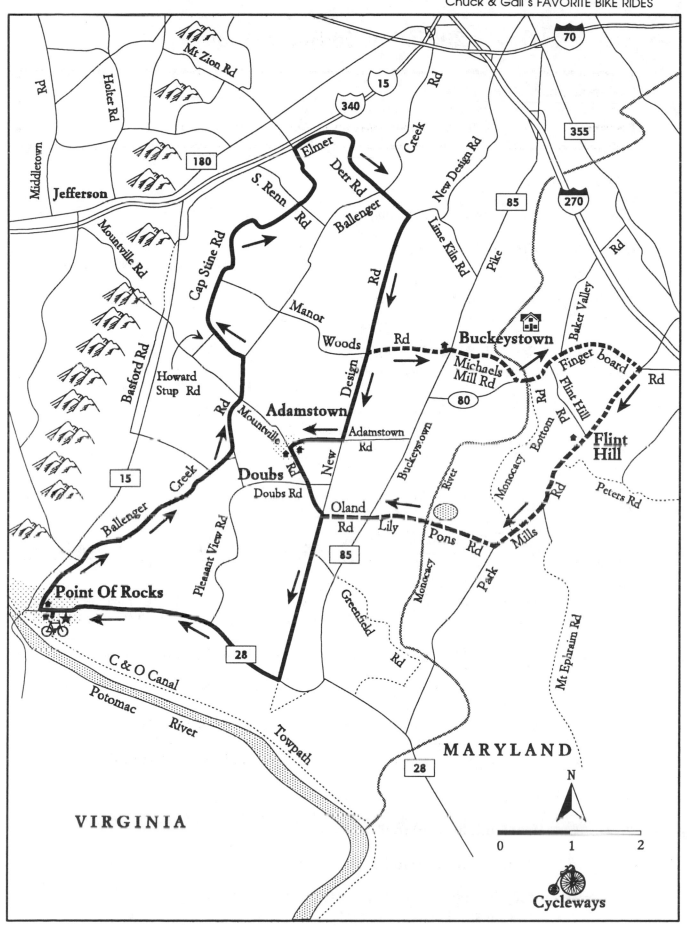

20. Hill Climber's Delight

Distance:	30 or **40** miles
Rating:	V; Paved roads with several climbs
Start:	Point of Rocks Train Station in Point of Rocks, Md.

40 Mile Ride

0.0	L	Rte 28 from parking lot		24.5	BR	Main St (unmarked) at SS in **Middletown** (Store)
0.3	L	Rte 15 at T ⊗		24.7	R	South Church St, Rte 17, at TL
0.7	R	672, Lovettsville Rd in Va.; becomes 673 in **Lovettsville** (Store)		25.3	L	Old Middletown Rd
7.0	R	Rte 287, Berlin Pike ⊗ (Store/Food); becomes Rte 17, Petersville Rd in **Brunswick, Md.**		25.7	R	Roy Schafer Rd
				26.2	L	Bussard Rd
				26.7	R	Old Middletown Rd at T
10.9	S	79, Petersville Rd at TL (Store/Food 0.2 mile to R on 464)		30.7	L	180 (unmarked) at T in **Jefferson** (Store)
				*☞		
12.7	L	180 at T		31.1	R	Lander Rd (Food)
13.0	R	Catholic Church Rd		31.3	L	Mountville Rd after Rte 340 (Store/Food)
☜*						
15.7	L	Gapland Rd (Store in **Burkittsville**-closed Sunday)		33.3	R	Basford Rd, just before Rte 15 on downhill
18.1	R	Arnoldstown Rd at top of climb (Water, Restrooms)		36.5	R	Ballenger Creek Rd at T
20.3	L	Picnic Woods Rd at T		40.0	L	Rte 28 (unmarked) at T in **Point of Rocks** (Store)
22.8	R	Bidle Rd; becomes Walnut St		40.2	R	into train station parking lot

---

* 30 Mile Ride

15.7	R	Gapland Rd
17.9	S	383, Broad Run Rd at St Marks Rd
20.2	L	180, Jefferson Pike (Store at mile 20.9) (Pick up cues in 0.8 miles at mile 31.1 on the 40 mile ride – *☞)

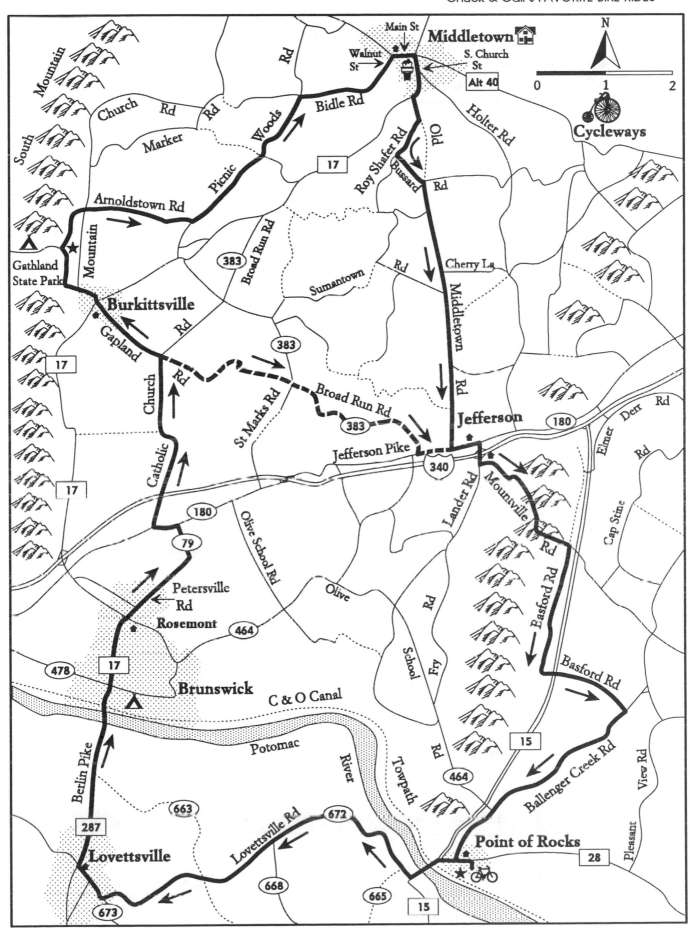

21. Catoctin Climber

Distance:	47 or **48** miles
Rating:	V: Paved roads
Start:	Waverly Elementary School in Frederick, Md.

49 Mile Ride

0.0	L	Waverly Dr from school
0.2	L	Shookstown Rd (unmarked) at T
0.6	L	Bowers Rd
1.6	R	Rte 40 at T (use shoulder)
5.1	L	Hollow Rd at Rosebud Ct on the downhill; then ...
5.1	R	Hollow Rd (unmarked) at SS
6.3	S	Hollow Rd at Rte 40
7.4	R	Harmony Rd; **Caution**-SS at bottom of hill
10.1	R	Wolfsville Rd (unmarked) at T; then ...
10.1	R	17, Wolfsville Rd after bridge (Store at mile 13.4-closed Sunday)
15.0	R	Stottlemeyer Rd in **Wolfsville** (Store-closed Sunday)
15.2	L	Brandenburg Hollow Rd
18.0	R	Garfield Rd (unmarked) at T
18.7	L	Stottlemeyer Rd at T; becomes Foxville-Deerfield Rd at Rte 77
21.6	BR	Foxville-Deerfield Rd at Herman Hauver Rd
	🚃*	
21.7	BL	Foxville-Deerfield Rd
22.2	BR	Foxville-Deerfield Rd at Foxville Church Rd

25.8	R	550 at T; becomes Church St in **Thurmont** (Food & Stores); becomes 806
30.8	R	Frederick St (unmarked) at Park La & Water St
31.2	L	Moser Rd (Food)
32.9	R	Hessong Bridge Rd
	*☞	
37.1	S	Hessong Bridge Rd at SS at Angleberger Rd (Store at mile 37.3 in **Lewistown**)
39.0	S	Hansonville Rd at Rte 15
39.1	R	Mountaindale Rd
39.5	L	Masser Rd
41.2	L	Opossumtown Pike (unmarked) at T
41.3	R	Opossumtown Pike
42.1	R	Walter Martz Rd
43.3	R	Walter Martz Rd at Poole Jones Rd
44.2	S	Rocky Springs Rd
44.8	L	Rocky Springs Rd at Indian Springs Rd
46.3	R	Kemps Lane
47.5	L	Shookstown Rd at T
47.8	R	Waverly Dr (unmarked)
48.0	R	into school parking lot

---

* 47 Mile Ride

21.7	BR	Manahan Rd into park
22.5	R	Park Central Rd (unmarked) at SS
26.2	R	Rte 77, Foxville Rd at T (Water at Visitors Center)
26.4	L	Catoctin Hollow Rd

32.9	R	Rte 15 ⊗; use shoulder
33.6	L	806
33.9	R	Blacks Mill Rd
35.1	R	Hessong Bridge Rd (Pick up cues in 1.5 miles at mile 37.1 on the 49 mile ride – *☞)

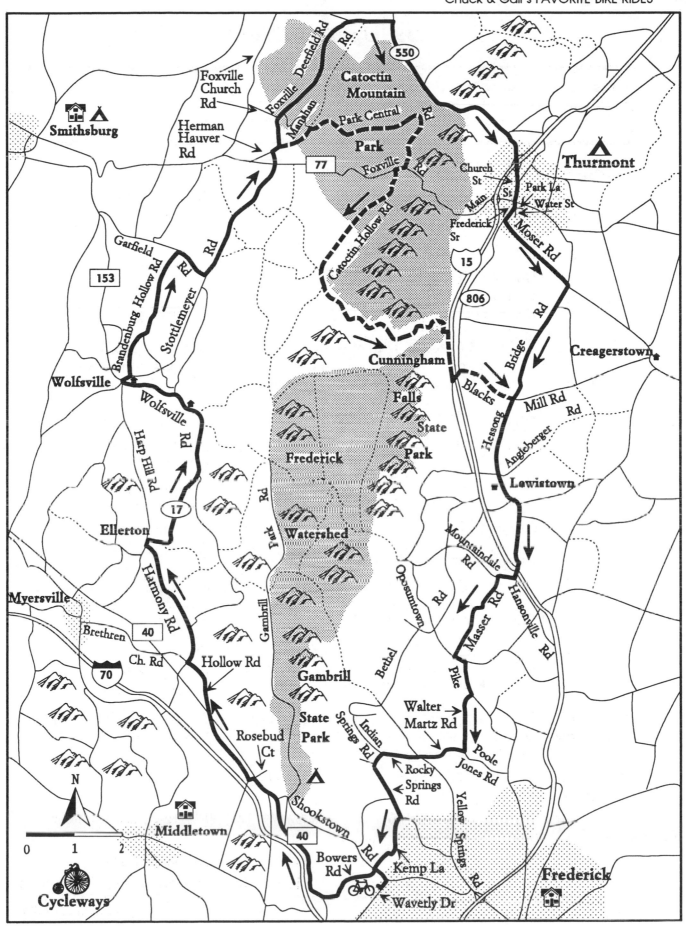

22. Up The Creek

Distance:	**13** or 15 miles
Rating:	IV; Mostly unpaved roads
Start:	Bethel Lutheran Evangelical Church in Bethel, Md.

13 Mile Ride

0.0   S   Putman Rd (paved) toward mountains

1.4   L   Mountaindale Rd at T (Store)

1.5   L   Mountaindale Rd at Putman Rd at Y (becomes unpaved in the watershed)

2.6   BR   Right Hand Fork Rd at Y past reservoir (not well marked)

5.4   The blue blazed Catoctin Trail crosses and goes to the right. If you follow it for 0.1 mile, leave your bike at the clearing and walk another 0.1 mile down the narrow foot trail, you come to a nice rocky overlook.

☞ *

7.2   L   Step Creek Rd (unmarked - the first maintained gravel road to the left; the microwave tower is in sight to the right); becomes Left Hand Fork Rd; follow it downhill and out of the watershed; becomes paved Mountaindale Rd

11.9   R   Mountaindale Rd at SS

12.0   R   Putman Rd (Store)

13.4   L   into parking lot

---

* 15 Mile Ride

8.3   S   Gambrill Park Rd (paved) at Mink Farm Rd

9.3   L   Delauter Rd (unpaved) (long downhill)

10.7   R   Step Creek Rd (unmarked) at T after ford; becomes Left Hand Fork Rd; becomes paved Mountaindale Rd

13.4   R   Mountaindale Rd at SS

13.5   R   Putman Rd (Store)

14.9   L   into parking lot

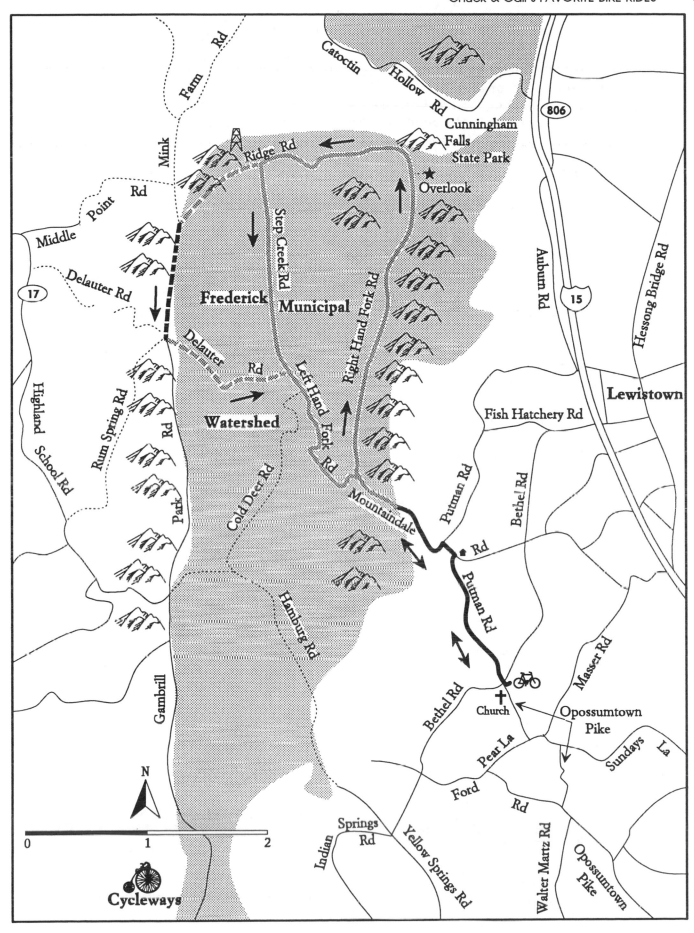

Catoctin Hollow Rd

806

Cunningham Falls State Park

Farm Rd

Mink

Ridge Rd

★ Overlook

Auburn Rd

15

Hessong Bridge Rd

Middle Point Rd

Step Creek Rd

Frederick Municipal

Right Hand Fork Rd

Lewistown

17

Delauter Rd

Delauter Rd

Fish Hatchery Rd

Highland School Rd

Rum Spring Rd

Left Hand Fork Rd

Watershed

Putman Rd

Bethel Rd

Park

Cold Deer Rd

Mountaindale

Rd

Putman Rd

Masser Rd

Gambrill

Hamburg Rd

Church ✝

Opossumtown Pike

Sundays La

Bethel Rd

Pear La

N

Ford Rd

Walter Martz Rd

Opossumtown Pike

Springs Rd

0   1   2

Indian

Yellow Springs Rd

Cycleways

23. Bridges To The Past

> **Distance:** 19 or **30** miles
> **Rating:** III or IV; Paved roads
> **Start:** Thurmont Community Park in Thurmont, Md.

30 Mile Ride (IV)

0.0	L	Frederick St, 806 from park
0.1	S	Park La at SS at Water St; follow road as it bends to the left and becomes Center St
0.3	R	Main St at SS
0.4	L	Carroll St
1.0	L	Apples Church Rd; becomes Roddy Rd
2.9	R	Old Kiln Rd
5.4	R	76, Motters Station Rd (unmarked) at T
6.3	BR	76, Motters Station Rd; becomes Longs Mill Rd
🖛*		
10.8	L	Legore Bridge Rd
12.2	R	Legore Bridge Rd (unmarked) at Legore Rd at T, after stone bridge
14.1	R	Steiner Smith Rd; becomes Dublin Rd
16.9	R	Links Bridge Rd (Spring on left)
17.4	L	Ramsburg Rd (unmarked); 1st left
19.5	L	Old Frederick Rd at T
19.8	R	Utica Rd
20.9	R	Hessong Bridge Rd at T (Store at mile 21.6 in **Lewistown**)
21.6	S	Hessong Bridge Rd at Angelberger Rd
23.3	L	Blacks Mill Rd (unmarked), 1st cross road, after metal bridge
24.4	R	806, Catoctin Furnace Rd (unmarked) at T
25.2	R	Kelly's Store Rd
27.0	L	Hessong Bridge Rd (unmarked) at SS
27.9	L	Moser Rd at SS
29.7	R	Frederick St, 806 at SS in **Thurmont**
29.9	L	into Community Park

* 19 Mile Ride (III)

12.4	BL	Longs Mill Rd at New Cut Rd
13.7	S	Blacks Mill Rd in **Creagerstown** (Store)
15.2	R	Layman Rd
17.0	R	Hessong Bridge Rd at T
17.4	L	Moser Rd at SS
19.2	R	Frederick St, 806 at SS in **Thurmont**
19.4	L	into Community Park

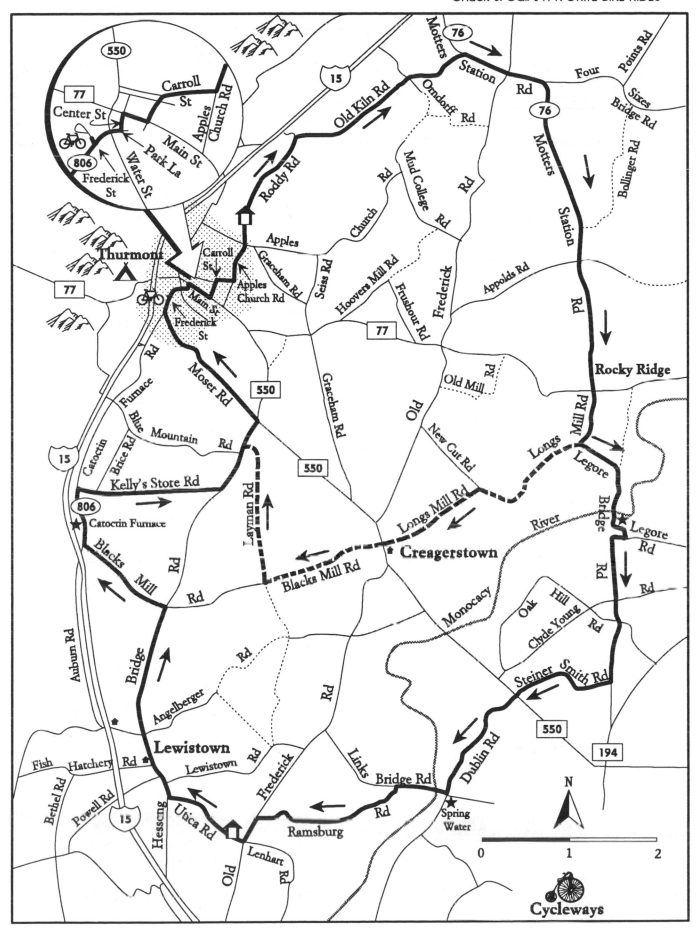

Cycleways

24. Leisurely Pursuits

Distance:	**36** miles
Rating:	III; Paved roads
Start:	Thurmont Community Park in Thurmont, Md.

36 Mile Ride

0.0	L	Frederick St from park
0.1	S	Park La at SS at Water St; follow road as it bends to the left and becomes Center St
0.3	R	Main St at SS
0.4	L	Carroll St
1.0	L	Apples Church Rd at SS
1.3	R	Apples Church Rd at Roddy Rd
1.4	BL	Apples Church Rd at Graceham Rd
3.8	R	Mud College Rd at T
5.0	L	Old Frederick Rd at T
7.2	R	76, Motters Station Rd (unmarked) at SS
7.6	BL	Four Points Rd as 76 swings right
8.6	L	Four Points Rd (unmarked), 1st left
9.7	R	Keysville Rd at SS
9.8	L	Simmons Rd
10.6	L	Toms Creek Church Rd (unmarked); 2nd left, at church
12.0	R	Rte 140 (unmarked) at T
12.5	L	Bollinger School Rd
14.3	L	Bullfrog Rd
15.2	L	Harney Rd at SS
15.5	R	Bullfrog Rd (unmarked) at sign toward Mason Dixon (Mason Dixon Dairy is 0.4 miles to R on unmarked Mason Dixon Rd - mile 16.2)
18.0	R	Business 15 at T; cross over Rte 15
18.3	L	Bullfrog Rd
20.8	L	Pumping Station Rd (unmarked) at SS
21.6	L	Middle Creek Rd
22.2	R	Wenschhof Rd
23.5	L	Tract Rd at SS (Food at mile 25.1)
25.8	L	Rte 140 (unmarked) at T (Store) (Store at mile 26.1)
26.3	R	Mountain View Rd (unmarked; sharp right at WW1 statue) in **Emmitsburg** (Food ahead at TL)
26.5	BL	Annandale Rd
27.5	BL	Annandale Rd at Hampton Valley Rd
28.9	BR	through iron gate into college as road swings left; follow road across campus
29.1	L/R	at SS, toward tin-sided gym
29.2	L	through parking lot around front of gym
29.3	R	exiting parking lot through gate onto St Anthony's Rd (unmarked)
30.6	S	Orndorff Rd at Rte 15
31.2	R	Old Kiln Rd at SS
32.8	L	Roddy Rd at T
34.7	R	Carroll St at SS in **Thurmont**
35.3	R	Main St, 77
35.4	L	Center St; becomes Park La as road bends to right
35.6	S	Frederick St at SS
35.7	R	into Community Park

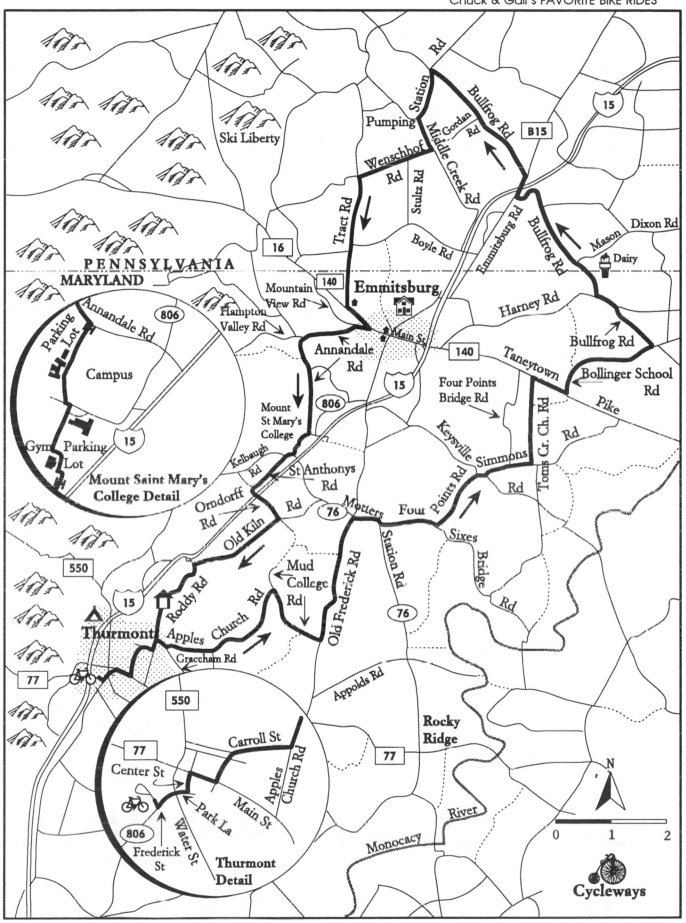

Ski Liberty

PENNSYLVANIA
MARYLAND

Station Rd

Bullfrog Rd

15

B15

Pumping

Gordan Rd

Middle Creek Rd

Wenschhof Rd

Stultz Rd

Tract Rd

16

Boyle Rd

Emmitsburg Rd

Bullfrog Rd

Mason

Dixon Rd

Dairy

140

Mountain View Rd

Emmitsburg

Flampton Valley Rd

Harney Rd

Bullfrog Rd

Annandale Rd

Main St

140

Taneytown

Bollinger School Rd

806

Annandale Rd

15

Pike

Four Points Bridge Rd

Parking Lot

Annandale Rd

806

Campus

Keysville

Simmons

Toms Cr. Ch. Rd

Rd

Gym   Parking Lot

15

Mount Saint Mary's
College Detail

Mount St Mary's College

Kelbaugh Rd

St Anthonys Rd

Orndorff Rd

Old Kiln Rd

76

Motters

Four Points Rd

Sixes

Bridge

Rd

550

Mud College Rd

Station Rd

15

Roddy Rd

Old Frederick Rd

76

Thurmont

Apples   Church Rd

77

Graccham Rd

Appolds Rd

Rocky Ridge

550

77

Carroll St

77

Center St

Apples Church Rd

Main St

77

Park La

806

Water St

River

Frederick St

Monocacy

Thurmont Detail

N

0   1   2

Cycleways

25. The High Water Mark

Distance:	8 or 20 miles
Rating:	III; Paved roads
Start:	Cyclorama Center in Gettysburg, Pa.

8 Mile Ride

0.0	L	Taneytown Rd from Cyclorama; becomes S Washington St (Town Traffic)
0.9	L	W Middle St, Rte 116 at 2nd TL
1.5 ☎*	L	W Confederate Ave (unmarked) at 2nd TL at top of hill
4.4	S	S Confederate Ave at Bus 15; becomes Sedgewick Ave then Hancock Ave
7.3	BL	at Y at Pennsylvania Monument (unmarked Hancock Ave)
8.0	R	At SS at T and into parking lot
8.1		Arrive at parking lot

* 20 Mile Ride

3.6	R	Millerstown Rd (unmarked), first crossroad, at SS; becomes Pumping Station Rd
7.7	L	Bullfrog Rd after Cunningham Rd (not well marked)
10.1	R	Bus 15, Emmitsburg Rd at T
10.5	L	Bullfrog Rd after Rte 15
12.2	L	Mason Dixon Rd (unmarked, at sign to Mason Dixon) (ice cream at Mason Dixon Dairy at mile 12.6 - closed Sundays and Saturday afternoons)
13.8	L	Barlow Rd
16.0	L	Rte 134, Taneytown Rd (unmarked) at T
17.8	L	Wright Ave, 1st crossroads past Rte 15, to enter battlefield
18.4	R	Sedgewick Ave at SS; becomes Hancock Ave
19.7	BL	at Y toward Pennsylvania Monument (unmarked Hancock Ave)
20.4	R	at SS at T and into parking lot
20.5		arrive at parking lot

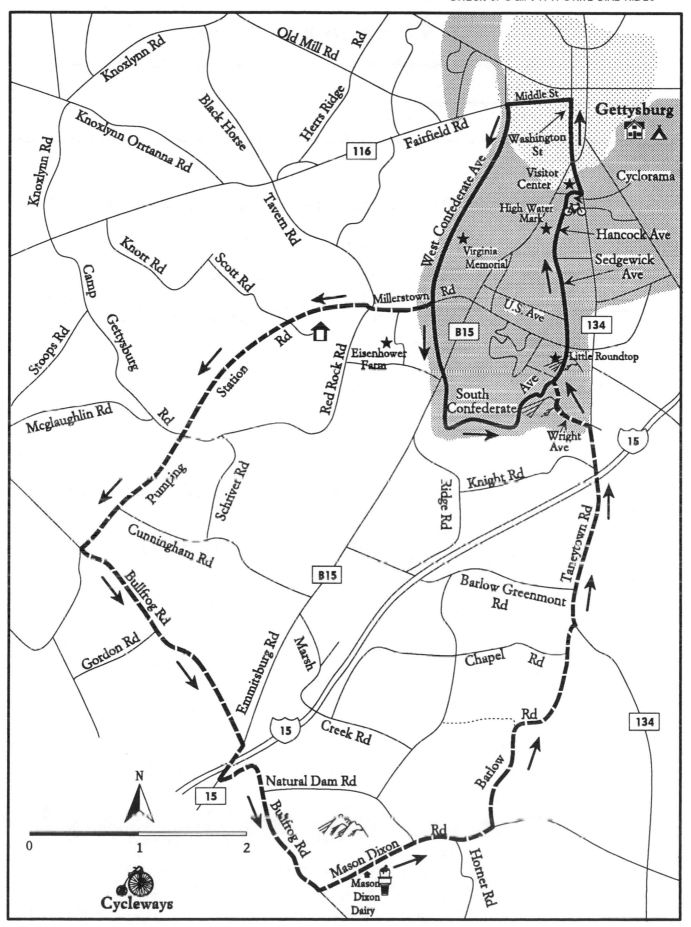

26. The Orchard Tour

Distance:	**29** or 37 miles
Rating:	III; Paved roads
Start:	Cyclorama Center in Gettysburg, Pa.

29 Mile Ride

0.0	L	Taneytown Rd, Rte 134 from Cyclorama (Town Traffic)
0.9	L	W Middle St, Rte 116
2.1	R	Old Mill Rd at State Police
4.3	L	Knoxlyn Rd (unmarked) at T
6.1	R	Knoxlyn-Orrtanna Rd at T
7.3	R	Railroad La, before steep hill
9.6	L	Orrtanna Rd at T
9.8	R	towards Orrtanna, before RR
10.2	R	Mt Carmel Rd at RR tracks (Store on right 0.4 mile ahead-closed Sundays)
11.0	R	Mt Carmel Rd at T
12.3	L	Orrtanna Rd at Y at SS
13.3	L	Old Rte 30 at T; **Cashtown**
13.4	R	High St (unmarked); 1st R
14.1	S	Cashtown Rd at Rte 30
15.3	L	Boyer Nursery Rd
18.0	R	Narrows Rd, Rte 234 (unmarked) at T; becomes High St in **Arendtsville**
18.9	L	Main St, Rte 234 (Store)
19.0	R	Gettysburg St
19.3	L	Cherry St
20.1	R	Ziegler Mill Rd
21.5	R	Russell Tavern Rd
24.8	L	Mummasburg Rd at T (unmarked)
27.2	L	Lincoln Ave at T in **Gettysburg**
27.4	R	N Washington St (unmarked); becomes Rte 134
28.7	R	into Cyclorama parking lot

* 37 Mile Ride

18.9	L	into store at Main St
18.9	R	High St, Rte 234 from store
19.5	R	Brysonia Rd
20.4	BR	Quaker Valley Rd (unmarked) as main road bears left
23.8	L	Rte 34, Carlisle Rd (unmarked) at T
23.9	R	Orchard La (unmarked)
25.8	R	Center Mills Rd at T
26.9	R	Old Carlisle Rd at T
29.7	BL	394, Table Rock Rd (unmarked) at Y
30.1	S	Table Rock Rd (unmarked) as 394 bears left
34.7	L	Rte 34, Biglersville Rd ⊗
35.3	R	Broadway in **Gettysburg**
35.4	L	N Washington St (unmarked); becomes Rte 134
36.9	R	into Cyclorama parking lot

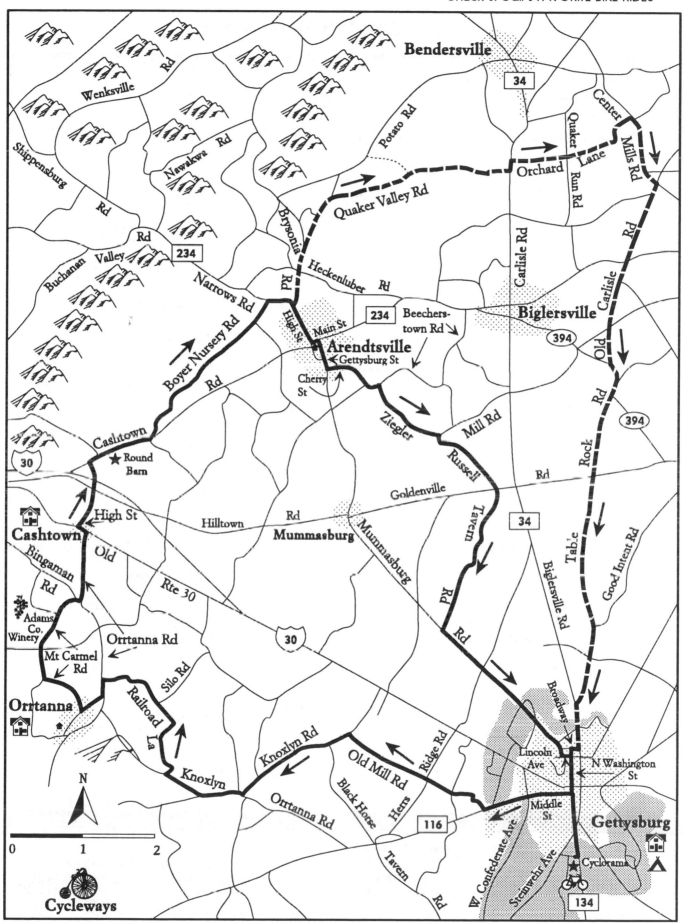

27. Small Towns Tour

Distance:	30, **37** or 42 miles
Rating:	IV; Paved roads
Start:	Westminster Elementary School in Westminster, Md.

37 Mile Ride

0.0	L	Uniontown Rd from school	17.6	L	Harney Rd at T
0.2	R	Royer Rd	18.4	L	W Baltimore St in **Taneytown** ⊗
0.7	L	Rte 140 (⊗; use shoulder)			☛*
1.3	R	Hughes Shop Rd	18.8	R	Rte 194 at TL (Food, Store)
4.5	L	Pleasant Valley Rd at SS			☛**
4.7	R	Halter Rd in **Pleasant Valley** (Store-closed Sunday)	19.4	BL	Crouse Mill Rd
			24.0	L	Middleburg Rd
			**☛		
8.3	L	Mayberry Rd (Store to right in **Silver Run**)	24.6	R	Bucher John Rd; becomes W Locust St in **Union Bridge**
10.4	R	Babylon Rd	27.3	L	Main St (Food, Store)
10.4	L	Krump Station Rd	27.8	S	Union Bridge Rd (unmarked) at Rte 75
11.6	S	at Stone Rd	28.1	R	Bark Hill Rd
11.7	L	Krump Station Rd at T	30.8	R	Middleburg Rd
13.8	S	Teeter Rd at Rte 194	31.4	S	Uniontown Rd in **Uniontown**
14.7	L	Ruggles Rd	36.7	R	into school parking lot
15.7	L	Walnut Grove Rd at T			

* 30 Mile Ride

18.8	S	E Baltimore St at Rte 194 (Food, Store)	24.5	L	Uniontown Rd at T in **Uniontown**
19.1	BR	Trevanion Rd; becomes 84	29.7	R	into school parking lot

** 42 Mile Ride

20.7	R	Keysville Rd	26.4	L	Detour Rd at T in **Detour** (Store)
24.2	S	Keysville Rd at Keysville Bruceville/Keysville Fred. Co. at SS (**Caution-RR tracks on long downhill**)	28.3	S	Middleburg Rd at Rte 194 (Store) (Pick up cues in 2.0 miles at mile 24.6 on the 37 mile ride – **☛)

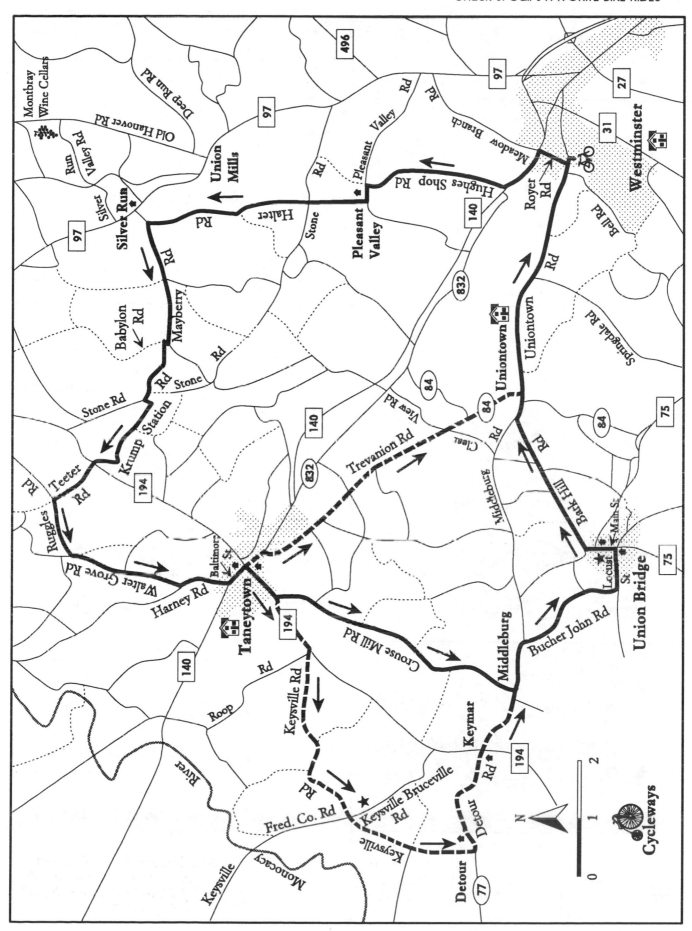

Cycleways

28. When Rail Was King

Distance:	Up to **40** miles roundtrip
Rating:	I; Unpaved rail-trail
Start:	Trail's southern end in Cockeysville, Md.

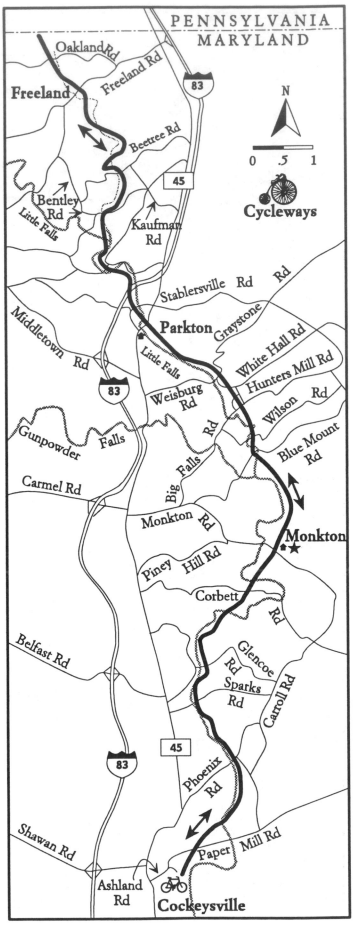

29. Rails No More

Distance: Up to **27** miles roundtrip
Rating: I; Paved rail-trail
Start: Park & Ride lot near the trail's southern end in Arnold, Md.

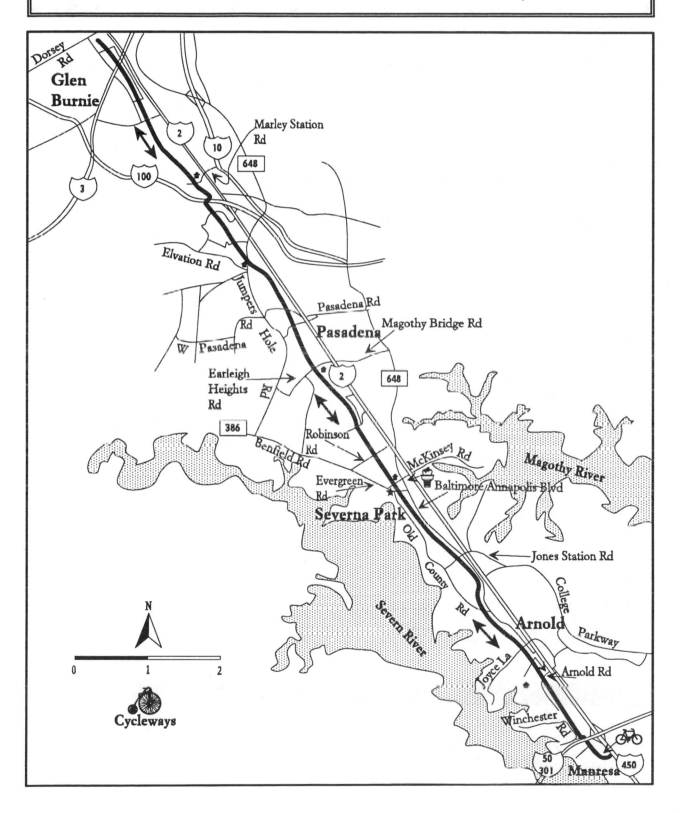

30. Capital for a Day

Distance:	15 or **29** miles
Rating:	IV; Paved roads
Start:	Sherwood Elementary School in Sandy Spring, Md.

29 Mile Ride

0.0	L	Rte 108 ⊗ from parking lot
0.3	L	Brooke Rd (Store)
2.5	L	New Hampshire Ave at SS
2.6	R	Haviland Mill Rd
☞ *		
5.6	R	Brighton Dam Rd at T
5.7	L	Nichols Dr
6.4	L	Highland Rd at T
7.2	L	Triadelphia Mill Rd
8.8	R	Green Bridge Rd at bottom of hill at T
8.9	L	Triadelphia Mill Rd; becomes Triadelphia Rd
12.7	L	Roxbury Rd
14.3	L	Roxbury Rd at T at Dorsey Mill Rd
14.8	L	Rte 97 at T (⊗; use shoulder)
16.3	R	Jennings Chapel Rd
16.6	L	Howard Chapel Rd
18.9	R	Sundown Rd (unmarked) at T
19.3	L	Zion Rd
22.1	L	Brookeville Rd
24.4	R	Georgia Ave, Rte 97 at SS
24.6	R	Georgia Ave, Rte 97 at top of hill in **Brookeville**
25.1	L	Goldmine Rd
26.7	R	Chandlee Mill Rd on the downhill
27.9	R	Brooke Rd at T
29.1	R	Rte 108 ⊗ in **Sandy Spring** (Store)
29.4	R	into school parking lot

* 15 Mile Ride

5.6	L	Brighton Dam Rd at T
10.4	L	Rte 97 in **Brookeville**
11.0	L	Goldmine Rd
12.6	R	Chandlee Mill Rd on the downhill
13.8	R	Brooke Rd at T
15.0	R	Rte 108 ⊗ in **Sandy Spring** (Store)
15.3	R	into school parking lot

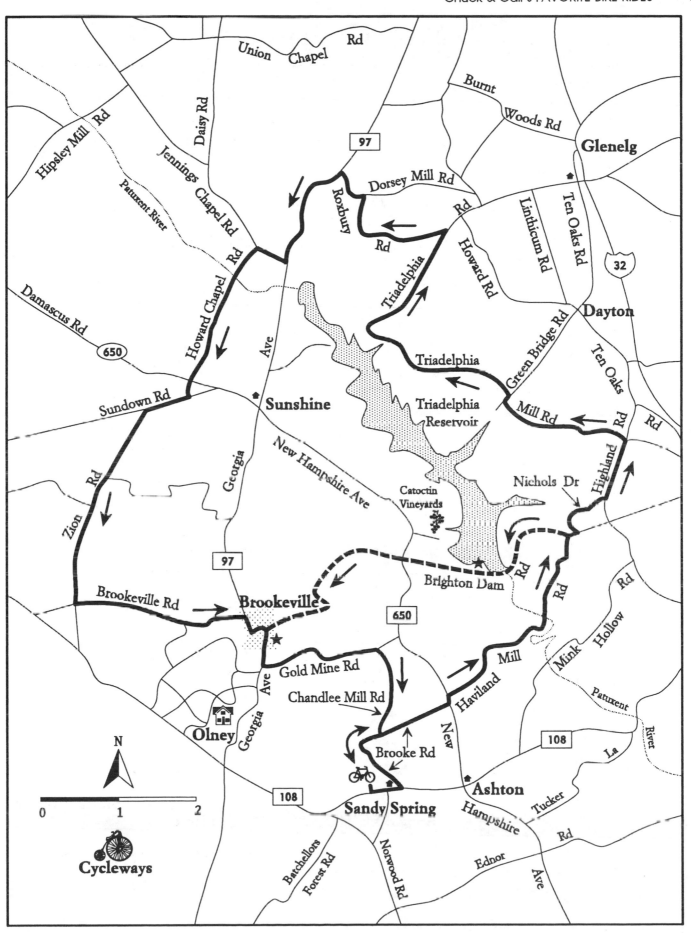

HORSE COUNTRY

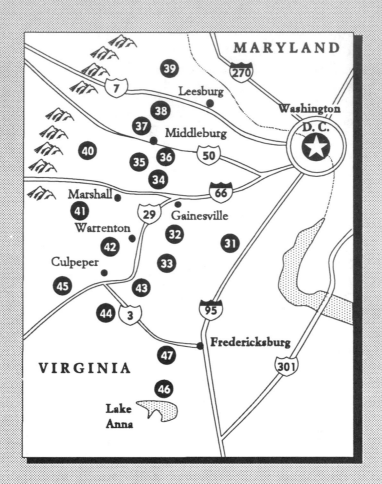

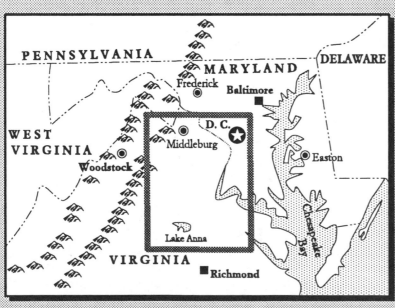

Lying west of Washington, just beyond its grasp, exists a different world. There survives a place most of us city dwellers only dream about. People of untold wealth live in sprawling estates. Horse farms and fields abound. Quaint, rustic towns sit quietly underneath wooded ridges. Abandoned farms give way to forests. And miles of quiet road beckon.

Cyclists consider this diverse area one of the crown jewels of Mid-Atlantic cycling. Horse country offers picturesque towns, large estates, horse farms, vineyards, miles of country lanes and good views of the ridges and hills. The well-kept yet rustic appearance makes the area appear much further removed from metropolitan Washington than it is.

In the north lies hunt country, home to large horse farms and estates. To the south you cycle past working farms and through miles of woods and abandoned farms, where Civil War armies fought and marched. Along the western edge you meet the foothills and climbs of the Blue Ridge Mountains, which offer stiff challenges and good vistas.

Middleburg, the unofficial capital of hunt country, draws crowds of visitors on weekends. Its main street becomes jammed with traffic, yet its historic buildings, a grocery store with chandeliers, fine restaurants and a bakery provide tempting stops for cyclists. Near Middleburg the cyclist finds quiet country lanes, both paved and unpaved. Some of the most tranquil cycling is found on the many unpaved roads that weave throughout the countryside around the town.

North of Middleburg, Purcellville boasts many beautiful Victorian homes dating from the era when the W&OD Railroad brought people escaping Washington's summer heat. Now the W&OD Trail brings people escaping Washington's urban sprawl. Dotted around hunt country are many quaint villages and hamlets: Hillsboro, Waterford, Bluemont, The Plains and Unison, to name a few.

The entire village of Waterford is on the National Historic Register. Bluemont, nestled at the base of the Blue Ridge, was the original terminus of the W&OD Railroad. Marshall provides a good start for exploring the area near the Blue Ridge Mountains.

On the western edge of horse country you approach the Blue Ridge Mountains. Here you find several challenging yet beautiful rides. You can tackle long, stiff climbs onto the Blue Ridge, enjoying thrilling descents and fine views. One of the hardest rides in the book, *The Blue Ridger*, climbs to the top of the Blue Ridge Mountains and then follows its spine. You can ride into the foothills near Hume, Orlean, Flint Hill or Syria, climbing many long hills as you near the base of the Blue Ridge. While this area is tough, you are amply rewarded by the great scenery and quiet country roads.

The rolling plains around Culpeper, Remington and Nokesville offer delightful cycling through working farm country. This area became a staging ground for both armies during the Civil War, and many fierce battles and engagements took place here. For the finest vista found on any ride in the book, cycle to the top of Clark Mountain, a lookout used by General Robert E. Lee.

In the south of horse country the countryside flattens to gentle rolling plains and farm country. Near Fredericksburg you find miles of abandoned farms that have returned to woods. Lake Anna and its swimming beach beckons on hot summer days. Civil War enthusiasts can spend days exploring the battlefields of Chancellorsville, The Wilderness and Spotsylvania Courthouse.

31. Prince William Forest Park (12 miles; III)

Paved roads; starts at Pine Grove Picnic Area in Prince William Forest Park in Triangle, Va.: Take I-95 south to Route 619, Triangle. Go west on Route 619 for 0.2 mile. Turn right into the park and go 0.5 mile. Turn left into the Pine Grove Picnic Area.

Prince William Forest Park gives an example of how nature reclaims exhausted farmland when it is given a chance. Farmers had worked the area within the park since colonial days. Since becoming a park in 1933, a dense forest has grown up and covered the land. Admission to the park is $3.00 per car or $1.00 per bicyclist if you arrive by bicycle.

Within the park lies a nature center, picnic areas and camping grounds. The park has little traffic and offers a good place for family riding. Stronger cyclists often use the park for training loops.

The ride we describe uses the paved roads within the park. The southeastern part of the loop and the out-and-back section are hillier than the northern part of the loop.

Within the park are several unpaved fire roads open to cycling. We have shown these fire roads on the map, but have not mapped out any particular loops for you. The hiking trails are closed to cyclists. If you wish to explore, bring your mountain or hybrid bike and strike out on the fire roads. These provide several out-and-back unpaved rides which you can connect with sections of the paved roads.

32. West of Nokesville (30 or 43 miles; II)

Paved roads; starts at Brentsville Regional High School in Nokesville, Va.: Take I-66 west to exit 43A, Route 29 South in Gainesville. Go 0.4 mile and turn left onto Route 619, Linton Hall Road. Go 6.0 miles and turn right on Route 28. Go 3.2 miles and turn left on Route 652 in Nokesville at the traffic light. Go 2 miles, turn right on Aden Road and then left into the high school.

Once, when trying to describe the charms of the Nokesville area, a longtime area cyclist exclaimed, "the area is pure vanilla, and *everyone* loves vanilla!" Yes, vanilla it is. Nothing earth-shaking, but an area you always return to. And so it remains a favorite area for bicyclists.

The countryside features gently rolling terrain and wide-open space. This ride goes south from Nokesville through several small towns such as Aden and Elk Run. The variation shortens the ride by going through sleepy Bristersburg. Sometimes a country store and a place name on a map are the only evidence that a community exists.

33. Rural Pleasures (17, 30 or 46 miles; II)

Paved roads; H.M. Pearson Elementary School in Calverton, Va.: Take I-66 west to exit 43A, Route 29 South in Gainesville. Go 0.4 mile and turn left onto Route 619, Linton Hall Road. Go 6.0 miles and turn right on Route 28. Go 10 miles and turn right onto 603 in Calverton. Go 0.9 miles and turn right into the school.

We hate to admit it, but we associate riding these nice roads with exhaustion. Our introduction to this area was on club century rides, 100 mile excuses for masochism. Whenever we ride through Remington, we remember working hard to stay with an equally tired group of riders. We didn't *see* the interesting buildings and the sleepy town until we slowed down and rode on our own. At Casanova, we remember thinking about the start of the hills rather than the friendly general store that always welcomes cyclists.

This area has changed little over our cycling careers and we do enjoy returning, although at a pace slower than those century rides. You begin in a bucolic setting and find lovely rural roads on all the variations. All three rides visit Casanova Store and Neavils Mill, pleasant places for stops.

34. Through Bull Run Mountain (10, **16** or 26 miles; II or III)

Paved roads with 0.2 miles of unpaved road; starts at The Plains Library in The Plains, Va.: Take I-66 west to exit 31, Route 245 to The Plains. Follow Route 245 north for 1.3 miles and turn right on Route 55 at the T in The Plains. In 0.1 miles turn left on Route 626, Loudoun Avenue. Go 0.1 miles and turn left onto Route 804, Stuart Street, before the railroad tracks. Park along the railroad tracks.

Bull Run Mountain presented a barrier to east-west travel for the early settlers. During the Civil War, General Stonewall Jackson used the railroad through Thoroughfare Gap to move his troops to Manassas for the Battle of First Manassas. This was the first use of the railroads to transport troops during war. One year later Jackson led his troops by foot through the same gap to surprise the Union army in the Battle of Second Manassas.

On the first loop of this two loop ride, you cycle east from The Plains through Hopewell Gap. You then return via Thoroughfare Gap. A key section of road through Hopewell Gap was paved several years ago, opening the ride to skinny-tired bicycles. There are still 0.2 miles of unpaved road on this loop.

As you cycle into Thoroughfare Gap, you pass Beverley's Mill to your right, across I-66. Slave labor built the mill before 1749 with stone quarried from the mountain. The mill supplied food for five wars: French and Indian, Revolutionary, War of 1812, Mexican and Civil Wars.

Returning to The Plains, you find satisfying stops at the restaurant and nearby store. Good food is available in The Rail Stop, one of the village's two restaurants. After eating, decide whether or not you will ride the second 10 mile loop. On this loop you sample the charms of hunt country. You cycle past horse farms, a practice track and several large estates. If you only want a gentle, short ride, cycle just this loop.

Where do I go from here? The Plains, Va.

35. Horse Heaven (19, **27** or 34 miles; III or IV)

Paved Roads; starts at The Plains Library in The Plains, Va.: see directions in Ride #34.
    Most cyclists regard the area between The Plains, Middleburg and Marshall to be *the heart* of hunt country. Somewhat less hilly than the area north of Middleburg, this area offers a good introduction to the enchantment of scenic hunt country. We offer three loops of varying distance. Leaving The Plains (named White Plains before the Civil War), you cycle north to Middleburg which is the unofficial capital of hunt country. On the way you pass Piedmont Vineyards which is usually open for visitors and wine tasting. Middleburg offers several restaurants, a tasty bakery and a grocery store with chandeliers.
    The longer rides visit the town of Marshall, originally named Salem. On the longest ride you visit Rectortown and pass the home (private) of John Marshall, the famous Chief Justice.   All three rides pass elegant horse farms and offer good views of Bull Run Mountain to the east and the Blue Ridge Mountains to the west. After the ride, The Rail Stop restaurant in The Plains offers a congenial atmosphere and good fare.

36. The Hunt Scene (**14** or 22 miles; III & IV)

Mostly unpaved roads; Middleburg Elementary School in Middleburg, Va.: Take I-66 west to exit 31, Route 245 to The Plains. Follow Route 245 north for 1.3 miles and turn right on Route 55 at the T in The Plains. In 0.1 miles turn left on Route 626, Loudoun Avenue, and follow it 8.1 miles into Middleburg. Turn right on Route 50, Washington Street, and left onto Route 626, Madison Street, at the traffic light. Go 0.1 mile and turn right into the school.
    Scenic unpaved roads lie all around Middleburg. The area abounds with unpaved roads that pass working horse farms and estates. Passing the Middleburg shop that gives this ride its name, you explore the area immediately to the south of the town.
    On the shorter ride, you cycle by Meredyth Vineyards, one of the area's larger wineries and always a fine place for a visit. The longer ride explores the area to the east and north of Middleburg and goes near Swedenburg Estate Vineyard on Route 50. The longer ride is rather hilly with several long climbs and descents. The views, however, are superb. There are no stores on either of these two rides.

37. The Stable Tour (9, 14, **20** or 26 miles; III)

Mostly unpaved roads; starts at Banneker Elementary School in St. Louis, Va.: Take I-66 west to exit 31, Route 245 to The Plains. Follow Route 245 north for 1.3 miles and turn left on Route 55 at the T in The Plains. In 1.0 mile turn right onto 704. Go 1.8 miles and turn right onto 709 at T. Continue for 6.2 and turn left onto Route 50, John Mosby Highway at T. Follow for 2.1 miles and turn right onto 611, St. Louis Road. In 2.1 miles turn right onto 744, Snake Hill Road in St. Louis. In 0.2 miles turn right into the school.
    To discover the full flavor of hunt country, you have to get off the macadam and onto the dirt roads. On dirt you feel closer to the horses, the farms and the stables. You are more likely to meet people on horseback. This ride offers the opportunity to slow down a lot and really leave the city behind.
    Starting northwest of Middleburg, the ride explores the area between Middleburg and the base of the Blue Ridge Mountains. It passes many horse farms and stables and offers

good views of the mountains. You encounter most of the hills near the beginning and end of the ride. The longer rides flatten out somewhat in the middle.

The two longer rides visit Unison, a peaceful hamlet that is always a pleasure to visit. We have wanted to offer a ride through Unison for years. We got tired of waiting for the county to pave the roads through Unison and pulled out the wide-tired bikes. As a result, we were rewarded with one the prettiest rides on unpaved roads in the entire region.

38. Horse Hills (18, 31 or 43 miles; IV)

Paved roads; starts at Middleburg Elementary School in Middleburg, Va.: see directions in Ride #36.

Hill climbers savor the northern heart of hunt country between Middleburg and Purcellville. Flatlanders avoid it. Middleburg was a stagecoach stopover halfway between Alexandria, Va. and Winchester, Va. in the Shenandoah Valley. Today it has a quaint feel and many unique shops. Several restaurants and a local bakery offer places to celebrate the end of the ride or to prepare for it.

On this ride you pass many horse farms and large estates. You also climb many hills. The 31 mile ride runs directly to Purcellville before returning to Middleburg. The longest ride goes north to Round Hill and Hillsboro, offering fine views of the Blue Ridge Mountains. South of Purcellville, both longer rides pass through Lincoln, a town rich in Pennsylvania Quaker tradition. The shortest ride visits the village of Philomont with its attractive country store.

39. Waterford Wanderer (35 miles; IV)

Paved roads and a section of the paved W&OD Trail; starts at Loudoun Valley High School in Purcellville, Va.: Take Route 7 northwest to Purcellville. Exit onto Route 287 and turn left at the end of the exit ramp toward Purcellville. In 0.7 miles turn right onto Business 7, Hurry Byrd Highway at the T. Go 0.8 miles and turn right onto 727, Maple Avenue. In 0.4 miles turn right into the school.

Waterford is so picturesque that the entire town is on the National Historic Register. Its shaded streets encourage you to glide slowly through town, enjoying the interesting homes and buildings. Several other picturesque towns await you on this ride – Purcellville, Paeonian Springs, Taylorstown, Lovettsville and Hillsboro. You begin on the W&OD Trail and then use country roads for the rest of the ride.

Founded by Quakers, Waterford's citizens refused to send militia aid to the Revolutionary War. During the Civil War, Waterford sent troops to aid the Union while the rest of Virginia turned to the Confederacy. When the W&OD Railroad bypassed Waterford, the town become an attractive backwater

One of our favorite roads, Route 665, runs north from Waterford along the base of Catoctin Mountain. The hills on this road offer a great roller coaster ride. You enjoy sweeping downhill runs, coasting part way up the next hill before having to work again. A long, brown fence sits along the side of the road and marks one of the largest horse farms in the area. The work you do on this road is rewarded by fine views of the valley.

You return by cycling south along the base of Short Hill to Hillsboro. The town has attractive stone buildings and sits in a scenic spot in a gap in the ridge known as Short Hill. Hillsboro is the birthplace of the mother of those famous bicycle makers, Orville and Wilbur Wright.

40. The Blue Ridger (56 miles; V)

Paved roads with sections of busier roads; starts at Marshall Community Center in Marshall, Va.: Take I-66 west to exit 28, Routes 17/Business 17 to Marshall/Warrenton. Go North on Business 17 into Marshall for 0.7 miles. Go straight at Main Street and in 0.1 miles turn right into the community center.

What we remember most about this ride are the descents – 50+ mph full tuck descents, the kind where the eyes tear and where you want wrap-around sunglasses and dependable equipment. You work hard for these few moments of thrills, but the payback is worth it.

The Blue Ridger has a good blend of length, two hard climbs and screaming descents, as well as shorter hills and beautiful countryside and views. Since we published it in our first Virginia guidebook, this tough and scenic ride has become a classic among stronger cyclists.

Cycling north from Marshall, you ride through some of the prettiest countryside in Northern Virginia. Rokeby farms on Route 623 has its own airfield and is famous for its mares and stallions. All the time you keep the Blue Ridge Mountains in view as a reminder of where you will soon be cycling. The moderately hilly terrain warms you up for the climbs to come.

At Airmont you turn west to Bluemont, a hamlet tucked into the base of the ridge. You then climb onto the Blue Ridge. There are few reprieves on this climb as the road twists onto the ridge at Snickers Gap. Your final 1.2 miles of climbing confronts you as you turn onto Route 601 at the top of the gap.

Bloomfield, Airmont and Bluemont offer the last stores before the first climb and are good places to load up on energy. We recommend you take a short stop at Airmont and carry food with you. Then take a longer break atop the ridge on the side of the road, after the first climb.

You cycle south for 11 miles along the undulating spine of the ridge, occasionally getting good views. The descent to Ashby Gap and Route 50 twists and turns and takes good handling skills. If you need refueling, stop at the restaurant in the gap.

On Routes 50 and 17 near Paris you meet some high speed traffic. The fact that you are attempting this ride means that you probably have the skills to handle riding with traffic. The ride uses short portions of several busy roads (Routes 7, 17, and 50) to get on and off the Blue Ridge.

Heavily treed, the second climb on Route 688 never offers a clue where you are on it until near the top. It then offers good views and a thrilling descent. You plummet past Naked Mountain Vineyard and into Markham.

You then follow Route 55 and I-66 frontage roads back to Marshall. Several hills remain to challenge you. In time Marshal will appear and you can find refreshments to replenish lost fluids. And of course trade stories with your riding companions about how easy the ride was today and how strong you felt.

41. Tally Ho! (25 or 38 miles; IV)

Paved roads; starts at Marshall Community Center in Marshall, Va.: see directions in Ride #40.

Before Interstate 66 was built, you could not safely cycle the first nine miles of this ride to Markham. Today, the cars have abandoned Route 55, a scenic way into the heart of the Blue Ridge Mountains, for the parallel interstate. The town of Markham is a reminder of Northern Virginia's rural past. As recently as four years ago, VISTA Volunteers worked

Springtime in Virginia's horse country

to develop the water system. Most of the houses in town remain without running water.

You turn south at Markham and climb a long but mild grade with good vistas of the mountains around you. You then descend through the wide-open space of horse country and arrive at the placid hamlet of Hume.

From Hume the shorter ride travels on a newly paved road back to the I-66 frontage road (old Route 55) and Marshall. The longer ride seeks dense woods and many more hills. You turn north on Route 690 and cycle along the scenic but hilly west flank of Rappahannock Mountain to Marshall.

The roads on this longer ride appear unchanged from the Civil War when Jackson's army marched through the area before the Battle of Second Manassas. His men marched 60 miles in two days, completely around the Union Army. Be thankful for your modern bicycle when you ride these roads.

42. Blue Ridge Views (60 miles; V)

Paved roads; starts at the municipal parking lot in Warrenton, Va.: Take I-66 west to exit 43A, Route 29 South in Gainesville. Take Route 29 for 11.5 miles and exit on business 29/15 to Warrenton/Winchester. In 0.8 miles at the first traffic light turn left on Blackwell Road (becomes Alexandria Pike) toward downtown Warrenton. In 1.0 miles turn right onto Main Street toward business 211. In 0.1 mile turn left onto Ashby Street and follow it into the parking lot.

If you don't mind lots of hills, you will be rewarded by the scenery on this picturesque ride. On almost the entire ride you have good views of the Blue Ridge Mountains and its foothills. You cycle west from Warrenton through Orlean to Flint Hill and the apple orchards nestled at the base of the Blue Ridge. There you turn south and cycle through

Ben Venue to Rixeyville, encountering long hills and excellent views. From Rixeyville you return northeast to Warrenton through relatively flatter terrain, past well-kept estates.

This ride illustrates the growing popularity of cycling. On a hot day last summer four of us stopped at the isolated store in Ben Venue. As we waddled in with our cleated cycling shoes, the owners looked up, smiled, and immediately pointed the way to the cold juices.

43. Battle of Brandy Station (20 or 32 miles; II)

The 32 mile ride is paved and the 20 mile ride has mostly unpaved roads; starts at Margaret M. Pierce Elementary School in Remington, Va.: Take I-66 west to exit 43A, Route 29 South in Gainesville. Follow Route 29 for 24 miles to Remington and turn left onto business 29 into Remington, just past Route 28. Go 1.4 miles and turn right into the school.

The town of Brandy Station saw a fierce cavalry battle on June 9, 1863. Federal cavalry surprised J.E.B. Stuart and proved they had become the equal of the Confederate cavalry. Today, Brandy Station has become the site for another type of battle, the preservationists versus the developers.

Both rides begin in Remington which was known as Rappahannock Station during the Civil War. They travel through a lightly rolling plain that is a delight to cycle. On the longer ride (all paved) you ride through the small towns of Elkwood and Brandy Station. You will pass the scene of some of the fiercest fighting near Fleetwood Hill, just before reaching Brandy Station. You cross the Rappahannock River at Kelly's Ford, one of the crossings for the Federal Cavalry and a popular spot for fishermen and canoeists. You then return to Remington through easy terrain.

The shorter ride travels mainly on dirt roads. It travels easterly on Route 672, one of the approach routes of the Federal Cavalry. At mile 15.3 on Route 674, north of Kelly's Ford, you pass a large dirt parking lot to the right. If you go past the gate and cycle 0.4 mile along a dirt forest road, you come to a monument to Confederate John Pelham.

44. Lee's Lookout (47 or 51 miles; III or V)

Paved roads; starts at Floyd T. Binns School in Culpeper, Va.: Take I-66 west to exit 43A, Route 29 South in Gainesville. Take Route 29 for 33.5 miles to the Culpeper exit, Business 15/29. Go into Culpeper for 3 miles and turn right on Main Street, Route 229 North. Go 0.4 miles and turn right on Radio Lane. Turn right into the school parking lot.

Dominating the surrounding countryside, Clark Mountain was an important Confederate lookout during the Civil War. It offers the best view of the Virginia piedmont and was used several times by Robert E. Lee. Here in May 1864 he watched General Ulysses Grant's Union Army begin its march to the south. This marked the beginning of the end for the Confederacy. Within a year, Lee would surrender to Grant at Appomattox. To reach the view from the top of Clark Mountain on the longer ride you ascend a challenging two-mile grade. You ride through woods and fruit orchards on the climb, and, when you finally arrive on top, enjoy a tremendous panorama.

Culpeper saw a large amount of activity during the Civil War. Robert E. Lee's Army of Northern Virginia camped repeatedly in the area. The Battle of Cedar Mountain in 1862, west of Mitchell, was the opening battle in the campaign that led to the battles of Second Manassas and Antietam. Brandy Station, north of the ride, saw a fierce cavalry battle in 1863. The Union Army camped around Stevensburg in the winter before Grant's final campaign. The stores in Rapidan and on Route 522 make pleasant rest stops.

View of the Blue Ridge Mountains on the *Base of Old Rag* ride

45. Base of Old Rag (28 or 40 miles; III)

Paved roads; starts at Waverly Yowell Middle School in Madison, Va.: Take I-66 west to exit 43A, Route 29 South in Gainesville. Follow Route 29 for 55 miles. Turn right onto Business 29 toward Route 231 North into Madison. Go 0.9 miles and turn left into the school at Route 231 North.

On this ride you taste the Blue Ridge Mountains without meeting its long hills. You ride north to Haywood which boasts one of the smallest post offices in Virginia. From Haywood you turn toward the Blue Ridge Mountains and cycle along two beautiful mountain streams, the Robinson River and the Rose River. You arrive in the town of Syria at the base of Old Rag Mountain. Graves Mountain Lodge in Syria offers a delectable weekend buffet. However, it does get busy and reservations are recommended. From here, you can continue west for 1.7 miles, following signs to Rose River Vineyards.

You return to Haywood by cycling next to a very pretty section of the Robinson River. You then cycle through wooded countryside, around a large foothill and again over the Robinson River, eventually returning to Madison. The shorter ride cuts off the section along the mountain streams on the way to Syria, the most scenic part of the ride.

46. Thru the Big Woods to Lake Anna (46 or 52 miles; II)

Paved roads; starts at Spotsylvania County Courthouse in Spotsylvania, Va.: Take I-95 south to Route 1 North towards Fredericksburg. Go 1.3 miles and turn left on Route 208. Go 6 miles into Spotsylvania and turn left into the county courthouse.

Head for this ride on a hot day. It was known as "gold hill" in the last century due to extensive mining activity. Locals now call it "the big woods." Lake Anna State Park on the shores of Lake Anna is your destination as you wander through the big woods. Lake

Anna is free for cyclists and costs $3.00 per car. It offers swimming, picnicking and a visitor center with exhibits about the area. Warmed by a nuclear power plant a few miles away, Lake Anna boasts the only heated lake in Virginia.

The swimming at Lake Anna and the shade found along the way make this ride attractive on a hot summer day. The only stores are passed after you leave the lake, not before. The longer ride crosses two arms of the lake before joining the main ride on its return to Spotsylvania. You pass Spotsylvania Courthouse Battlefield Park (water, exhibit and $1.00 entrance fee) just before returning to the start.

47. Stonewall's Last Ride (6 or 13 miles; II)

Longer Ride – paved & unpaved roads; shorter ride – paved roads; starts in Chancellorsville Battlefield Park Visitor Center in Chancellorsville, Va.: Take I-95 south to Rte 3 West toward Culpeper. Follow for 8.3 miles and turn right into the Visitor Center.

As you cycle past Wilderness Church on your ride around Chancellorsville Battlefield, stop for a moment and try to picture the scene at six p.m. on May 2, 1862. The Union soldiers were cooking dinner and not expecting any more fighting that day. Suddenly, wild animals, flushed from the woods by Confederate troops, began bounding into the clearing past the startled Union soldiers. The animals were followed by 26,000 confederate soldiers charging down the Orange Turnpike and out of the dense woods along the road.

In May 1863, Robert E. Lee engineered his greatest victory over the Union Forces at Chancellorsville, Virginia. Although outnumbered, he sent General Thomas "Stonewall" Jackson and the greater part of his army on a 12-mile march around the Union forces. Stonewall Jackson attacked in the evening and caught the Union army by surprise.

The National Park Service preserves Jackson's route mostly as it was at the time of the battle, a dirt road through dense woods. Beginning at the visitor center, you first cycle on paved roads. The shorter ride stays on paved roads and bypasses most of Jackson's march.

At mile 9.4 on the longer ride we deviate from Jackson's route by turning south on Brock Road, Route, 613 and then left onto Route 600, a mostly dirt road. Jackson continued north on Brock Road and then east on the Orange Turnpike, the present Route 3, to begin his attack. Our variation bypasses new development and a long section on busy Route 3.

When you reach busy Route 3, you turn right and ride one mile on the dirt shoulder to return to the visitor center. The Confederates began their charge to your left and continued east along Route 3, rolling over the Union forces. In a short distance you pass Wilderness Church on the north side of the road. Only the late hour of the attack and the arrival of darkness prevented a complete Union defeat.

Although a great victory for the South, the battle was a costly one. Later that evening, while scouting between the lines of the two armies, Jackson was mistakenly shot by his own men. When he died eight days later, the South lost one its best generals. As you turn left into the battlefield at the finish of the ride, pause for a moment. There stands a solitary stone monument to Jackson, at the place he fell.

31. Prince William Forest Park

Distance:	**12** miles
Rating:	III; Paved roads
Start:	Pine Grove Picnic Area in Prince William Forest Park in Triangle, Va.

12 Mile Ride

0.0	R	from Pine Grove Picnic area
0.1	R	to Camping & Nature Center
1.3	BR	at road fork to "Carter Day Camp"
2.1	BR	follow sign to Scenic Drive; Nature Center to left
9.3	R	to HQ & park exit at stop sign
10.5	BL	to Park exit
11.7	L	to Park HQ at stop sign
11.8	L	into Pine Grove Picnic area

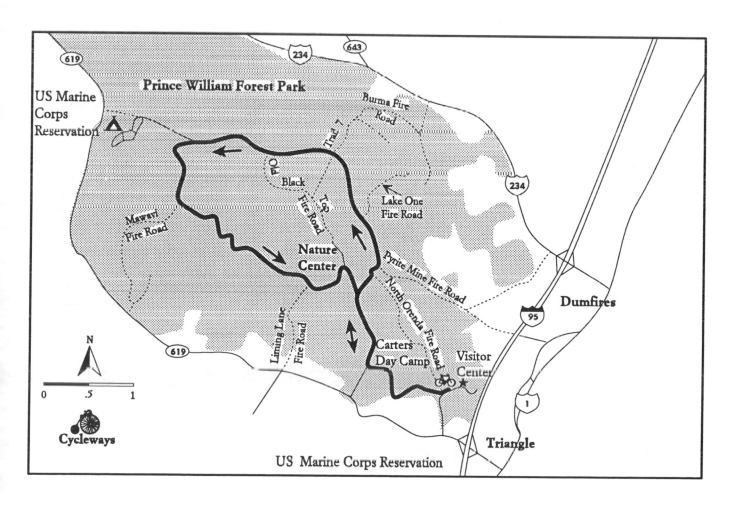

32. West of Nokesville

Distance: 30 or **43** miles
Rating: II; Paved roads
Start: Brentsville Regional High School in Nokesville, Va.

---

43 Mile Ride

0.0	L	646, Aden Rd from parking lot	25.6	L	616
				*☞	
3.7	R	611, Fleetwood Dr (Store)	30.6	S	603 at stop sign in **Calverton** (Store)
7.0	R	611 at T	33.7	R	667 at T
8.8	BL	612	33.9	L	603 at T (Store at mile 35.7)
☜*					
14.2	R	610/612 and immediately	37.4	R	652
14.2	BR	610 at 612	38.7	R	604, Burwell Rd at T
17.0	L	616 at T	38.8	L	652, Fitzwater Dr
17.2	R	610 (Store-closed Sundays) in **Somerville**	43.0	R	646 at T
			43.1	L	into school parking lot
21.6	R	806 (Store) in **Elk Run**			

---

* 30 Mile Ride

9.6	R	609 from 612
11.4	L	806 at SS in **Bristersburg**
12.0	R	616 (Pick up cues in 5.0 miles at mile 30.6 on the 43 mile ride – *☞)

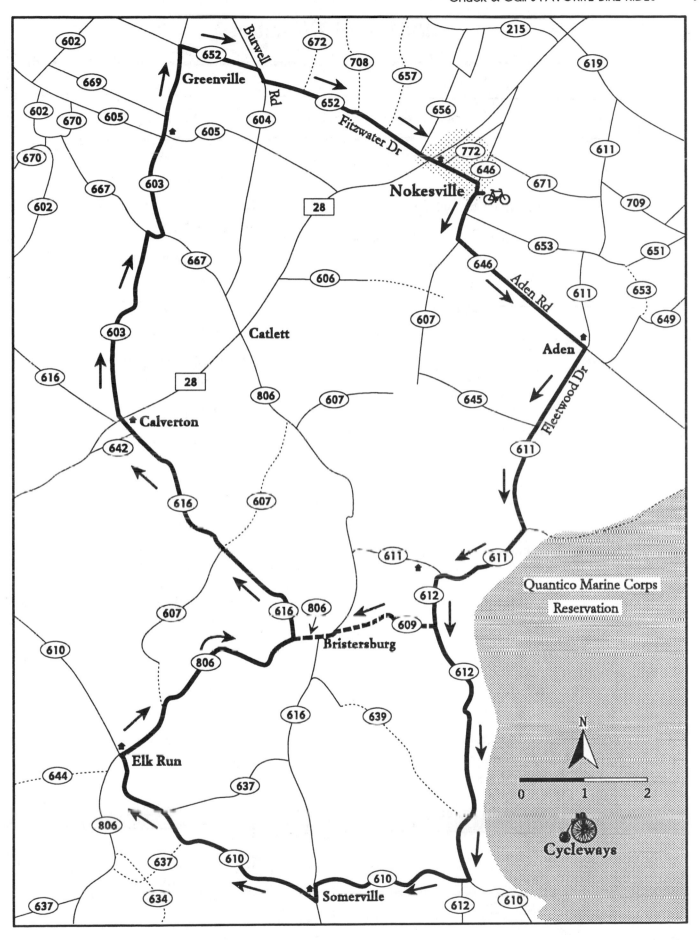

33. Rural Pleasures

Distance:	17, **30**, or 46 miles
Rating:	II; Paved roads
Start:	H.M. Pearson Elementary School in Calverton, Va.

30 Mile Ride

0.0	L	603 from school parking lot		21.1	L	747 (unmarked) to cross RR tracks at **Casanova** (Store)
0.9	S	616 at Rte 28 in **Calverton**		*☞		
5.9	R	806 at T		21.1	L	602 immediately after RR tracks
☞**						
9.9	R	610 in **Elkrun** (Store)		24.6	R	602/670 (unmarked) to cross creek
13.8	S	649		24.7	BR	670 (unmarked) at **Neavil's Mill**
**☞						
16.6	R	663, Balls Mill Rd (unmarked) at T		25.2	R	667 at Y
18.8	L	643 at T		27.4	R	603
20.0	R	616		29.7	L	into school parking lot

* 17 Mile Ride

0.0	L	603 from school parking lot		3.8	R	747 (unmarked) to cross RR tracks in **Casanova** (Store) (Pick up cues immediately at mile 21.1 on the 30 mile ride – *☞)
0.9	R	Rte 28 ⊗				
1.0	R	616				

** 46 Mile Ride

12.8	R	637 (Store at Rte 17 at mile 14.6)		27.9	R	661 at SS in **Bealeton**
				27.9	L	805 after RR tracks
15.6	R	637 at 634		30.5	L	602 at T
17.6	R	651 at SS		31.1	L	610 at T
24.3	R	Franklin St, 656, in **Remington** after RR tracks (Stores)		31.2	R	602 (Store) in **Midland**
24.4	R	656		31.9	L	649 at T (Pick up cues in 1.9 miles at mile 16.6 on the 30 mile ride – **☞)

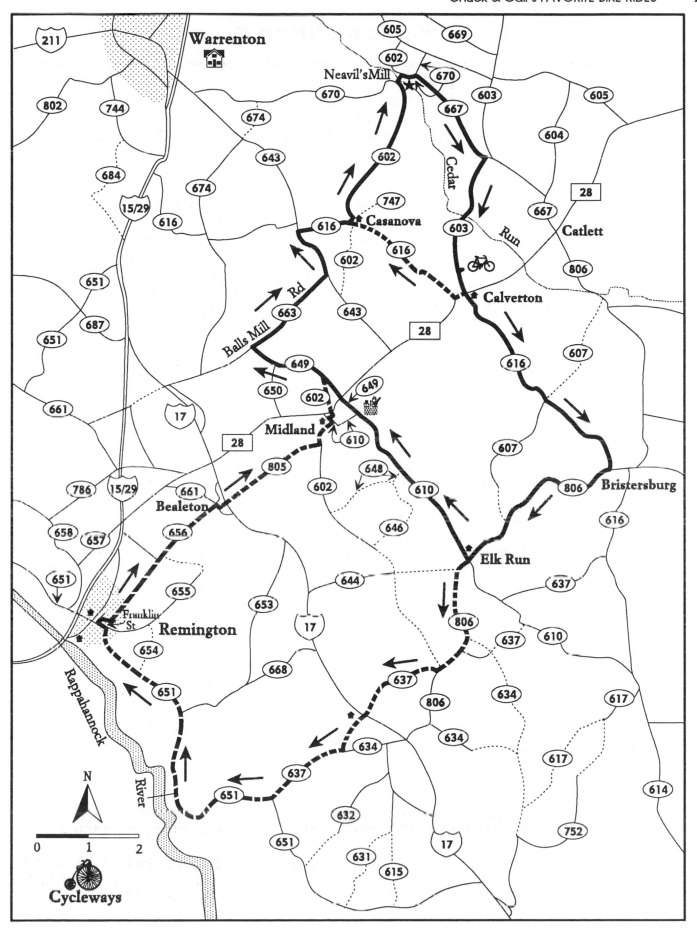

34. Through Bull Run Mountain

Distance:	10, **16** or 26 miles
Rating:	II or III; Paved roads with 0.2 miles of unpaved road
Start:	The Plains Library in The Plains, Va.

16 Mile Ride (III)

0.0	L	804, Stuart St with the RR tracks at your back	5.3	R	681, Antioch Rd
			8.5	R	55, John Marshall Hwy at T
0.1	L	626, Loudoun Ave at T: Walk bike!			
			15.9	R	626, Loudoun Ave in **The Plains**
0.1	R	601, Hopewell Rd, after RR tracks; there are 0.2 miles of unpaved road just before the next turn)	16.1	L	804, Stuart St
			16.2		Arrive at the library

10 Mile Ride (II)

0.0	L	804, Stuart St with the RR tracks at your back	6.6	R	707
			7.9	BR	704
0.1	R	626, Loudoun Ave at T			
			8.5	L	55 (unmarked) at T
0.2	R	55, Main St at T			
			9.6	L	626, Loudoun Ave in **The Plains**
0.3	L	245			
2.1	R	750	9.7	L	804, Stuart St
3.6	R	709 at T	9.8		Arrive at the library

26 Mile Ride: Combine these two loops into one ride

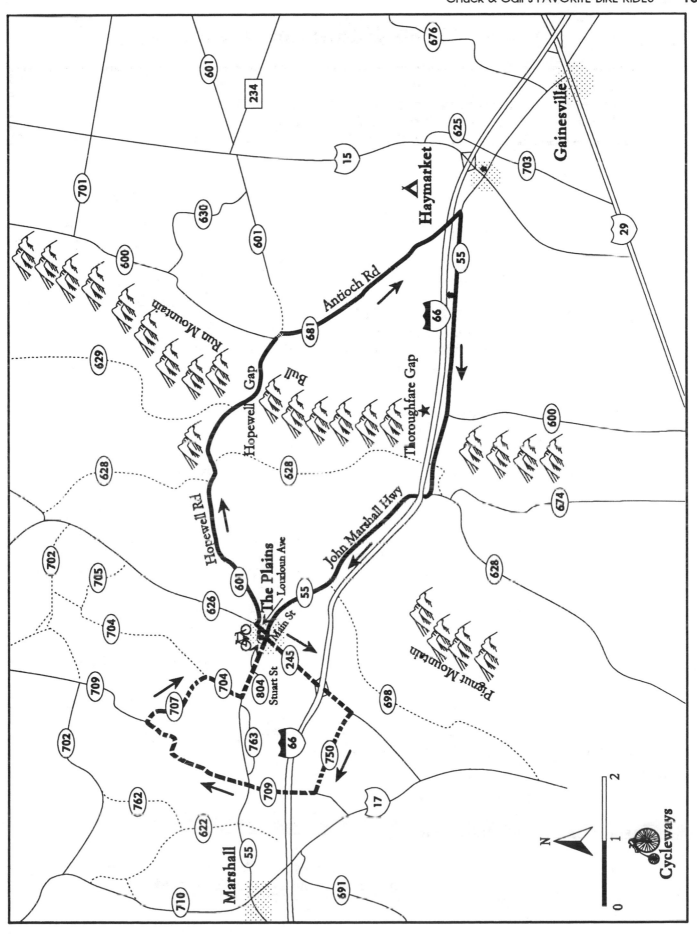

35. Horse Heaven

Distance: 19, **27** or 34 miles
Rating: III or IV; Paved roads
Start: The Plains Library in The Plains, Va.

27 Mile Ride (III)

0.0	L	804, Stuart St with RR at your back
0.1	L	626, Loudoun Ave at T; Walk bike!
8.0	L	Rte 50, Washington St at T in **Middleburg** ⊗ (Food, Store 0.1 mile to right at Pendleton St
9.2	L	709, Zulla Rd
☎*		
14.1	R	702
☎**		
17.5	L	710, Rectortown Rd at T

20.5	L	55, Main St in **Marshall** (Store)
**☞		
22.5	R	709
23.5	L	750
25.1	L	245 (unmarked) at T
26.8	R	55 at T in **The Plains** (Food)
26.9	L	626, Loudoun Ave (Store)
27.0	L	804, at RR tracks
27.1		Arrive at parking

* 19 Mile Ride (III)

15.4	L	707
16.7	BR	704
17.3	L	55 (unmarked) at T

18.4	L	626, Loudoun Ave in **The Plains** (Food, Store)
18.5	L	804, at RR tracks
18.6		Arrive at parking

** 34 Mile Ride (IV)

17.5	R	710, Rectortown Rd at T
18.9	L	713 in **Rectortown** (Store)
22.5	L	F185 just before Rte 17/55; becomes 55 in **Marshall** (Food/Stores) (Pick up cues in 6.7 miles at mile 22.5 on the 27 mile ride – **☞)

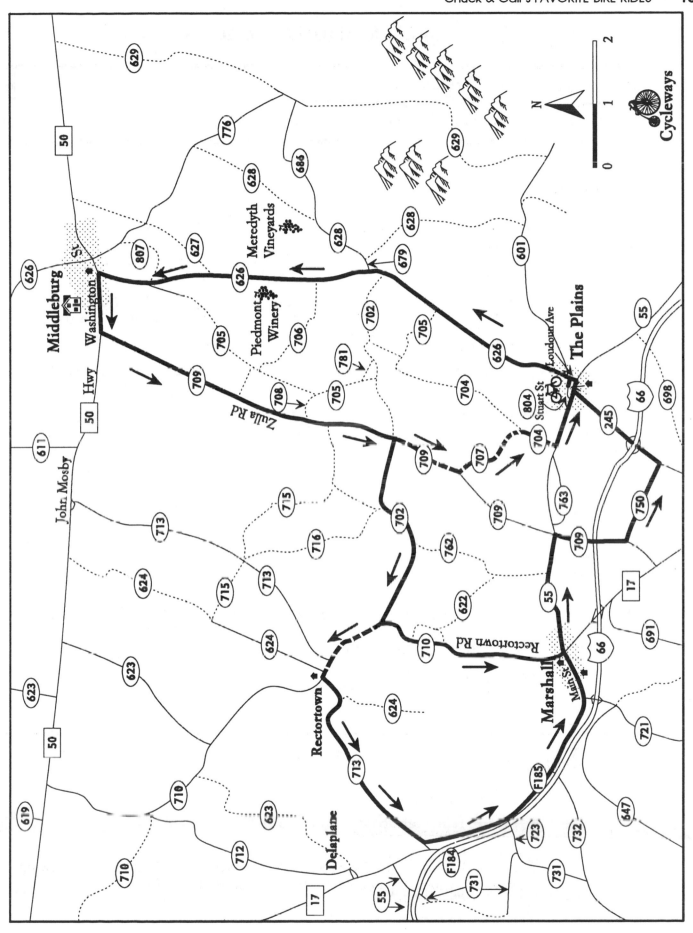

36. The Hunt Scene

Distance:	14 or 22 miles
Rating:	III or IV; Mostly unpaved roads
Start:	Middleburg Elementary School in Middleburg, Va.

14 Mile Ride (III)

0.0	L	626, Madison St from parking lot
0.1	R	Washington St, Rte 50 at TL
0.3	L	626, Plains Rd
1.1	R	705; becomes unpaved
4.4	L	705 at 708 at T
5.5	L	702 (unmarked) at T
7.6	L	paved 626
8.1	R	679; becomes 628 ☎*
9.2	L	unpaved 628; Meredith Vineyards on left in 0.4 miles
11.7	L	paved 776, Landmark School Rd at SS
14.2	S	626, Madison St at TL
14.3	R	into school parking lot

* 22 Mile Ride (IV)

9.2	S	paved 686
11.4	BL	629; becomes unpaved
15.5	L	Rte 50, John Mosby Hwy at T ⊗; use unpaved shoulder
15.8	R	unpaved 629, Cobb House Rd
16.9	L	paved 734, Snickersville Tpke at T
17.1	L	unpaved 627, Macsville Rd
19.6	R	Rte 50, John Mosby Hwy at T ⊗; use unpaved shoulder
19.9	L	unpaved 627, Parson Rd
21.3	R	paved 776, Landmark School Rd at SS
22.3	S	626, Madison St at TL
22.4	R	into school parking lot

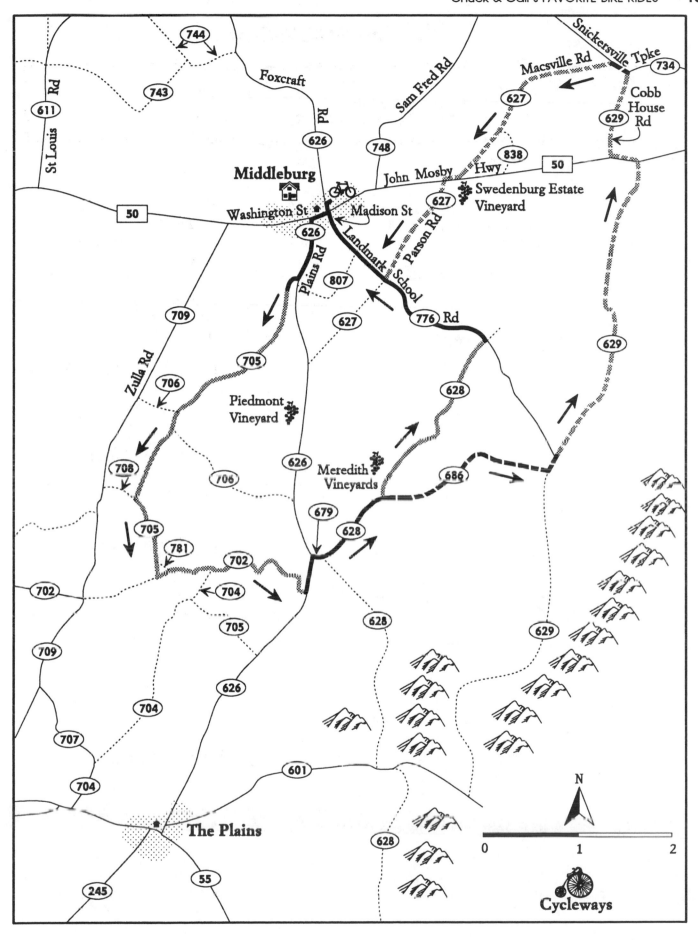

37. The Stable Tour

Distance:	9, 14, **20** or 26 miles
Rating:	III; Mostly unpaved roads
Start:	Banneker Elementary School in St Louis, Va.

20 Mile Ride

0.0	R	744, Snake Hill Rd from parking lot; becomes unpaved		12.3	R	739, Austin Grove Rd
				13.7	R	626, Foggy Bottom Rd at T
1.6	R	743, Millville Rd; becomes Welbourne Rd		14.7	L	paved 719, Airmont Rd at T
☛*				15.0	R	626, Bloomfield Rd (Store); becomes unpaved
☛**						
6.1	BR	paved 743, Millville Rd at 623, Willisville Rd; becomes unpaved at 719		**☛		
				17.2	R	630, Unison Rd in **Unison** at T (Store)
8.7	R	619, Trappe Rd at T		†☛		
11.7	L	765, Ridgeside Rd		18.5	BL	790, Newlin Mill Rd
☛†				20.0	L	744, Snake Hill Rd
				20.4	R	into school

* 9 Mile Ride

5.6	R	630, Quaker Lane		8.8	L	744, Snake Hill Rd
7.3	R	790, Newlin Mill Rd at T		9.2	R	into school

** 14 Mile Ride

6.1	R	623, Willisville Rd
9.1	R	626, Bloomfield Rd (Pick up cues in 1.4 miles at mile 17.2 on the 20 mile ride – **☛)

† 26 Mile Ride

14.1	L	626, Foggy Bottom Rd at T		17.7	L	719, Airmont Rd at T (paved)
15.2	S	759, Hollow Oak Rd		18.4	R	700, Woodtrail Rd (unpaved) (Store 0.1 mile ahead in **Airmont**)
15.7	R	831, Yellow Schoolhouse Rd at T				
16.7	L	779, Ebenezer Church Rd at T		20.8	R	630, Unison Rd at T (Store at mile 22.5 (Pick up cues in 3.0 miles at mile 18.5 on the 20 mile ride – †☛)

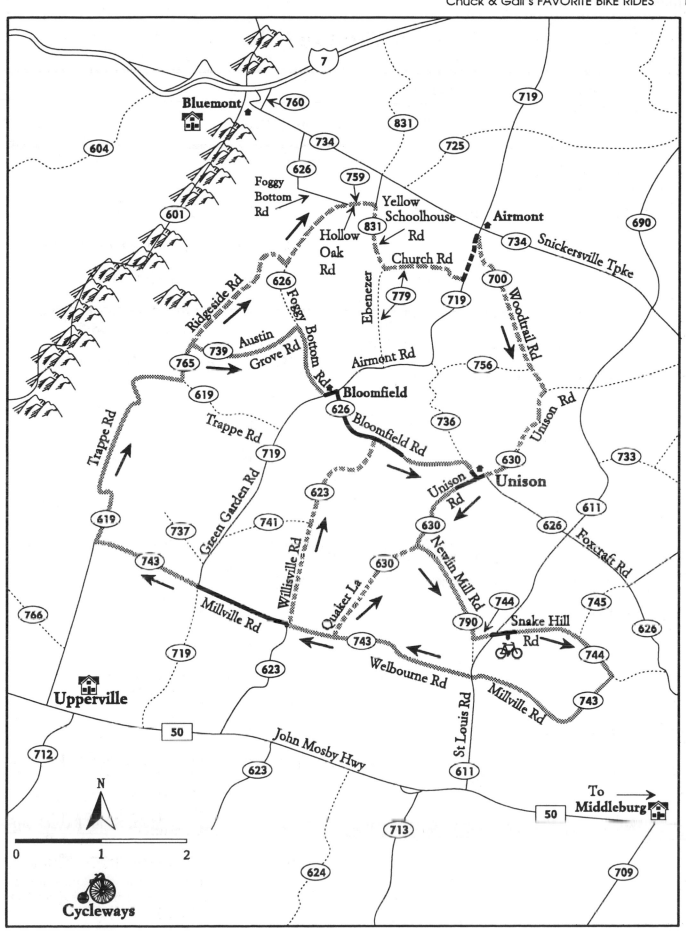

38. Horse Hills

Distance:	18, **31** or 43 miles
Rating:	IV; Paved roads
Start:	Middleburg Elementary School in Middleburg, Va.

31 Mile Ride

0.0	R	626, Foxcroft Rd from school parking lot		21.5	L	731, Water Mill Rd
				23.7	L	734, Snickersville Tpke at T
4.8	R	611, St Louis Rd		*☞		
🐎*				26.5	R	748, Sam Fred Rd
🐎**						
8.6	S	690, Silcott Springs Rd; becomes S 32nd St in **Purcellville**		29.9	R	Rte 50, John Mosby Hwy (unmarked) at SS ⊗
				30.4	R	Jay St in **Middleburg**
14.2	R	Bus 7, Main St (Store)		30.5	L	T1202, Marshall St
**☞						
15.2	R	722, S Maple Ave (Store, Food); becomes Lincoln Rd		30.7	R	626 (unmarked) at SS
20.8	R	728, North Fork Rd at T		30.8	R	into school parking lot

* 18 Mile Ride

8.6	R	734, Snickersville Tpke (Store at mile 9.5) (Pick up cues in 5.2 miles at mile 26.5 on the 31 mile ride – *☞)

** 43 Mile Ride

8.6	L	734, Snickersville Tpke		21.3	L	812, Gaver Mill Rd at 718
11.0	R	719, Airmont Rd in **Airmont** (Store)		21.6	R	690, Hillsboro Rd (unmarked) at T
14.6	S	719, Woodgrove Rd at Bus 7 in **Round Hill** (Stores)		24.3	L	711, Allder School Rd
				25.6	R	611, Purcellville Rd at SS, becomes Hatcher Ave in **Purcellville**
19.5	R	719, Stony Point Rd at 751, Cider Mill Rd				
20.8	R	Rte 9 (unmarked) at T in **Hillsboro** ⊗ (Store)		27.1	L	Bus 7, Main St at T (Pick up cues in 0.5 miles at 15.2 on the 31 mile ride – *☞)
21.1	R	812				

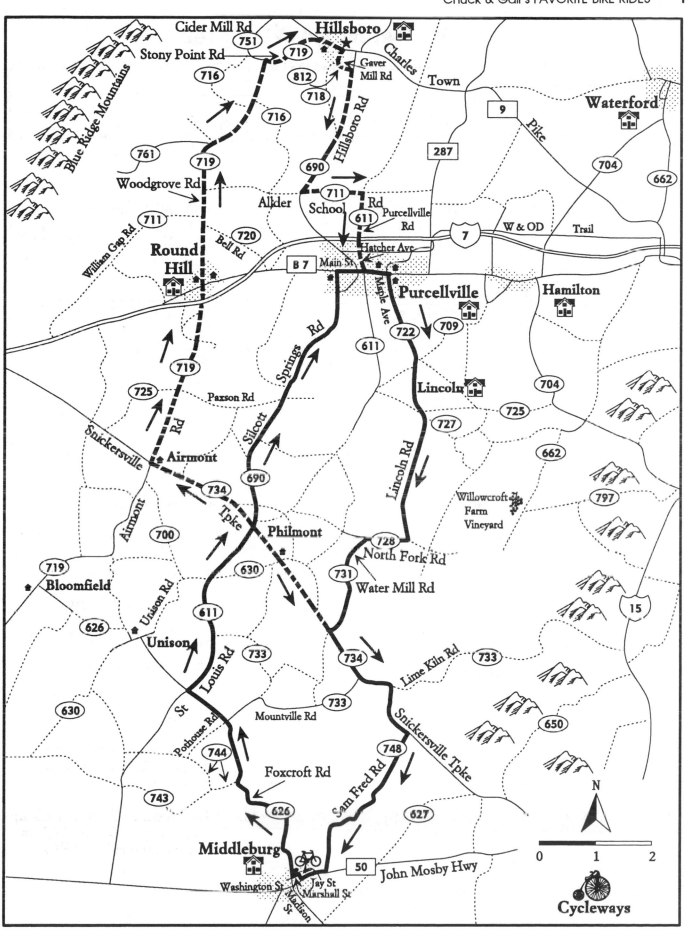

39. Waterford Wanderer

Distance:	35 miles
Rating:	IV; Paved roads and a section of the paved W&OD Trail
Start:	Loudoun Valley High School in Purcellville, Va.

35 Mile Ride

0.0	R	722 from parking lot and **Immediately Right** onto W&OD trail; follow W&OD Trail signs
4.7	L	662, Simpson Circle in **Paeonian Springs**
4.9	R	Rte 9, Charlestown Pike at SS ⊗
5.0	L	662, Clarkes Gap Rd
7.4	L	662, Factory St at 665 in **Waterford**; becomes Second St (Store)
7.8	R	698, Water St at Y
8.0	BL	665, Loyalty Rd
13.4	L	663, Taylorstown Rd at T in **Taylorstown** (Store); becomes 668
15.4	L	672, Lovettsville Rd at T; becomes E Broadway, 673, in **Lovettsville**
19.1	S	673, W Broadway at Rte 287, N Berlin Pike (Food/Store); becomes Irish Corner Rd; becomes 690, Mountain Rd
25.3	R	690, Mountain Rd at 693, Morrisonville Rd
28.6	R	Rte 9, Charlestown Pike at T ⊗
28.9	L	812 in **Hillsboro** (Store 0.2 mile ahead on Rte 9)
29.1	L	812, Gaver Mill Rd at 718
29.4	R	690, Hillsboro Rd (unmarked) at T
32.0	L	711, Allder School Rd
33.3	R	611, Purcellville Rd
34.7	L	onto W&OD Trail (Water)
35.4	R	at 1st cross road into parking lot

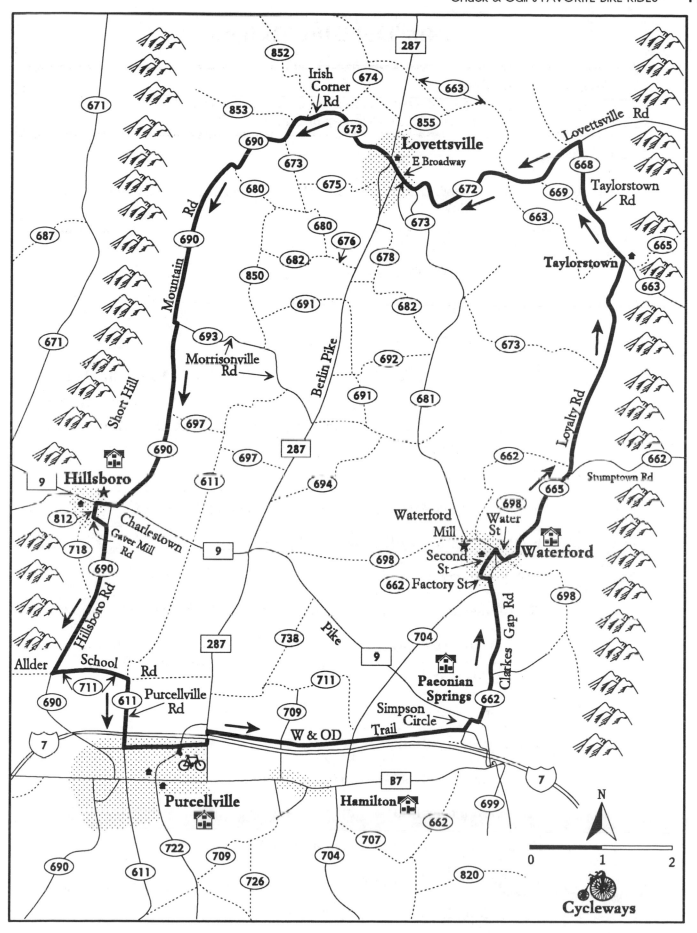

40. The Blue Ridger

Distance:	**56** miles
Rating:	V; Paved roads with sections of busier roads
Start:	Marshall Community Center in Marshall, Va.

56 Mile Ride

0.0	R	710, Rectortown Rd from parking lot (Store at mile 4.3 in **Rectortown**-closed Sunday)
6.6	R	623; becomes No 6 Rd
10.3	L	Rte 50, John Mosby Hwy (unmarked) at T ⊗
10.7	R	623, Willisville Rd
12.3	BL	743, Millville Rd
13.6	R	719, Green Garden Rd; becomes Airmont Rd (Store in **Bloomfield** at mile 16.8)
20.3	L	734, Snickersville Tpke in **Airmont** (Store) (Also a store in **Bluemont** at mile 23.5 at the start of the first climb)
24.2	L	Rte 7 at T ⊗ (keep climbing)
24.8	L	601, Blue Ridge Mountain Rd at top of gap (keep climbing)
36.1	L	Rte 50, John Mosby Hwy at SS ⊗ (Food)
36.8	R	759 into **Paris**
37.2	R	701 (unmarked) in front of gas station and the Ashby Inn
37.9	R	Rte 17 (unmarked) at T ⊗
39.3	R	688 (2nd climb)
46.1	L	55, after crossing under I-66
50.3	R	731 at T; 55 goes left
50.4	L	F184, immediately after crossing under I-66
52.4	L	723 to cross over I-66
52.5	R	F185 at T; becomes Main St in **Marshall**
55.8	L	710, Rectortown Rd (Store)
55.9	R	into parking lot

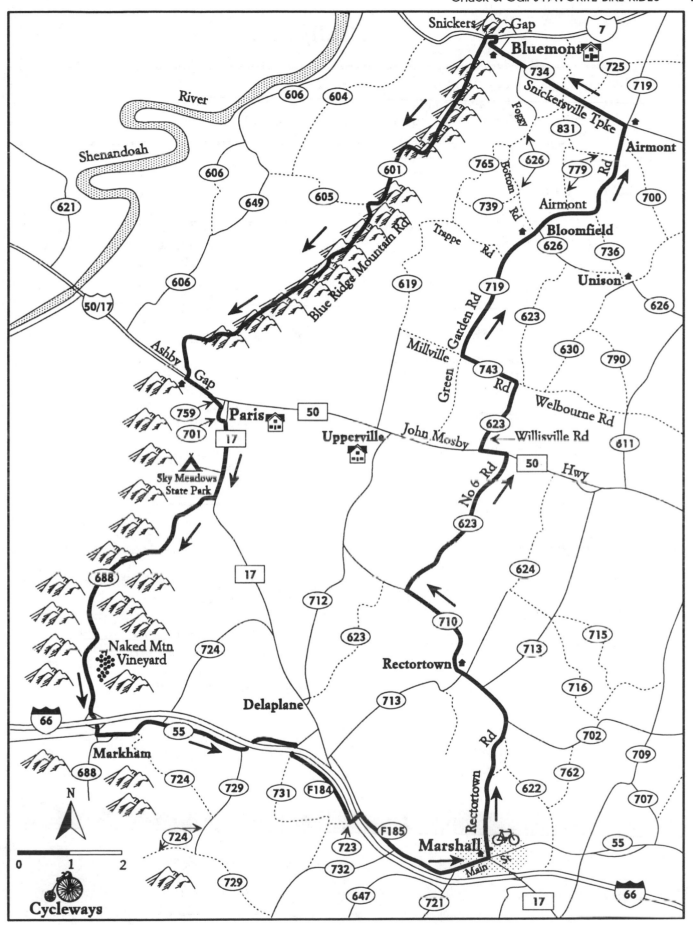

41. Tally Ho!

Distance:	**25** or **38** miles
Rating:	IV; Paved roads
Start:	Marshall Community Center in Marshall, Va.

25 Mile Ride

0.0	L	710, Rectortown Rd from parking lot		9.4	L	757 in **Markham**; becomes 688 (Store in **Hume** at mile 15.2)
0.1	R	Main St, 55 at SS; becomes F185		15.3	L	635 in **Hume**
3.3	L	723, crossing I-66		18.5	L	732
3.4	R	F184 immediately after crossing I-66		23.1	R	F185 at T; becomes 55, Main St in **Marshall**
5.4	R	731 at SS		25.2	L	710, Rectortown Rd
5.5	L	55 after crossing under I-66		25.3	R	into parking lot

* 38 Mile Ride

19.5	R	647 at SS		36.6	L	Rte 17 at T ⊗; becomes Bus 17 at I-66
20.9	L	733				
21.6	S	738		37.8	S	710, Rectortown Rd in **Marshall**
27.2	S	689		37.9	R	into parking lot
27.9	L	691				

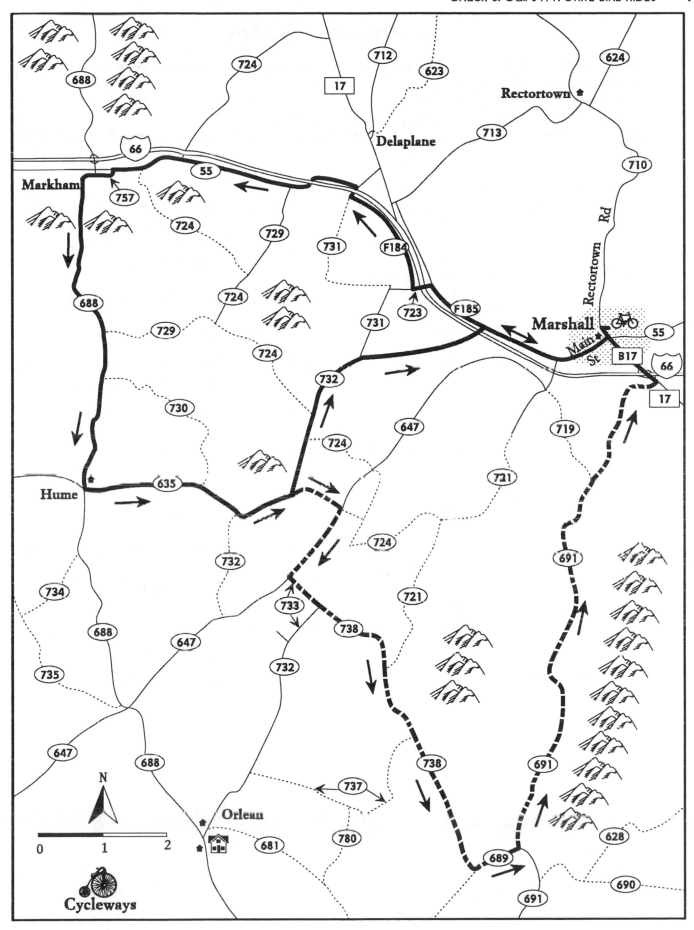

42. Blue Ridge Views

Distance:	**60** miles
Rating:	V; Paved roads
Start:	Municipal parking lot in Warrenton, Va.

60 Mile Ride

0.0	S	Ashby St from the north end of the parking lot	32.2	L	729 at 618 at T (Store at mile 35.2)
0.1	L	Waterloo St at SS	35.7	BL	729 at 615
0.8	S	Rte 211 at TL	36.3	L	627 toward Rixeyville
0.9	R	Rappahannock St	38.3	S	640
0.9	L	Waterloo Rd at SS; becomes 678	42.4	R	Rte 229 (unmarked) at T (⊗) in **Rixeyville** (Store)
4.9	L	691	42.7	L	640
7.1	R	688 at SS (Store, closed Sunday, at mile 12.6 in **Orlean**)	45.8	S	625
			49.1	S	621
15.3	L	647	50.1	R	623 at T
23.1	L	Rte 522 (unmarked) at T in **Flint Hill** (Store, Food)	53.0	R	802 at T (Store at mile 55.1); becomes Culpeper St in **Warrenton**
23.5	L	729 toward Ben Venue (Store at mile 27.1 at Rte 211)	60.1	L	Franklin St
			60.2	R	into parking lot

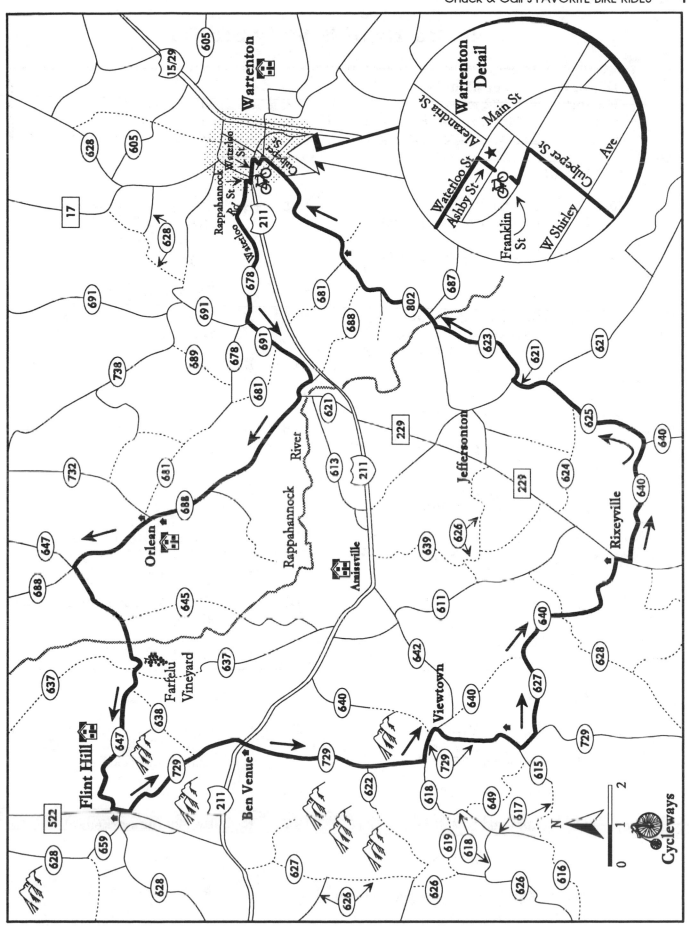

43. Battle of Brandy Station

Distance:	20 or **32** miles
Rating:	II; 32 mile ride is paved, 20 mile ride has mostly unpaved roads
Start:	Margaret M. Pierce Elementary School in Remington, Va.

32 Mile Ride

0.0	R	Bus 29, James Madison Hwy from school parking lot
1.1 ☞*	L	673 after crossing river
3.3	R	674
4.9	L	678 just before RR tracks in Elkwood (Store to right at Rte 15/29 - closed Sunday)
5.2	R	676 at SS
5.3	S	685 (unmarked) at Rte 15/29
7.6	L	663 (unmarked) at SS; cross Rte 15/29
7.8	L	762 (unmarked) at T in **Brandy Station**
7.9	R	669 (Store)
8.0	R	700
8.2	BL	663
8.5	BL	663 at 684 (Store to left on Rte 3 at mile 12.4 in **Stevensburg**-closed Sunday)
15.4	L	647 at T in **Batna**
19.3	R	Rte 3 (unmarked) at SS in **Lignum**
19.4	L	647
20.3	R	610
20.8	L	620 (Store at mile 22.5); stay on 620 past several side roads and turns
26.7	L	651 at T
31.3	R	656, Franklin St after RR tracks in **Remington**
31.5	L	Bowen St
31.6	R	James Madison Hwy, Bus 29 at SS
31.7	L	into school parking lot

* 20 Mile Ride

3.3	S	unpaved 673
4.3	R	unpaved 675
6.6	L	paved 669 at T
8.7	L	unpaved 672
13.2	S	paved 620 at SS
13.4	S	unpaved 674 ; Kelly's Ford to right with nice views of the Rappahannock River
16.5	R	paved 673
18.7	R	Bus 29 (unmarked) at T
19.8	L	into school parking lot

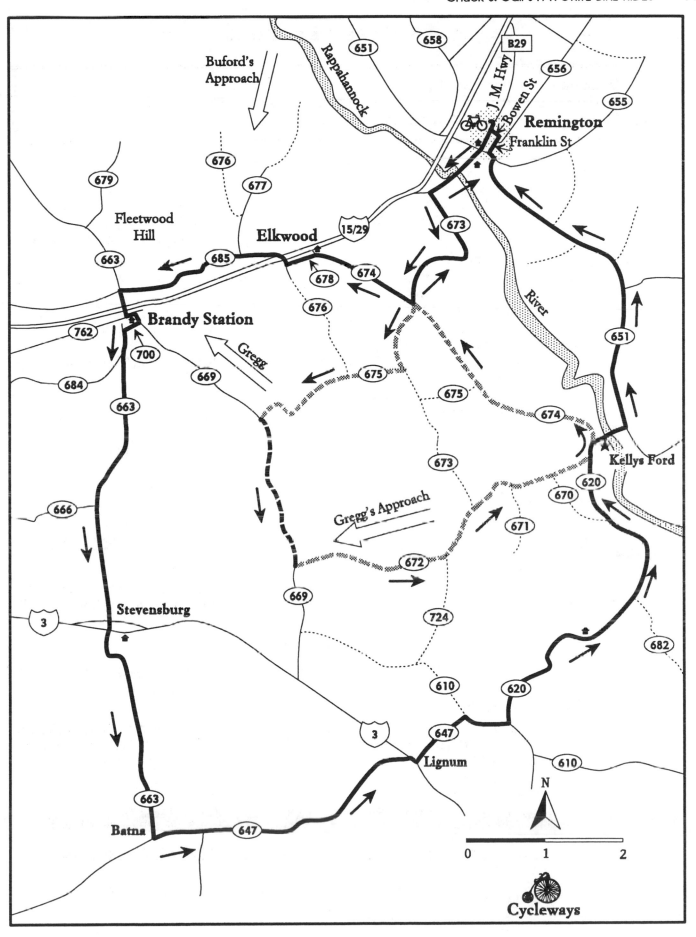

44. Lee's Lookout

Distance:	**47** or 51 miles
Rating:	III; V with climb to top of Clark Mountain; Paved roads
Start:	Floyd T. Binns School in Culpeper, Va.

47 Mile Ride

0.0	L	Radio Lane from parking lot
0.1	R	Main St at T
0.2	L	Grandview Ave and immediately
0.2	L	Old Rixeyville Rd; becomes West St
1.2	L	Davis St at the Courthouse
1.4	R	East St at second TL
2.0	L	Orange Rd at SS
2.1	L	Fredericksburg Rd, Rtes 3/522 at TL ⊗
3.9	R	658, just past Rte 522
4.6	R	656 on the downhill
5.4	L	652 at T
7.1	R	617 at SS
8.3	L	Rte 522 just before RR tracks ⊗ (Store at mile 8.5)
8.9	S	615 (Store to right on Rte 614 at mile 16.2 in **Rapidan**)
17.5	L	627, Clark's Mountain Rd

* For the extra 4 miles, turn Left on 697, Moormont Rd at mile 19.5, ride to the top of Clark Mountain for a terrific vista, and return to Rte 627)

22.8	L	617, Everonia Rd
23.9	L	Rte 522, Zachory Taylor Hwy at SS ⊗
24.6	R	663, True Blue Rd
27.2	L	611, Racoon Ford Rd at T
29.7	R	Rte 522 (unmarked) at T ⊗ (Store at mile 29.9)
30.8	R	647 after crossing Rapidan River
36.4	L	663 at SS (Store 0.1 mile to right at Rte 3, mile 39.5)
41.2	L	666
44.4	L	667, after Rtes 15/29; becomes Nalles Mill Rd
46.3	L	Bus 29, James Madison Hwy ⊗
47.0	R	Hendrick St
47.3	L	Radio Lane
47.4	L	into school parking lot

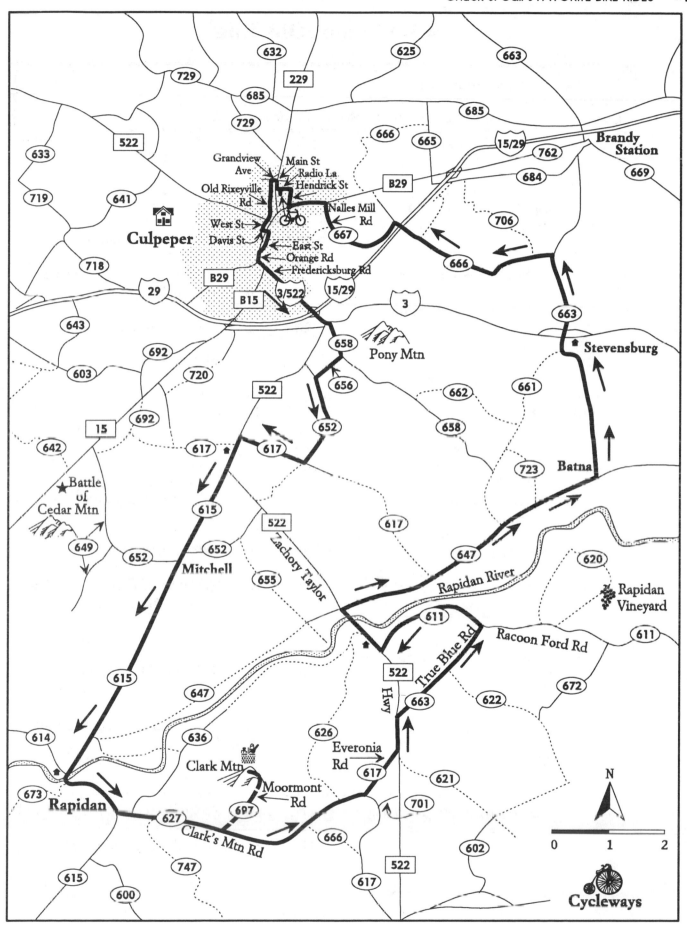

45. Base of Old Rag

Distance:	28 or **40** miles
Rating:	III; Paved roads
Start:	Waverly Yowell Middle School in Madison, Va.

40 Mile Ride

0.0	S	out of parking lot and Bear Right onto Rte 231 at Yield sign
0.9	R	638 after crossing bridge
1.7	BR	638 (unmarked) at 653
3.0	L	603 at SS
5.7	L	609 at SS in **Haywood**
7.5	R	Rte 231 at T
8.0	L	670 (Store) in **Banco**
11.6	R	643/600 in **Syria** (Store-closed Sunday afternoons); Rose River Vineyard 1.7 miles ahead on 670 and 648; follow signs
11.9	R	600
13.6	L	670 at T
16.0	R	Rte 231 at yield sign (Store)
16.5	L	609
23.9	R	640 on the downhill after 607
24.3	L	612 at T
26.1	L	Rte 29 at T ⊗
26.2	R	631 in **Leon**
29.6	R	618
32.1	L	632 at T, crossing river
33.1	R	634 (unmarked) at T (Stores at mile 33.5 in **Oak Park**-closed Sunday and at mile 37.5)
38.7	R	634 at 616
39.9	S	634, Washington St at Rte 29 into **Madison**
40.1	R	Main St at T (Stores/Food)
40.4	R	into school parking lot

---

* 28 Mile Ride

5.7	R	609 at SS in **Haywood** (Pick up cues in 5.7 miles from mile 23.9 on the 40 mile ride – *☞)

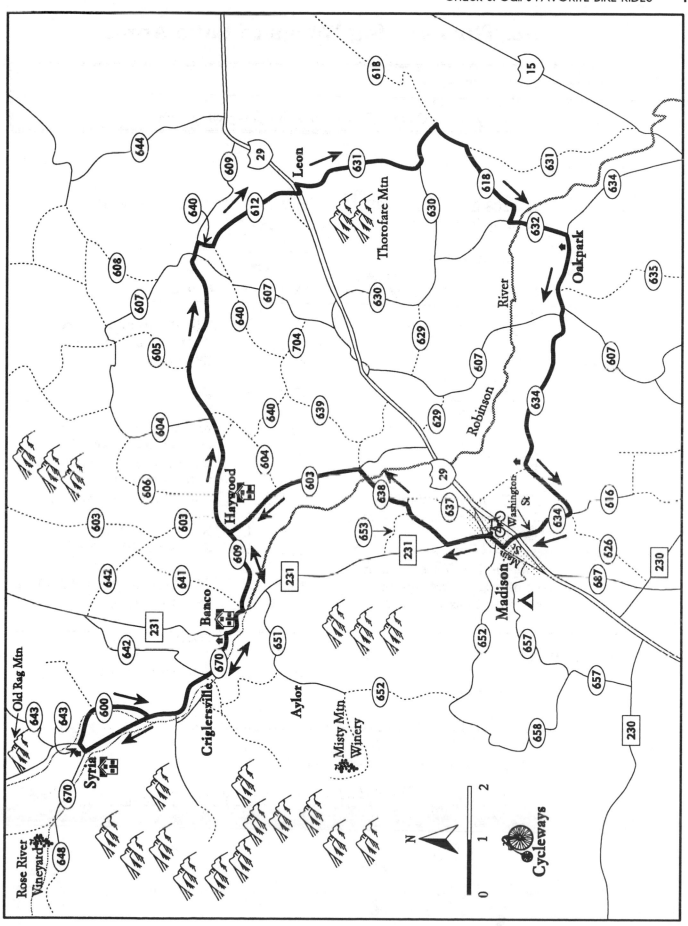

46. Thru the Big Woods to Lake Anna

Distance:	**46 or 52 miles**
Rating:	II; Paved roads
Start:	Spotsylvania County Courthouse in Spotsylvania, Va.

46 Mile Ride

0.0	L	Rte 208 from courthouse parking lot
0.1	R	613 at TL (Store)
0.6	L	608, Robert E Lee Dr
7.6	L	608/612 at T
7.9	L	612
12.0	R	606/612 at SS
12.9	BL	612
16.1	L	601
17.3	R	7000, into Lake Anna State Park; follow signs to Visitor Center
20.0		Arrive at Visitor Center (Water, Restrooms); Turn Around and reverse route to exit park
22.7	L	601 at park exit 🐴*
24.8	R	601 at 653 *☞
29.8	R	608 at T
30.7	BL	608 at 606 at Y (Store) (Store at mile 34.2-closed Sunday)
37.0	BL	612
40.3	R	613 at T (Store 0.1 mile to left); pass Spotsylvania Courthouse Battlefield at mile 44.0; Water & Restrooms in season)
45.9	L	Rte 208 at TL in **Spotsylvania** (Store)
46.0	R	742, into courthouse parking lot

* 52 Mile Ride

23.8	L	612 from 601 (Store at mile 24.3)
28.1	R	719 at SS toward **Paytes** (Store at mile 28.9)
29.9	S	652 (Store at mile 31.5-closed Sunday)
33.1	L	601 at T (Pick up cues in 3.1 miles at mile 29.8 on the 46 mile ride – *☞)

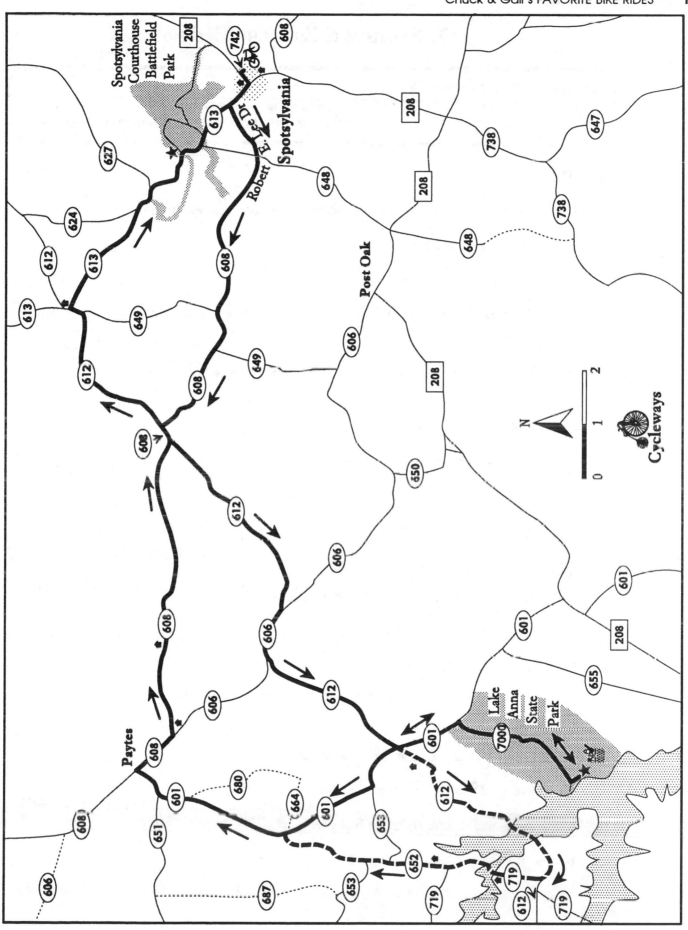

47. Stonewall's Last Ride

Distance:	6 or **13** miles
ating:	II; Long Ride - Paved & unpaved roads; Short Ride - Paved roads
Start:	Chancellorsville Battlefield Park Visitor Center in Chancellorsville, Va.

13 Mile Ride

0.0	R	Bullock Dr, exiting parking lot with Visitor Center on your left
0.8	R	610, Elys Ford Rd (unmarked) at T
1.5	S	Old Plank Rd at Rte 3
2.6	R	Furnace Rd (unmarked) into battlefield; 1st crossroad, at the Last Bivouac site
4.0	BL	Jackson Trail East (unmarked) at Y; becomes unpaved at Catherine Furnace
6.8	L	paved 613, Brock Rd (unmarked) at T
7.1	R	unpaved Jackson Trail West
9.4	R	paved 613, Brock Rd (unmarked) at SS
10.1	L	600; becomes unpaved then paved
11.9	R	621, Orange Plank Rd at T
12.1	R	Rte 3 at T ⊗; use unpaved shoulder
13.2	L	paved Bullock Rd into Battlefield
13.3	R	into Visitor Center

* 6 Mile Ride

4.0	BR	Sickles Dr at Y (Catherine Furnace to left)
4.9	BL	Stuart Dr at Y, toward Jackson Monument
5.8	S	Bullock Dr, crossing Rte 3
5.9	R	into Visitor Center

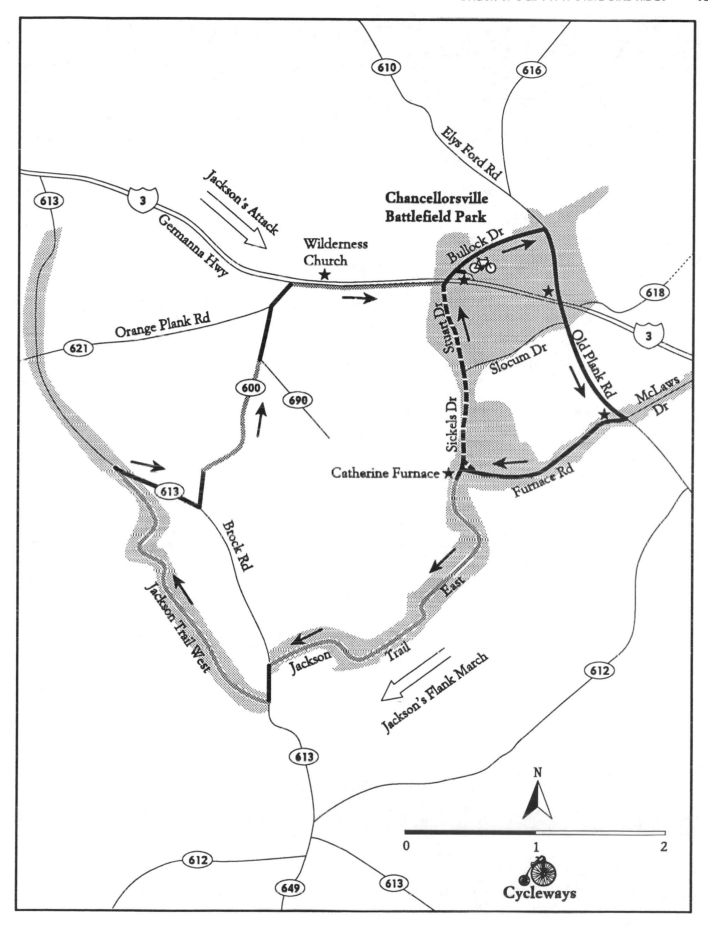

Chancellorsville
Battlefield Park

Wilderness
Church

Jackson's Attack

Germanna Hwy

Orange Plank Rd

Elys Ford Rd

Bullock Dr

Stuart Dr

Slocum Dr

Old Plank Rd

McLaws Dr

Sickels Dr

Catherine Furnace

Furnace Rd

Brock Rd

Jackson Trail West

Jackson   Trail   East

Jackson's Flank March

Cycleways

N

0   1   2

CHESAPEAKE TREASURES

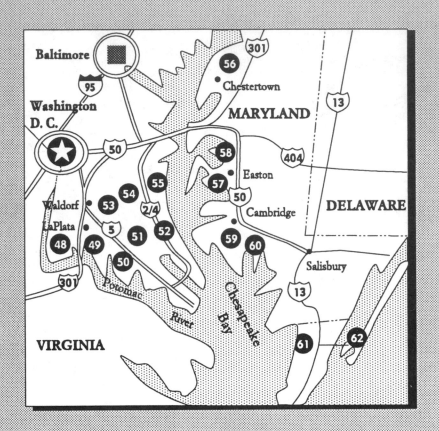

Imagine cycling on a narrow lane surrounded by water and marsh, past Worlds End Creek. Overhead are thousands of honking geese. A bald eagle perches on a gnarled tree. You glide through quaint fishing villages on narrow spits of land jutting into the Chesapeake Bay, isolated from all that mainstream America has to offer. You visit a bald cypress swamp and the island where the first Maryland settlers landed in 1634. Wild ponies ignore you as you ride within a few feet of them. You hear the clip-clop of horse's hooves as Amish farmers ride to market in their buggies. All this is Chesapeake Bay country, to the east and south of Washington, D.C. and Baltimore, Maryland.

The Chesapeake Bay, America's largest estuary, is famous for its crabbing, fishing, sailing and waterfowl. Many of the graceful towns on its shores date from colonial days and appear frozen in another time. Some of the first English settlements in America occurred on the bay's rivers and shores: Jamestown, Kent Island, and St. Mary's City. Lying within a two-hour drive of Washington, Baltimore and Philadelphia, the area is a popular recreation destination that attracts many city dwellers on the weekends.

On the western side of the Chesapeake Bay, cyclists find miles of quiet cycling roads south of Washington and Annapolis. Popular attractions are the Merkle Wildlife Sanctuary, the Battle Creek Cypress Swamp and the small Amish community near Charlotte Hall. Cyclists enjoy the rural roads around Maryland Point and Chapel Point. You can explore the countryside through which John Wilkes Booth fled. Most of the rides west of the bay feature good views of the bay's tributaries. Southern Maryland also has many acres planted in tobacco, a surprisingly pretty plant. Off-road cyclists enjoy the shaded dirt roads through Cedarville State Forest.

The Eastern Shore is the area's real draw. It has its own distinct personality, its own flavor. Here you find some of the region's most attractive bicycle rides. In the Easton area you visit quaint towns founded before the Revolutionary War and cross the Tred Avon River on the nation's oldest operating ferry. You can cycle through several well-known wildlife refuges: Blackwater and Chincoteague. South of Blackwater you can ride for miles through an open saltwater marsh to the forgotten town of Elliott. Near Chincoteague you ride to Saxis, a homey oystering town. North of Chestertown you visit Betterton, a resort town from the Victorian era.

The Eastern Shore offers the flattest cycling in the entire region. All the rides have the easiest rating, category I. In some counties the only hills are the bridges over the waterways. Just remember that the wind frequently blows hard here, adding a level of difficulty not expected on a flat ride. Once we had the wind shift on us and rode into a headwind for 56 miles of a 70 mile flat ride.

West of the bay you find more rolling terrain than the Eastern Shore. These rides have ratings of II or II/III. This is more difficult than a category I ride, but you will find no killer hills. The hills here are fewer and more gentle than those found in other chapters.

48. Around Maryland Point (23, **37** or 41 miles; II)

Paved roads; starts at the boat ramp at Smallwood State Park in Charles County, Md.: From I-95, Washington Beltway, take Route 210 South, Indian Head Highway. Continue for 14.0 miles and turn left onto Route 227. In 1.4 miles go straight onto Route 224. At T, turn left on Routes 225/224, then right in 0.4 miles to stay on Route 224. Go 4 miles and turn right on Sweden Point Road into the state park. In 0.3 miles turn right at the bottom of the hill toward the boat ramp. In 0.4 miles turn right into the parking lot.

Yes, roads this deserted and rural do lie this close to Washington, D.C.! The growth is getting closer, but the roads in western Charles County are still here, and are still quiet. On a recent spring day we rode tandems with friends on the these pleasant, rolling roads. We saw fox, deer, owl and several beaver dams. At our break on the Potomac River, we watched osprey fish in the river and a flock of grebes flying upriver. The silence of the road around Maryland Point, with its low traffic volume and miles of dense woods, is stunning.

You begin at the boat landing on Mattawoman Creek and head south into the most rural part of Charles County. If you ride the longer rides, carry food with you for a stop on the Potomac River. The store after the river is poorly stocked and not always open. The short ride cuts across the peninsula to historic Durham Church.

49. Booth's Escape (18 or 33 miles; II/III)

Paved roads; starts at Charles County Courthouse & Government Complex in LaPlata, Md.: From I-95, Washington Beltway, take exit 7A, Route 5, Branch Avenue South toward Waldorf. In Waldorf continue straight on Route 301 to LaPlata. Turn left on Route 6 East, E. Charles Street. In 0.3 miles turn left on Washington Street at the traffic light. Turn left on Baltimore Street behind the courthouse and right into the parking lot.

After assassinating Abraham Lincoln in 1865, John Wilkes Booth and co-conspirator David Herold fled Washington, D.C. to southern Maryland, a center of Confederate sympathy. At the steps of the Port Tobacco courthouse, the Union offered a reward for Booth's capture. There were no takers, and Booth fled into Virginia.

On this ride you explore the roads and peninsulas south of LaPlata. Aside from several historical markers to Booth's escape route, little evidence of that troubled time remains. Early in the ride you pass the reconstructed Port Tobacco courthouse, now a museum open Saturday afternoons. Take a few moments to enjoy the view from St. Ignatius Church on Chapel Point where a Catholic Church has stood since 1642.

The longer ride heads to Popes Creek where you can enjoy one of the seafood restaurants on the Potomac River's edge. You then explore the roads around Allens Fresh, which drains Zekiah Swamp. The longer ride uses the shoulders of several busy roads, one with heavy traffic.

50. Blessing of the Fleet (29 miles; II)

Paved roads; starts at Chopticon High School in Morganza, Md.: From I-95, Washington Beltway, take exit 7A, Route 5, Branch Avenue South toward Waldorf. Follow for 12.2 miles and turn left on Route 205, Mattawoman Beantown Road. Go 3.2 miles and turn left on Route 5 at the Gateway Plaza. Continue for 17.3 miles and turn right at 235 to remain on Route 5. In 4.7 miles turn right on Route 242. Go 1.3 miles and turn left into the school.

For 51 weekends of the year, the roads on Colton Point are void of most traffic. However, if you ride them on the first weekend in October, expect to find crowds. The water fills with boats and the land with crowds. Every October people come to celebrate the first landing and the annual blessing of the fleet.

In 1634, the first English settlers in Maryland landed at St. Clement's Island, just offshore from Colton Point. They settled a few miles down the Potomac River at St. Mary's City. The large cross on St. Clement's Island commemorates the first landing.

At Colton Point, opposite the island, sits the St. Clement's Island Potomac Museum. The museum and the pier make an appealing picnic place. The return ride reminds you that tobacco was, and still is, the main cash crop of tidewater Maryland. Tobacco barns dot the farmlands, and during the summer tobacco plants stand shoulder high.

Harvested tobacco drying in the barn, southern Maryland

51. Hidden Amish (25 or 49 miles; II/III)

Paved roads; starts at T.C. Martin Elementary School in Bryantown, Md.: From I-95, Washington Beltway, take exit 7A, Route 5, Branch Avenue South toward Waldorf. Follow for 12.2 miles and turn left on Route 205, Mattawoman Beantown Road. Go 3.2 miles and turn left on Route 5 at the Gateway Plaza. In 4.9 miles turn right on Olivers Shop Road, Route 232 at the blinking light in Bryantown. Go 0.9 miles and turn right into the school.

Most people associate the Amish with Lancaster County, Pennsylvania, not Maryland. During the 1940s a small group of Amish farmers became disenchanted with the growth in Pennsylvania and moved to this rural retreat in southern Maryland. Most are still here, going to and from the market in New Market on Wednesdays and Saturdays and worship on Sundays.

This is a small community and sometimes you have to search to find the Amish. Watch for them on Ryceville Road, North Ryceville Road, Thompson Corner Road and Lockes Crossing Road. Look for farmhouses without electricity, German names, black buggies and dark clothes hanging on clothes lines.

The longer ride explores countryside to the south and east of New Market. It returns to New Market on quiet section of Route 6, a stretch that is somewhat hillier than the rest of the ride. Both rides put you for a short while on the wide shoulder of busy Route 5 in New Market. For a short distance you have high speed traffic next to you. Just be patient at the crossings and soon you will return to less-travelled roads.

52. The Bald Cypress Swamp (15 or 31 miles; III)

Paved roads including shoulders of busier roads; starts at Calvert Middle School in Prince Frederick, Md.: From I-95, Washington Beltway, take exit 11, Pennsylvania Avenue Route 4 South. Follow for 31 miles to Prince Frederick. Turn left on Armory Road at the MacDonalds restaurant. The school is on the right in 0.2 miles.

When you arrive at the Battle Creek Cypress Swamp, park your bike and walk the quarter-mile trail through the swamp. Here, you enter a primordial world. The giant bald cypress trees tower 100 feet overhead and block the sunlight. Their knobby "knees" stick upward from the swampy base, looking like something from a science fiction movie. Much of the Coastal Plain may have looked like this 100,000 years ago.

On this ride you explore the area to the south and west of Prince Frederick in Calvert County. The visitor center at the cypress swamp offers restrooms and water. On the longer ride you cycle to Broomes Island, home to an oyster fleet. The recently renovated Stoney's restaurant in Broomes Island offers a chance to enjoy the waterfront during lunch.

53. A Day in the Forest (6, 8 or 10 miles; II)

Unpaved gravel and forest roads; starts at the Charcoal Kiln parking lot in Cedarville State Forest in Brandywine, Md.: From I-95, Washington Beltway, take exit 7A, Route 5, Branch Avenue South toward Waldorf. Follow for 11.5 miles and turn left on Cedarville Road. In 2.4 miles turn right on Bee Oak Road. Go 1.7 miles and turn right on Forest Road at the stop sign. Follow unpaved Forest Road for 0.2 miles and turn right at the charcoal kiln parking lot.

Cycling through this lush forest, it is hard to imagine the area was once devoid of trees. The Indians burnt down the trees so they could hunt, and then the English settlers cut down the trees to plant tobacco. Today, the trees block the sunlight and offer cool respite on a hot day. Birds sing unseen among the dense vegetation. Fortunately for us, the State of Maryland purchased this former farmland in the 1930s for a forest demonstration area.

Cedarville State Forest, sitting just 15 miles south of Washington's Beltway in southern Maryland, offers pleasant, easy riding on its unpaved forest roads. The smooth roads are particularly attractive to beginning mountain bikers and riders of hybrid bikes. Here you can sample an enjoyable ride through the forest without finding rocks or logs as obstacles. Most of the roads are open to bikes but closed to cars, insuring an even more enjoyable ride.

At this writing, the forest has no formal policy on bicyclists. The manager has said that the dirt roads are open to cyclists. He asks that cyclists do not use the single-track trails in the park due to the wet nature of several trails. This may change, but for now please stay off the narrower hiking trails unless you first check with a ranger.

Several roads have gates that cyclists simply ride around. On the Sunset Road (the eight mile ride) there are several "Do Not Enter" signs. According to the manager, these signs apply to cars but not cyclists. The area south of Sunset Road is open to hikers, cyclists and horseback riders, but not automobiles. Cedarville Pond in the southern end of the forest makes a nice picnic spot.

54. The Sanctuary (17 or 33 miles; II/III)

Paved roads with 0.4 miles of gravel road on the longer ride; starts at Mattaponi Elementary School in Rosaryville, Md: From I-95, Washington Beltway, take Route 4 South/East toward Upper Marlboro. Go 2.9 miles and exit right onto Route 223, Woodyard Road. Bear right in 2.5 miles onto Rosaryville Road at the traffic light. In 2.8 miles continue straight onto Old Indian Road at Route 301, Crain Highway. Bear left in 0.3 miles on Duley Station Road. Go 0.4 miles and turn right into the school.

Ride into the Merkle Wildlife Sanctuary in the late fall and you find geese blanketing the fields. Thousands of Canadian Geese spend the winter here, in the largest wildlife refuge on the western shore of the Chesapeake Bay. The sanctuary makes a pleasant destination and offers a good view of the grounds when you enter. Also, you can refill your water bottles and use the restrooms at the visitor center.

The longer ride visits the remains of Nottingham. Nottingham was once a bustling port where ocean going vessels unloaded their goods. The British invasion force landed here in 1814 during the War of 1812. They then defeated the defending American forces in the Battle of Bladensburg and burned Washington, D.C. Today, little of Nottingham remains.

The destination of the longer ride is a landing on the Patuxent River. The landing makes a relaxing picnic spot. Both rides pass a farm on Molly Berry Road where you sometimes see bison and other exotic animals.

55. A New Deale (31 or 43 miles; II)

Paved roads; starts at Davidsonville Elementary School in Davidsonville, Md.: Take Route 50 east. Exit onto Route 424 south toward Davidsonville. Go 3.3 miles and turn right on Route 214. In 0.7 miles turn right into the school.

The Happy Harbor Inn in Deale, as weather beaten as ever, still serves modest but tasty seafood at the water's edge. As far as we know, it has been there forever. On several happy occasions, we have filled several tables with cyclists. We now get reports that Suzy's restaurant, in a marina a little south of the Happy Harbor, welcomes cyclists too. We don't always ride to eat, it just seems that way.

Anyway, these roads in southern Anne Arundel County and northern Calvert County still draw cyclists from the nearby cities. These rides are old standbys, always to be counted on for a satisfying ride. And how much nicer it is when a waterfront restaurant awaits. The longer ride gets a little hillier and visits the western shore of the Chesapeake Bay. Both rides return on mostly quiet roads that occasionally use sections of busier ones.

56. Lunch on the Sassafras (32 or 42 miles; II)

Paved roads; starts at Chestertown Landing in Chestertown, Md.: Take Route 50 east over the Chesapeake Bay Bridge onto the Eastern Shore. Go straight at Route 301 for 5.8 miles and turn left on Route 213, Centerville Road. Follow for 17.8 miles into Chestertown. Turn left on Cross Street, 289 at the traffic light. Go 0.1 miles and turn left on High Street. Proceed 0.3 miles to the landing.

What better destination than Betterton, Maryland's only public beach on the Chesapeake Bay's Eastern Shore? Rural Kent County sits on the Eastern Shore and offers miles of attractive roads. Chestertown, a gem of a town with a colonial town square and quaint buildings, is an ideal place to begin and end a ride. You begin on the Chester River and head north to the Sassafras River, riding through the farmland along the way. In places, Kent County looks like Maryland's answer to Iowa: corn, corn and more corn.

Betterton grew as a resort community at the turn of the century. Its architecture certainly recalls that era. Since there are no stores in Betterton, buy food in Still Pond and carry it to Betterton. There you can eat on the beach or on the pier. The longer ride passes Vonnies, a restaurant long known to cyclists, at the crossroads of Harmony Corner. Turners Creek Park on the Sassafras River provides another place for a break or picnic lunch.

57. The First Eastern Shore Ride (26 or 34 miles; I)

Paved roads; starts at the municipal parking lot on Dover Street next to the police station in Easton, Md.: Take 50 east over the Chesapeake Bay Bridge onto the Eastern Shore to Easton. Turn right on Route 322 toward Easton, St. Michaels and Oxford. In 0.4 miles turn left at the sign to Easton on unmarked Washington Street. Follow Washington Street south into downtown Easton and turn right on Dover Street just past the courthouse. Turn left into the parking lot just past the police station.

Just about everyone rides some variation of this ride on their first visit to the Eastern Shore. The flat terrain and attractive towns are irresistible to most cyclists. You visit distinctive small towns and use the oldest remaining ferry in the country. It is no wonder that cyclists continue to flock here.

The ride runs south from Easton on country roads. The ruined church at Route 50 is that of White Marsh Church, built around 1685. You then ride into Oxford on the Route 333 bicycle lanes. For a more direct but busier ride, turn right on Route 333 in Easton and ride the bicycle lanes directly to Oxford. This variation is several miles shorter, but has much more traffic.

Oxford, on the Tred Avon River, is a handsome small town with a tree-lined, 18th and 19th century appearance. Dating from 1668, Oxford was a busy port before the Revolutionary War. The village green on the riverfront makes a relaxing place to enjoy the ice cream available in the nearby market.

You cross the Tred Avon River on a ferry that has operated since 1760. The ferry ride costs $1.50 per bicyclist and operates year round except on Christmas Day. For the schedule of hours call the ferry at (410) 226-5408 or (410) 745-9023. In Royal Oak you can return directly to Easton on the bicycle lanes of Route 33 and other roads. Or you can visit St. Michaels before returning to Easton.

The longer ride visits bustling St. Michaels, a sparkling little town built around "the green" or St. Mary's Square. One of the best-known yachting centers on the East Coast, St. Michaels has been a shipbuilding center since the seventeenth century. Local legend has it that when the British shelled the town at night during the War of 1812, townspeople hung lanterns from the tops of trees and tricked the British into firing their cannons over the town.

Today St. Michaels is known for its seafood restaurants and shops. It also boasts the Chesapeake Bay Maritime Museum, which is located on the harbor at the end of Mill Street. The 16 acre museum traces the history of the bay and the waterman's life. The museum is open daily, except Mondays, from 10 a.m. to 4 p.m., and 10 a.m. to 5 p.m. in the summer.

58. The Little Red Schoolhouse (24 or **40** miles; I)

Paved roads; starts in the municipal parking lot on Dover Street next to the police station in Easton, Md.: see directions in Ride #57.

After riding the Oxford Ferry loop (Ride #57), cyclists often spend a second day in the attractive area north of Easton. Here, you follow country roads through mostly flat terrain and over several nice creeks. Your destination is indeed a little red schoolhouse.

At the schoolhouse, enjoy a picnic lunch and decide whether to ride the longer ride or head back to Easton. On the longer ride you ride to Wye Mill, home of the Wye Oak. At more than 450 years, it is the oldest white oak in the country. It was 100 years old when the first English settlers landed! Nearby, you can visit a restored grist mill that supplied George Washington's troops at Valley Forge. The pond across from the mill provides another restful picnic spot.

59. The Goose Gazer (7, **26** or 38 miles; I)

Paved roads; starts in Blackwater Wildlife Refuge foot trails parking lot in Cambridge, Md.: Take Route 50 east over the Chesapeake Bay bridge onto the Eastern Shore, through Easton, to Cambridge. Continue through Cambridge and turn right on Woods Road. Go 1 mile and turn right on Route 16, Cambridge Parkway. Go 1.8 miles, past the high school, and turn left onto Egypt Road at Chesapeake Street. Continue south on Egypt Road for 7 miles. Turn left onto Key Wallace Drive and go 0.3 miles. Turn right onto Wildlife Drive at the Blackwater Office. Bear left in 0.2 miles and continue 0.1 miles. Turn left into the foot trails parking lot.

During the fall, migrating geese fill the fields and sky. Geese flying overhead make so much racket that they drown out conversation. Blackwater Wildlife Refuge on the Eastern Shore lies on the Atlantic flyway, the goose's Route 66.

One-way Wildlife Drive at the beginning of the ride sets the tone for the whole day. While meandering through ponds and marshes, you will want to linger and look at the waterfowl. You will see many herons, egrets, ducks and geese. During the winter, chances are good you will see a bald eagle.

Vast marshes and wetlands dominate Dorchester County. The heart of the county is the scenic Blackwater National Wildlife Refuge, a 16,000 acre refuge established in 1932. The refuge is the chief wintering ground for the Canadian goose and a haven for endangered species such as the bald eagle and the Delmarva fox squirrel.

The short ride turns right from Wildlife Drive on public roads and returns to the start. Stop at the Visitor Center with its displays of the refuge's wildlife.

The two longer loops head south into the Lakes and Straits Neck district. The longest ride visits the isolated towns of Crapo, Wingate and Toddville. The land of this area is so low that it frequently floods. These fishing villages appear little changed by modern America and are unlikely to grow any time soon.

On the two longer rides you return to the wildlife refuge through a scenic, open marsh. The road through the marsh twists and turns as it seeks higher and dryer land. All around you are ponds, waterways and, during the autumn and winter, geese.

60. To the Ends of the Earth (28 or 60 miles; I)

Paved roads; starts at the Blackwater Wildlife Refuge foot trails parking lot in Cambridge, Md.: see directions in Ride #59.

As far as you can see, marsh stretches away from you. The smell of the marsh fills your nostrils. A high tide may cover the road with a few inches of water. An occasional egret or heron graces the water. Somewhere in the marsh grass hides the black rail, the most reclusive bird in North America.

The road through the marsh to Elliott ranks as one of our favorites in the region. It certainly is the most remote and wildest road we know. Elliott sits at the end of a spit of land. To reach it you cycle nine miles on a narrow, meandering road through open marshlands. Elliott feels like the town that time forgot, the town that modern life has mostly passed by. There are two small stores to buy food and a beach to enjoy land's end.

Outside of Elliott you pass a few small settlements but no stores or restaurants. Carry enough food and water with you when you leave Blackwater. The short ride bypasses the out-and-back section to Elliott and offers a quiet ride through pine forests and marshes. If you don't want to ride the entire 60 miles, cycle south toward Elliott and turn around whenever you want. For a 39 mile ride, begin in the town of Vienna and ride to Elliott and back.

Of the four times we have visited Elliott, twice we had fierce headwinds that made the return trip feel much longer than the trip out. We prefer to ride our tandem to Elliott since it punches through the wind better than a single bicycle. Better yet, visit Elliott on a day when there is little wind or invite strong friends whom you can draft.

61. Saxis-of-Pearl (29 or 49 miles; I)

Paved roads; starts at Arcadia High School in Oak Hall, Va. on Virginia's Eastern Shore: Take Route 50 east onto the Eastern Shore, to Salisbury, Md.. Follow Business 13 south past Salisbury State College to Route 13. Follow Route 13 south for 33 miles into Virginia and turn right into the high school, 1.5 miles after Route 175. Park in the back of the school.

The last few years have been hard for the oystermen of the Chesapeake Bay. They have struggled to work on the bay as their annual harvest of oysters has declined. The town of Saxis sits on the bay, isolated from the rest of Virginia by more than the marsh that separates it from the peninsula. Saxis still retains its fleet of oystering boats and an appearance of slow, easy living.

On the way to Saxis you pass through woodlands and several small towns. Then you cycle out to Saxis through the marsh. Here you usually see egrets, blue herons and cormorants. The boat ramp at the oyster fleet's harbor in Saxis makes a good lunch spot. After you return to firm ground, you can head straight back to your starting place. If you want greater mileage, meander north and east through the farmland and woodland that cover the area.

62. Land Across the Water (10 or 12 miles; I)

Paved bike paths closed to cars before 3 p.m. and an optional paved road; starts at Chincoteague Wildlife Refuge Visitor Center in Chincoteague, Va.: take Route 50 east onto the Eastern Shore, to Salisbury, Md.. Follow Business 13 past Salisbury State College to

Route 13. Follow Route 13 for 31.5 miles and turn left on Route 175 toward Chincoteague. Go 10 miles and turn left on Main Street. In 0.4 miles turn right on Maddox Boulevard, toward Assateague. Enter the wildlife refuge in 1.8 miles. Turn left into the visitors center parking lot 0.2 miles after the entrance station.

The Indians had it right when they called the island "Gingoteague" or "beautiful land across the water." While Chincoteague has become a crowded resort town, the Chincoteague Wildlife Refuge on nearby Assateague Island preserves the beautiful wild charms known to the Indians. Here in the Refuge you find the best bike trails in the region. We wish all bike trails were this nice!

The trails through the Refuge ($3.00 admission per car) display the island's charms and some of the tamest wild animals anywhere. Wild ponies graze in open meadows and allow you to ride close to them. Sika deer stand in the pine forests and watch you cycle by. Blue herons and snowy egrets fish in shallow water channels, oblivious to you. In the autumn Canadian and snow geese fill the large ponds and open fields. At the beaches on the Atlantic Ocean you 'can walk onto the sand dunes and watch the ocean's waves crash ashore.

All the bike trails in the refuge are traffic free until 3:00 p.m. when Wildlife Drive opens to cars. A one-mile bike trail connects the town of Chincoteague with the refuge. This allows you to start your ride in town and miss the admission booths. Just remember, as irresistible as those "adorable" wild ponies are, don't feed or pet them.

An early morning ride in Chincoteague Wildlife Refuge, Va.

48. Around Maryland Point

Distance:	23, **37** or 41 miles
Rating:	II; Paved roads
Start:	Boat ramp at Smallwood State Park in Charles County, Md.

37 Mile Ride

0.0	L	from parking lot toward park entrance
0.4	L	Sweden Point Rd at T
0.7	R	224 (unmarked) at SS
5.6	R	224 at 344
☞*		
20.5	R	6 at T
21.2		Arrive at the Potomac; Turn Around
21.9	S	6 at 224 (Store at mile 23.3)
26.9	R	425
☞**		
*☞		
30.3	L	425 at Durham Church Rd
31.7	S	425 at 6 (Store to right 0.1 mile on 6 in **Ironsides**)
31.8	L	Smallwood Church Rd
36.0	R	224 (unmarked) at T
36.6	L	Sweden Point Rd into Smallwood State Park
36.9	R	toward boat ramp at bottom of hill
37.3	R	into parking lot

* 23 Mile Ride

10.3	L	Liverpool Point Rd; becomes Baptist Church Rd (Store at mile 10.6)
14.6	L	425 (unmarked) at T (Pick up cues in 1.6 miles at mile 30.3 on the 37 mile ride – * ☞)

** 41 Mile Ride

30.3	S	Durham Church Rd (**Caution**: dangerous curve in 1 mile)
31.8	R	Rte 6 at T (unmarked)
32.7	L	Annapolis Woods Rd
35.6	L	Poorhouse Rd
37.7	S	484, Pisgah Rd (Store)
39.3	L	Sweden Point Rd
40.2	S	Sweden Point Rd into park
40.5	R	toward boat ramp at bottom of hill
40.9	R	into parking lot

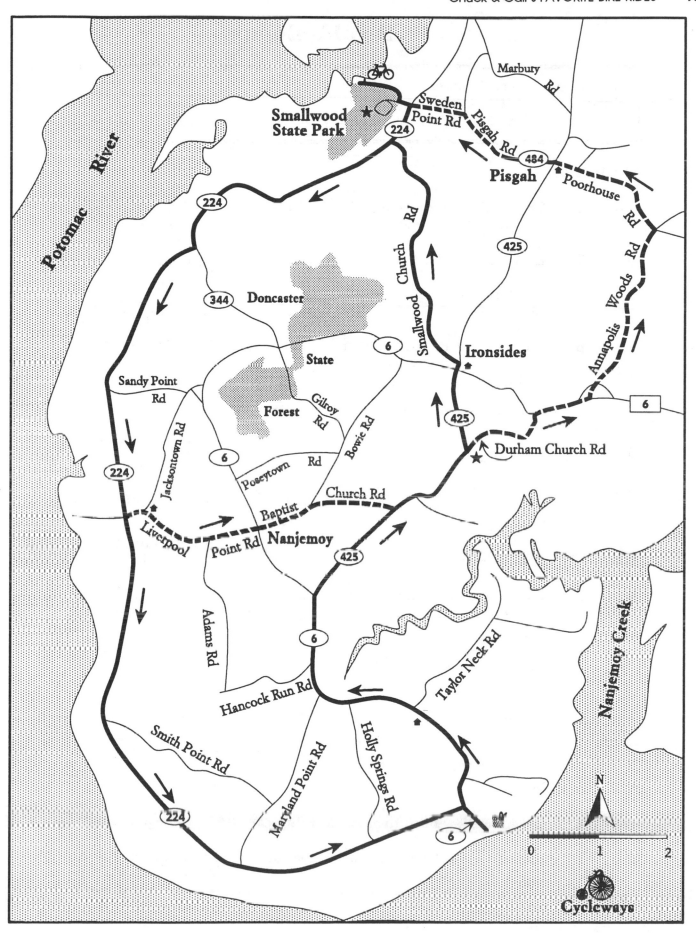

Smallwood State Park

Potomac River

Marbury Rd

Sweden Point Rd

Pisgah Rd

Pisgah

Poorhouse Rd

224

224

344

Doncaster

Smallwood Church Rd

Ironsides

425

484

425

Annapolis Woods Rd

6

State

Gilroy Rd

Sandy Point Rd

Jacksontown Rd

Forest

Bowie Rd

6

Poseytown Rd

Church Rd

6

Baptist

Durham Church Rd

224

Liverpool Point Rd **Nanjemoy**

425

Adams Rd

6

Smith Point Rd

Maryland Point Rd

Hancock Run Rd

Holly Springs Rd

Taylor Neck Rd

Nanjemoy Creek

224

6

N

0   1   2

Cycleways

49. Booth's Escape

Distance:	18 or **33** miles
Rating:	II/III; Paved roads
Start:	Charles County Courthouse & Government Complex in LaPlata, Md.

33 Mile Ride

0.0	L	Church St with courthouse on your left
0.1	R	E Charles St at T (⊗)
0.3	S	Rte 6 at Rte 301 (⊗ - use shoulder)
2.5	BL	Chapel Point Rd (Store); Port Tobacco Courthouse on right at mile 2.9
6.4 🏞*	L	Chapel Point Rd at SS
8.3	BR	Irving Rd
8.8	R	Rte 301 (⊗ - use shoulder)
9.3	L	Mt Air Rd
9.4	R	Faulkner Rd
9.9	R	Popes Creek Rd (unmarked) (Store at Rte 301, Food in Popes Creek at mile 13.0)
15.1	L	Edge Hill Rd (unmarked) at T
16.0	L	Rte 301 (⊗ - use shoulder)
16.4	R	Rte 234 at blinking light (use shoulder)
18.0	R	Penns Hill Rd after Allens Fresh
19.9	L	Newport Church Rd at T
21.5	R	Penns Hill Rd at T
24.1	L	Cooksey Rd
26.2	L	Rte 6 (unmarked) at T (use shoulder)
27.9	L	Bel Alton-Newtown Rd
28.0 *☞	R	Springfield-Newtown Rd
30.7	R	St Marys Ave (unmarked) at SS before Rte 301 (Food)
32.5	R	E Charles St at T in **LaPlata**
32.6	L	Washington St at TL
32.7	L	Baltimore St into parking lot behind courthouse

---

* 18 Mile Ride

8.6	S	Bel Alton-Newtown Rd at Rte 301 (Stores)
12.9	L	Springhill-Newtown Rd (Pick up cues in 2.7 miles at mile 30.7 on the 33 mile ride – *☞)

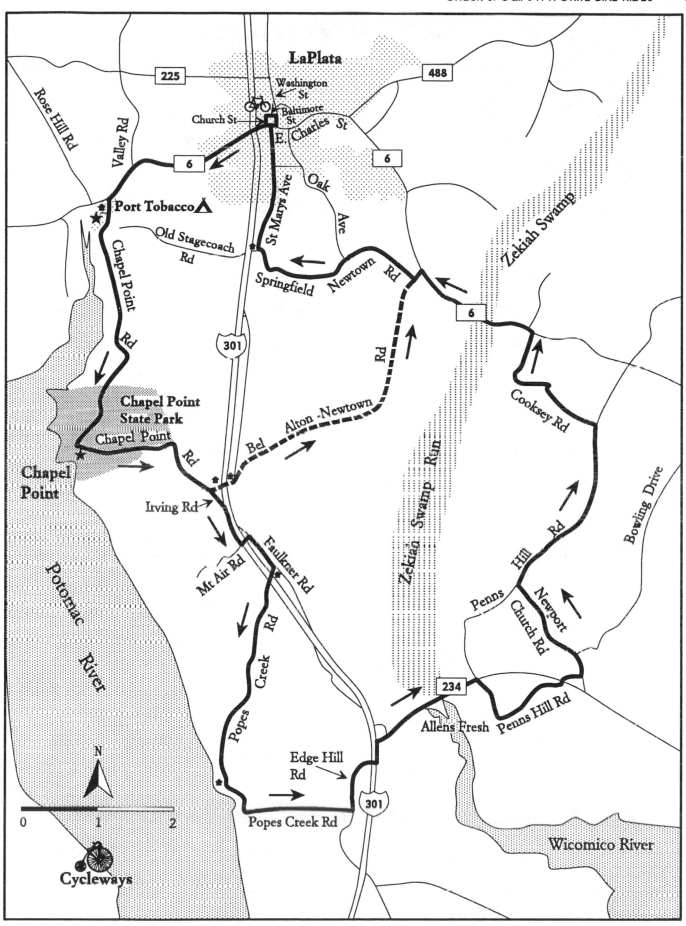

50. Blessing of the Fleet

Distance:	**29** miles
Rating:	II; Paved roads
Start:	Chopticon High School in Morganza, Md.

29 Mile Ride

0.0	L	242, Colton Point Rd from parking lot (Store, Food at Rte 234)
4.6	L	470, Oakley Rd
8.4	L	242 at SS, Colton Point Rd (Store) (Store at mile 9.5 and 11.3)
11.4	L	Point Breeze Rd at T in **Colton Point**
11.5		Arrive St Clement's Island Potomac Museum (Water)
11.7	L	Bayview Rd
11.9	R	242 at SS (Store)
16.2	L	239, Bushwood Wharf Rd (Store on 242 just ahead)
17.5	R	Bushwood Rd (nice view and store straight ahead)
20.7	L	Dynard Hurry Rd at T; becomes Chaptico Hurry Rd
24.7	R	238 at SS in **Chaptico** (Store, Food)
27.5	R	Dr Johnson Rd
29.4	R	242 at T
29.4	L	into parking lot

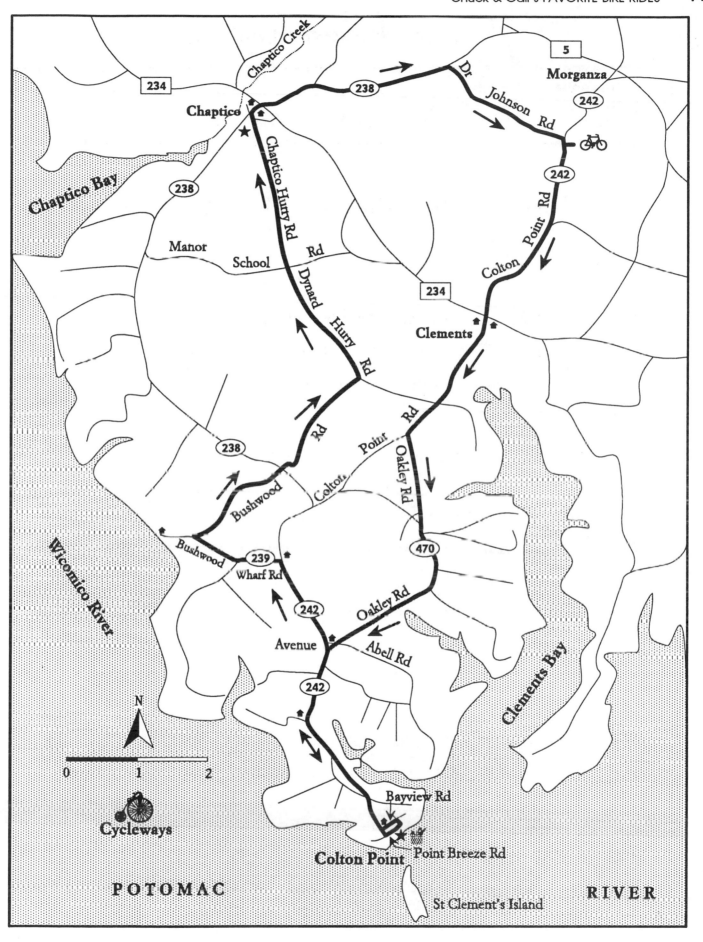

234

Chaptico Creek

238

5

Morganza

242

Chaptico

★

238

Chaptico Bay

Chaptico Hurry Rd

Johnson Rd

242

Colton Point Rd

238

Manor

School Rd

Dynard Hurry Rd

234

Clements

Wicomico River

238

Bushwood Rd

Colton Point Rd

Oakley Rd

470

239

Bushwood Wharf Rd

242

Avenue

Oakley Rd

Abell Rd

Clements Bay

242

N

0   1   2

Cycleways

242

Bayview Rd

Colton Point

Point Breeze Rd

St Clement's Island

POTOMAC   **R I V E R**

51. Hidden Amish

Distance:	25 or **49** miles
Rating:	II/III; Paved roads
Start:	T.C. Martin Elementary School in Bryantown, Md.

49 Mile Ride

0.0	R	232, Olivers Shop Rd from parking lot; becomes Trinity Church Rd at Rte 6 (Store)
9.3	L	Ryceville Rd
11.6	L	N Ryceville Rd
14.7	L	Thompson Corner Rd (unmarked), 236, at T
15.0	R	Lockes Crossing Rd
16.9	R	Old Rte 5 at T (Store on left at Sunoco station, mile 18.7)
19.4	R	Baptist Church Rd
24.5	L	238 (unmarked) at T
26.3	R	Dr Johnson Rd
28.3	L	242 (unmarked) at T; becomes Morganza Turner Rd at Rte 5
32.8	S	6 at Rte 235 (Store)
38.6	L	6 at T at All Faith Church Rd
41.2	R	Rte 5 (⊗ - use shoulder) (Store)
41.5	L	Charlotte Hall School Rd
41.7	R	Old Rte 5 (on left is Ye Coole Springs, a good place for a picnic lunch)
43.2	L	Oaks Rd
45.9	R	Oaks Rd at Keech Rd at SS
48.0	R	Olivers Shop Rd at T
49.4	L	into school parking lot

* 25 Mile Ride

16.7	L	Rte 5 at T (⊗ - use shoulder)(Store on left at Rte 6 (Pick up cues in 0.5 mile at mile 41.5 on the 49 mile ride – *☞)

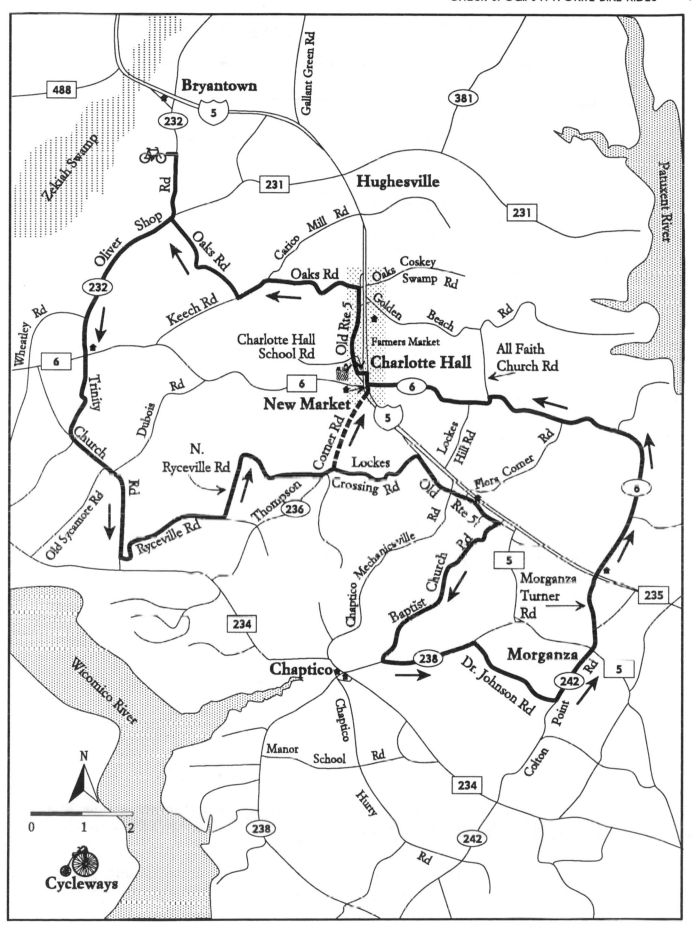

52. The Bald Cypress Swamp

Distance	15 or 31 miles
Rating:	III; Paved roads including shoulders of busier roads
Start:	Calvert Middle School in Prince Frederick, Md.

15 Mile Ride

0.0	R	Armory Rd from parking lot
0.8	L	765, Main St at T (Store at mile 0.9)
2.6	L	Rte 2/4 at T (⊗ - use shoulder)
3.3	R	506, Sixes Rd
5.2	L	Grays Rd
5.4 ☛*	R	into Battle Creek Cypress Swamp (Water, Restrooms)
5.4 *☛	L	Grays Rd from Swamp entrance
5.6	L	506, Sixes Rd at T
7.5	R	508, Adelina Rd
8.6	BR	Rte 231 (⊗ - use shoulder) (Store on right at mile 8.8)
9.6	L	Barstow Rd in **Barstow**
12.0	BR	Stokley Rd at Leitchs Wharf Rd
14.1	R	Rte 2/4 at TL (⊗ - use shoulder)
14.7	L	Armory Rd (Food)
14.9	R	into school parking lot

* 31 Mile Ride

5.4	R	Grays Rd from Swamp entrance
8.4	R	Broomes Island Rd, 264 at T (unmarked) (Store at mile 10.7)
13.4	L	Oyster House Rd (one way); Arrive at Stoney's Restaurant at mile 13.5
13.7	R	Broomes Island Rd at T, 264 (Store)
18.9	L	Grays Rd (Pick up cues in 3.2 miles at mile 5.6 on the 15 mile ride – *☛)

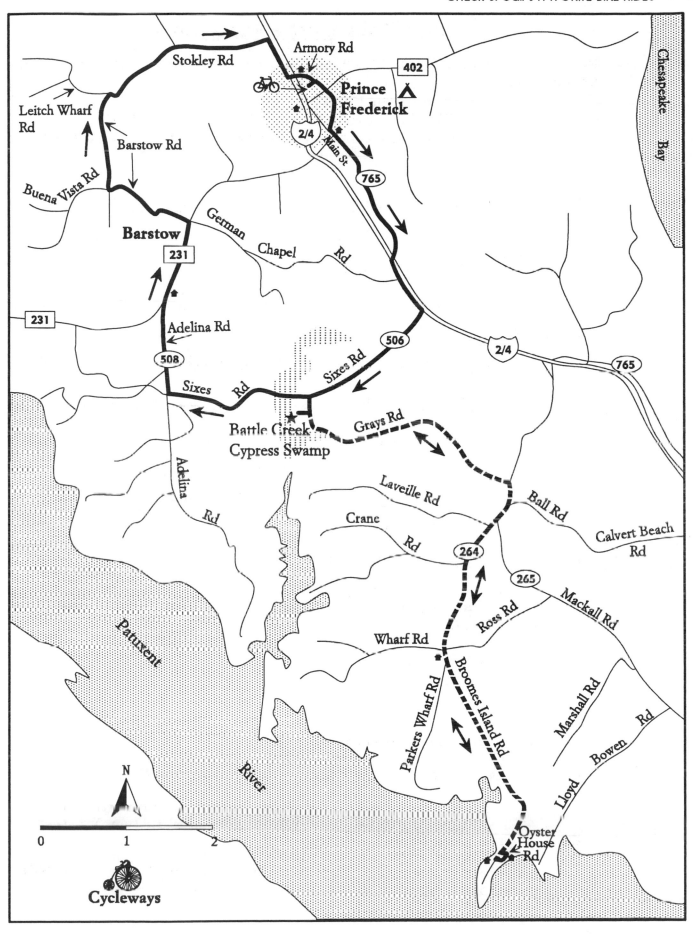

Chesapeake Bay

Armory Rd

Prince Frederick

402

Stokley Rd

Leitch Wharf Rd

Barstow Rd

Buena Vista Rd

2/4

Main St

765

Barstow

German Chapel Rd

231

506

2/4

765

231

Adelina Rd

508

Sixes Rd

Sixes   Rd

Battle Creek Cypress Swamp

Grays Rd

Adelina   Rd

Laveille Rd

Ball Rd

Crane   Rd

264

Calvert Beach Rd

265

Mackall Rd

Patuxent

Ross Rd

Wharf Rd

Parkers Wharf Rd

Broomes Island Rd

Marshall Rd

River

Lloyd   Bowen   Rd

N

Oyster House Rd

0   1   2

Cycleways

53. A Day in the Forest

Distance:	**6**, 8 or 10 miles
Rating:	II; Unpaved gravel and forest roads
Start:	Charcoal Kiln parking lot in Cedarville State Forest in Brandywine, Md.

6 Mile Ride

0.0	R	Forest Rd from parking lot	2.4	R	unmarked road at T
0.1	L	unmarked road just past bridge	2.5	R	first road on right after reentering woods
0.7	R	Cross Rd (unmarked) at T	2.8	BL	as road narrows at beaver pond; walk across foot bridge and continue on road
0.7	BL	Mistletoe Rd at Y (unmarked)			
			3.2	S	at gate at unmarked Forest Rd
1.7	L	Forest Rd at T			
1.8	L	into parking lot at pond; continue straight past gate (brown blazed Plantation Trail) following road up the hill	3.6	R	Brown/Green blazed road
			4.1 ☞*	L	Forest Rd (unmarked) at T
			5.6	L	into parking lot

* 8 mile Ride

5.5	L	Sunset Rd	7.1	L	at first unmarked road
6.3	L	dirt road at fish hatchery (go past Do Not Enter sign)	7.8	BR	Sunset Rd (unmarked)
			8.1	L	Forest Rd at T
6.7	BL	at Y at cross road	8.2	L	into parking lot

** 10 mile Ride

8.2	L	from parking lot	9.4	BR	at Able Rd at Y, toward houses
8.4	R	Loop Rd			
			9.5	L	Forest Rd (unmarked) at T
8.5	BL	at water tower; continue straight, crossing stream; follow road around campground	10.2	R	into parking lot

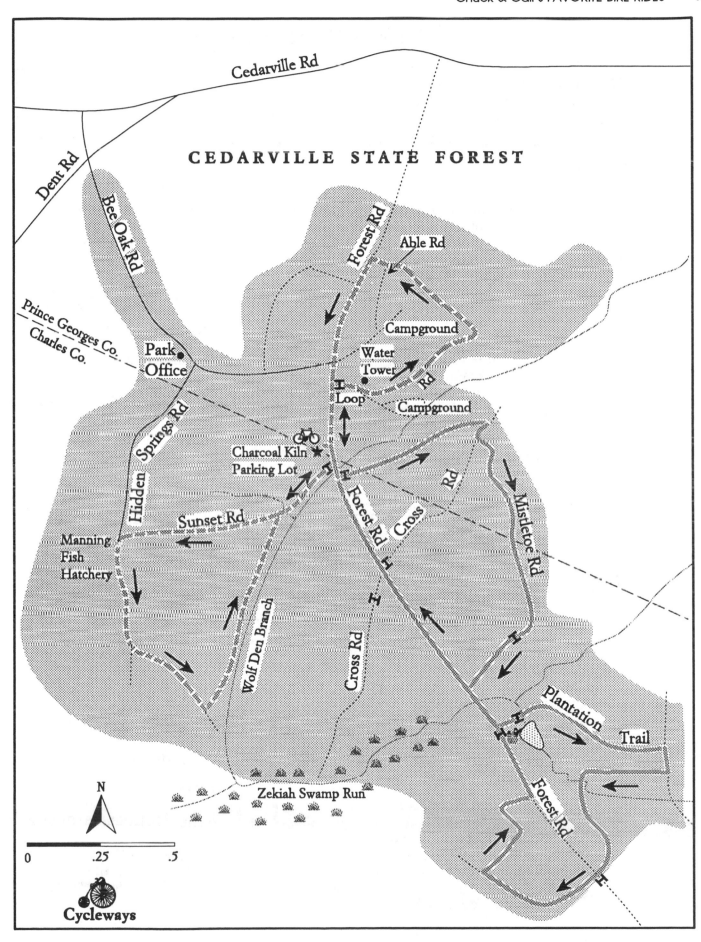

CEDARVILLE STATE FOREST

Cedarville Rd

Dent Rd

Bee Oak Rd

Prince Georges Co.
Charles Co.

Park
Office

Forest Rd

Able Rd

Campground

Water
Tower

Loop

Campground

Rd

Hidden Springs Rd

Charcoal Kiln
Parking Lot

Cross Rd

Forest Rd

Mistletoe Rd

Sunset Rd

Manning
Fish
Hatchery

Wolf Den Branch

Cross Rd

Plantation

Trail

Forest Rd

N

Zekiah Swamp Run

0   .25   .5

Cycleways

54. The Sanctuary

Distance:	17 or 33 miles
Rating:	II/III; Paved roads; 0.4 miles of optional gravel road on the longer ride
Start:	Mattaponi Elementary School in Rosaryville, Md.

17 Mile Ride

0.0	R	Duley Station Rd from parking lot	10.2	L	Croom Rd at T (Store)
0.1	L	Duley Station Rd at Cheltenham Rd at T	10.8	R	Candy Hill Rd
			12.0	R	Molly Berry Rd at T
			*☞		
2.6	R	Croom Rd at T (Store at mile 2.8 in **Croom**)	12.4	BR	Molly Berry Rd at North Keys Rd
3.0	L	St Thomas Church Rd; becomes Fenno Rd	13.5	L	Van Brady Rd
5.9	L	into **Merkle Wildlife Sanctuary**; follow road to visitor center and back to entrance (Water; restrooms)	16.1	S	Van Brady Rd at Van Brady Rd
			16.4	R	Old Indian Head Rd at T
			16.6	R	Cheltenham Rd
7.8	L	Fenno Rd (unmarked) at T to exit Sanctuary	16.9	L	Duley Station Rd
☜*					
8.6	R	Nottingham Rd at T	17.0	R	into school parking lot

* 33 Mile Ride

8.6	L	Nottingham Rd at T	18.7	R	into Patuxent River Park boating area; Continue on gravel road to pier and picnic tables. Turn Around.
9.7	R	Tanyard Rd in **Nottingham**			
11.6	S	Brooks Church Rd	19.1	L	Magruder's Landing Rd (unmarked) to exit park
12.0	BL	Baden Naylor Rd at Y	20.3	R	Croom Rd at T
13.2	L	Nelson Perrie Rd	20.5	L	Baden Westwood Rd
14.5	R	Bald Eagle School Rd	23.9	R	Baden Naylor Rd at T
15.8	L	Baden Westwood Rd at T	26.3	BL	Molly Berry Rd (Pick up cues in 2.1 miles at mile 12.4 on the 17 mile ride – *☞)
17.3	R	Croom Rd at T			
17.5	L	Magruder's Ferry Rd			

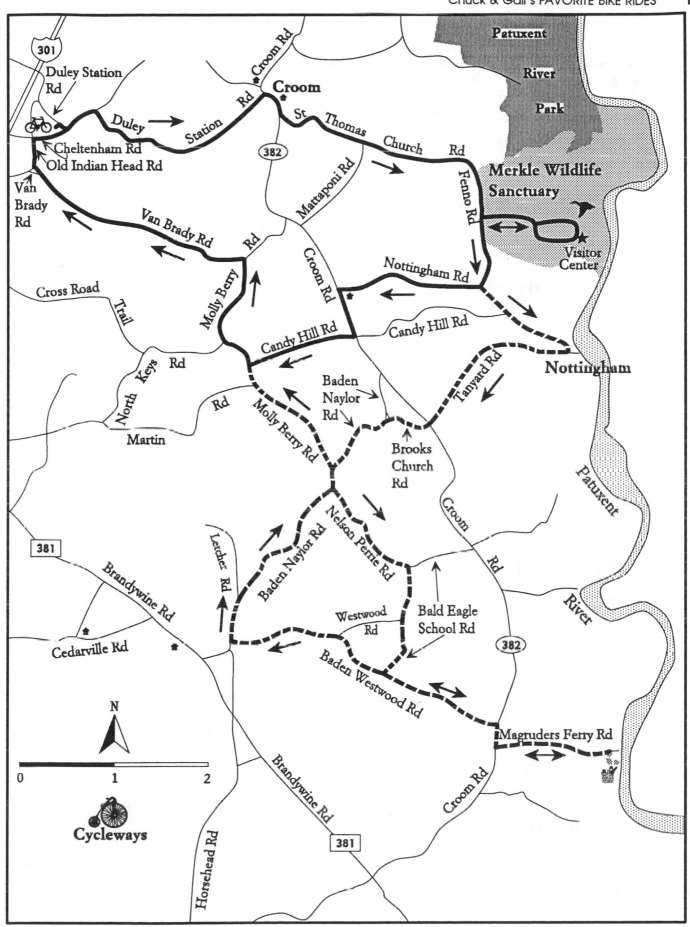

55. A New Deale

Distance	31 or **43** miles
Rating:	II; Paved roads
Start:	Davidsonville Elementary School in Davidsonville, Md.

43 Mile Ride

0.0	S	Queen Anne Bridge Rd, crossing Rte 214 from school
1.1	L	Wayson Rd
2.3	L	Harwood Rd at T
4.7	R	Rte 2 at T (⊗ - use shoulder)
5.4	L	Owensville Sudley Rd
9.3	L	Sudley Rd
10.5	R	Muddy Creek Rd at T
10.7	R	Swamp Circle Rd
12.6	R	Deale Rd, 256 at T (Store to left)
13.6 ☜*	L	256, Deale Rd at T (Food)
14.8	L	Franklin Gibson Rd
16.2	L	Leitch Rd
17.2	R	Town Point Rd at T; becomes Fairhaven Rd at SS
20.2	R	261, Friendship Rd at T (Store at Rte 2); becomes Sansbury Rd

22.3	R	Wilson Rd
23.8	R	Jewell Rd at T
24.1	L	McKendree Rd
25.9	L	258 at SS
26.7	L	Fisher Station Rd
28.7	L	Fisher Station Rd to cross Rte 4; becomes Lower Pindle Rd (unmarked)
29.7	R	Lower Pindle Rd (unmarked) at Mallard La at T
30.6 *☞	L	Pindell Rd; becomes Plummer La; becomes Sands Rd at Rte 4
39.1	L	Harwood Rd at T
40.5	BR	Queen Anne Bridge Rd at Patuxent River Rd
42.4	R	Rte 214 at SS
42.5	L	into school

* 31 Mile Ride

15.8	R	Rte 2 at T
16.2	L	258 at TL
16.8	R	Brooks Woods Rd
19.6	S	Grenock Rd, 259, at SS

19.7	L	408 at T
21.3	R	Ed Prout Rd
23.1	R	Sands Rd at T (Pick up cues in 4 miles at mile 39.1 on the 43 mile ride – *☞)

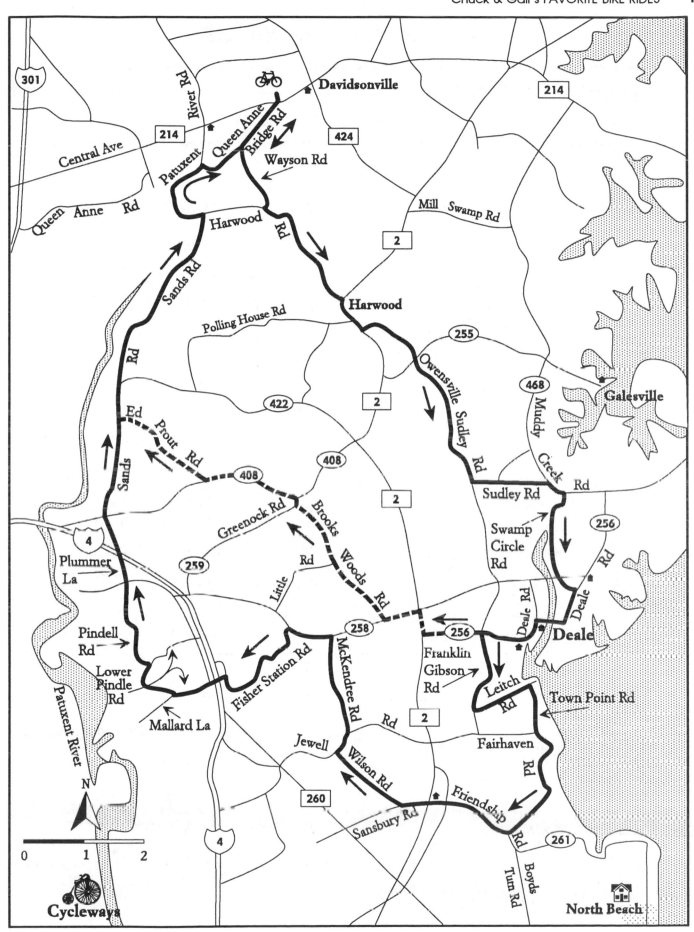

56. Lunch on the Sassafras

Distance:	**32** or 42 miles
Rating:	II; Paved roads
Start:	Chestertown Landing in Chestertown, Md.

32 Mile Ride

0.0	S	High St with Chester River at your back
1.2	R	Rte 291 (use shoulder)
5.0 ☜*	L	Perkins Hill Rd
5.8	L	Perkins Hill Rd at Stryckning Rd
7.8	R	Rte 213 at T (use shoulder)
8.3	L	292
12.0	S	Main St in **Still Pond** (Store); becomes Trustee St
12.3 *☞	L	Rosedale Cannery Rd at T
13.8	L	Royal Swan Rd as SS
14.1	R	292 (unmarked) at T; becomes Main St in **Betterton**
15.6	L	Ericsson Ave (unmarked, at beach); follow up hill (Good views from jetty; restrooms, snack bar in season)
16.2	R	Howell Point Rd at T
17.0	L	Clark Rd
18.6	R	Still Pond Neck Rd at SS
19.1	L	Still Pond Creek Rd
20.7	BR	Still Pond Creek Rd (unmarked) at Bessicks Corner Rd; becomes Montabello Lake Rd
23.9	L	297, Smithville Rd (unmarked) at T (Stores to R at mile 25.1 at Rte 298)
25.8	R	Porters Grove Worton Rd
27.9	L	514 (unmarked) at T (Store on right at mile 30.0)
30.4	L	Rte 20 at T in **Chestertown**; becomes High St
31.7		Arrive at Chestertown Landing

*42 Mile Ride

5.8	S	Stryckning Rd at Perkins Hill Rd
6.8	S	Morgnec Rd at SS
9.7	L	298, Browntown Rd (unmarked, after Kennedyville Rd) (Food/Store at mile 13.3)
14.6	R	Turners Creek Rd
17.2		Arrive Turner's Creek Park (Water, restrooms in season); Turn Around
18.6	R	Bloomfield Rd
21.1	R	566 at T (use shoulder)
21.9	BR	Medders Rd
22.1	BR	Rosedale Cannery Rd (Store 0.2 mile to left in **Still Pond**) (Pick up cues in 1.6 miles at mile 13.8 on the 32 mile ride – *☞)

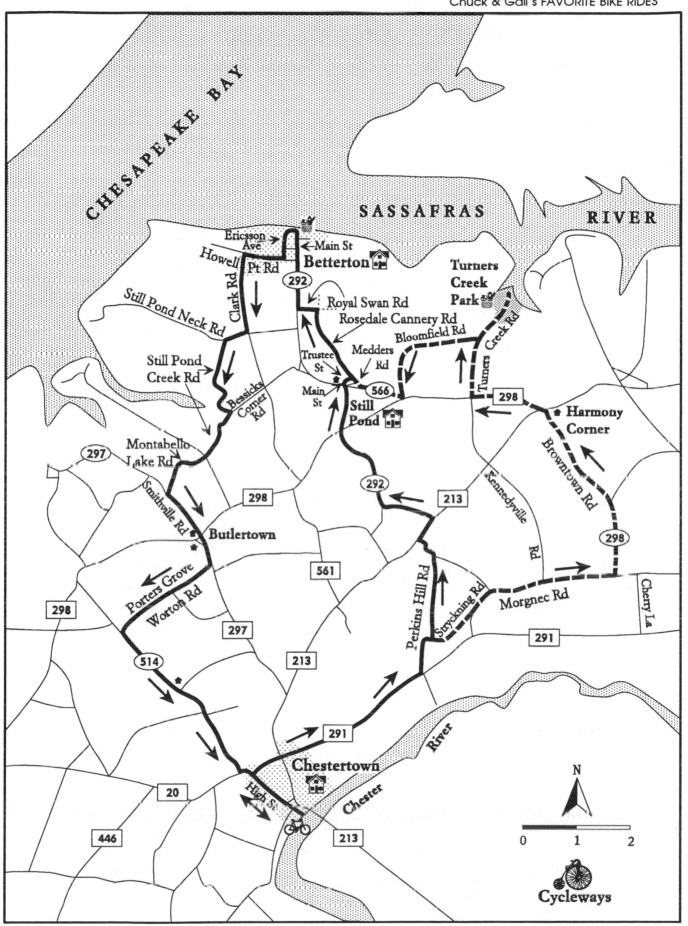

CHESAPEAKE BAY

SASSAFRAS RIVER

Ericsson Ave
Main St
Betterton
Howell Pt Rd
292
Clark Rd
Still Pond Neck Rd
Royal Swan Rd
Rosedale Cannery Rd
Bloomfield Rd
Turners Creek Park
Turners Creek Rd
Still Pond Creek Rd
Trustee St
Medders Rd
566
Main St
Still Pond
Bessicks Corner Rd
298
Harmony Corner
Montabello Lake Rd
297
292
213
Kennedyville Rd
Browntown Rd
Smithville Rd
298
Butlertown
561
298
Porters Grove
Worton Rd
Perkins Hill Rd
Stryckning Rd
Morgnec Rd
Cherry La
298
297
291
514
213
291
Chestertown
River
20
High St
Chester River
446
213

N

0   1   2

Cycleways

57. The First Eastern Shore Ride

Distance	**26** or 34 miles
Rating:	I; Paved roads
Start:	Muncipal parking lot on Dover St next to police station in Easton, Md.

26 Mile Ride

0.0	R	Dover St from north side of the parking lot with police station on your right
0.1	R	West St (unmarked) at SS
0.2	L	Glenwood Ave
0.2	R	S Washington St at T
1.1	L	Dutchman's Lane
1.7	S	Dutchman's Lane at Rte 50
3.6	R	Manadier Rd at T
4.6	BR	Manadier Rd at Boston Cliff Rd; becomes Hole in the Wall Rd
7.4	S	Almshouse Rd at Rte 50 (Church ruins on right)
10.1	L	Rte 333 (unmarked) at SS toward Oxford-Bellevue ferry (Store) (⊗, use bike lane)

13.5		Enter **Oxford**; Rte 333 becomes Morris St (Stores, Food)
14.5		Cross the Tred Avon River on the ferry ($1.50 for bikes)
14.5	S	Bellevue Rd (main road) from the ferry landing
🚲*		
17.8	R	329 at T in **Royal Oak** (Store)
20.1	R	Rte 33 at T (⊗, use bike lane) (Store at mile 20.4)
*☞		
22.8	L	370
22.9	R	Glebe Rd
25.3	S	Glebe Rd at Easton Parkway; becomes Washington St in **Easton**
26.3	R	Dover St, just past courthouse
26.4	L	into parking lot

* 34 Mile Ride

17.8	L	329 at T in **Royal Oak** (Store)
18.9	L	Rte 33 at T (⊗, use bike lane); becomes Talbot St in **St Michaels**; (Stores/Food)
22.1	R	Mills St toward Maritime Museum (Store)

22.3		Arrive Maritime Museum; Turn Around
22.5	L	Talbot St, becomes Rte 33 (⊗, use bike lane) (Pick up cues in 8.1 miles at mile 22.8 on the 26 mile ride – *☞)

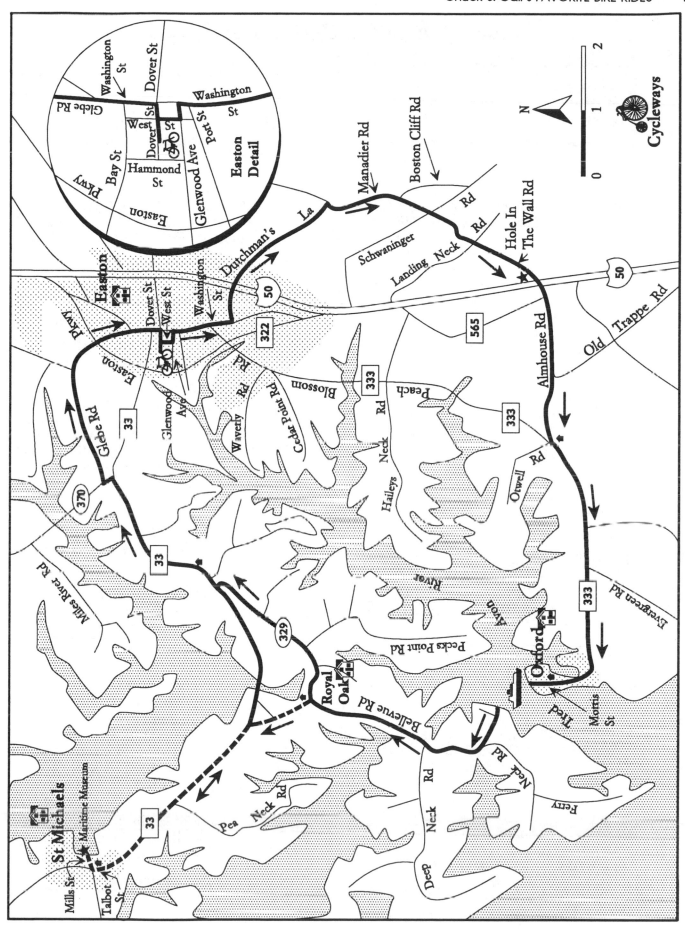

58. The Little Red Schoolhouse

Distance	24 or 40 miles
Rating:	I; Paved roads
Start:	Muncipal parking lot on Dover St next to police station in Easton, Md.

40 Mile Ride

0.0	R	Dover St from north side of parking lot with police station on your right
0.1	L	West St (unmarked) at SS
0.2	R	Bay St at T
0.3	L	Washington St at TL
0.5	S	Glebe Rd at TL
3.6	R	370 (unmarked) at T
5.1	L	Miles River Rd after bridge
5.5	R	Marengo Rd
7.4	R	Gregory Rd at T
8.7	L	Tunis Mills Rd at SS
9.2	R	at first paved road to remain on Tunis Mills Rd (unmarked); cross bridge over Leeds Creek
9.7	R	Cooperville Rd
11.0	R	Bruffs Island Rd (unmarked) at T
11.7	L	Bruffs Island Rd (unmarked) at Gregory Rd; becomes Todds Corner Rd
13.3	R	Little Park Rd (sign turned)
14.8	S	Sharp Rd
16.4	L	662 (unmarked) at T, toward Bay Bridge
17.0		Little Red Schoolhouse on left

(**For 24 Mile Ride** turn around here and pick up cues at mile 34.9 below — *☞)

18.3	S	662 at Rte 50 (Store at mile 20.2 in **Skipton**)
20.6	R	Rte 50 (⊗ - use shoulder)
21.1	L	662
24.0		Wye Oak on left
24.2	R	404 (unmarked) across from Wye Mills Market (Store) in **Wye Mills**; Wye Mill Grist Mill on left just past store; pond opposite mill
25.2	S	Rte 404 at Rte 50 (⊗)
25.7	R	Newtown Rd
28.7	R	Skipton Cordova Rd (unmarked) at T
29.3	L	662 (unmarked) at T in **Skipton** (Store)
31.3	S	662 at Rte 50
*☞		
34.9	R	Hailem School Rd
35.9	L	Goldsborough Neck Rd at SS
37.8	L	Glebe Rd at T; becomes Washington St in **Easton**
39.5	R	Dover St just past courthouse
39.6	L	into parking lot

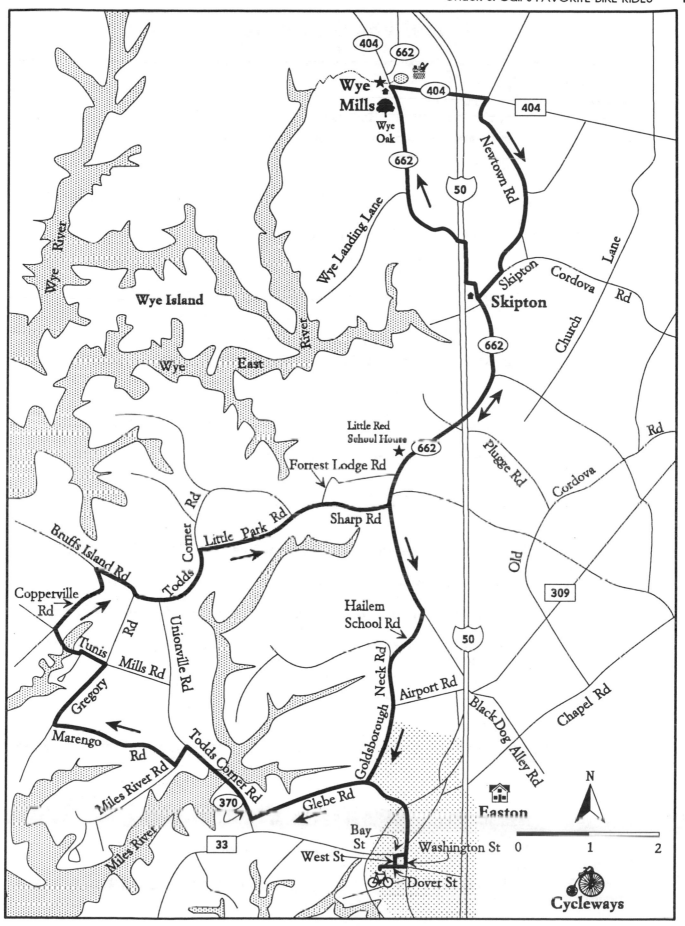

59. The Goose Gazer

Distance:	7, **26** or 38 miles
Rating:	I; Paved roads
Start:	Blackwater Wildlife Refuge foot trails parking lot in Cambridge, Md.

26 Mile Ride

0.0	BR	from parking lot
0.1	L	Wildlife Dr (unmarked) at SS; begin one way drive
2.3 ☞ *	L	to 335
3.3	L	335 (unmarked) at T to leave wildlife refuge (Store at mile 6.9)
8.9 ☞ **	L	336 at T (Store at mile 13.3)
13.8 ** ☞	L	Andrews Rd; becomes Robbins Rd then Maple Dam Rd
24.2	L	Key Wallace Dr
25.2	L	Wildlife Dr to enter wildlife refuge at Blackwater Refuge Office
25.5	BL	toward foot trails and observation tower
25.6	BL	into parking lot

* 7 Mile Ride

3.3	R	335 (unmarked) at T to leave wildlife refuge
3.6	R	Key Wallace Drive
4.6		Blackwater National Wildlife Refuge Visitors Center to right (Water, restrooms)
6.1	R	Wildlife Dr at Blackwater Refuge Office
6.4	BL	toward foot trails and observation tower
6.5	BL	into parking lot

** 38 Mile Ride

21.0	L	Farm Creek Rd (Store) in **Wingate**
22.7	L	Toddville Rd (unmarked) at SS (Store)
24.2	R	Wesley Church Rd at T; becomes Andrews Rd
28.6	R	Robbins Rd at T; becomes Maple Dam Rd (Pick up cues in 8.4 miles at mile 24.2 on the 26 mile ride – ** ☞)

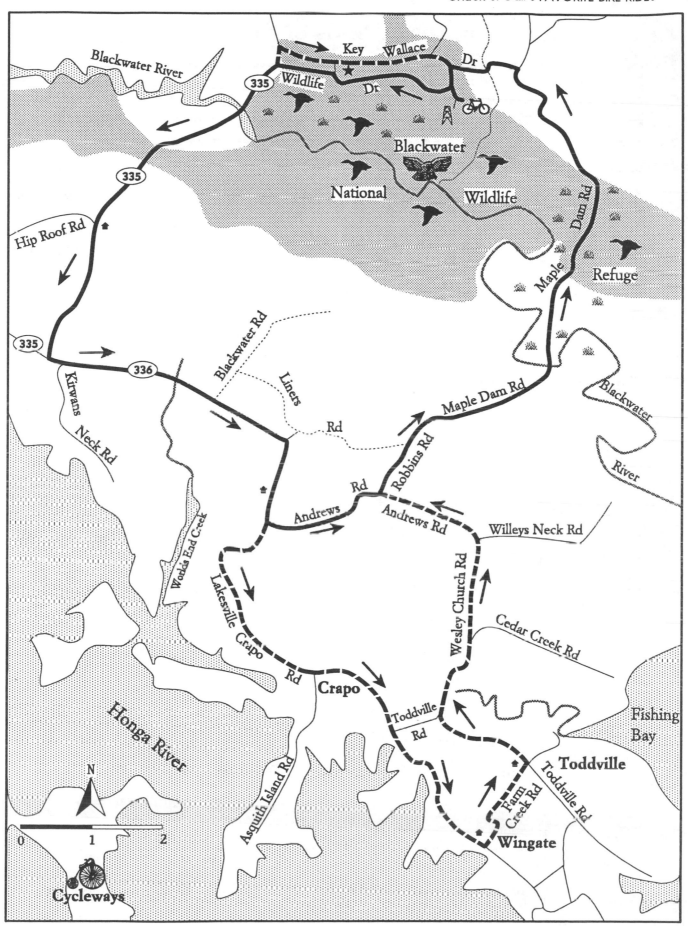

60. To the Ends of the Earth

Distance:	28 or **60** miles
Rating:	I; Paved roads
Start:	Blackwater Wildlife Refuge foot trails parking lot in Cambridge, Md.

60 Mile Ride

0.0	BR	from parking lot
0.1	BR	toward Key Wallace Drive
0.4	R	Key Wallace Dr (unmarked) at T
1.5	L	Maple Dam Rd (unmarked) at T
1.8	R	Greenbriar Rd
4.3	L	Bucktown Rd at T and Bestpitch Ferry Rd
5.3	R	Decoursey Bridge Rd (unmarked); first paved road
10.5	R	Drawbridge Rd (unmarked) at T
12.9 ☞*	R	Griffith Neck Rd
13.3	L	Henrys Cross Rd
15.3	R	Elliott Island Rd (unmarked) at SS
28.5	BL	toward boat ramp in **Elliott** (Stores)
29.2		Arrive at boat dock and ramp; Turn Around
29.8	R	at SS in **Elliott** (Stores) (unmarked Elliott Island Rd)
43.0	L	Henrys Cross Rd
45.0 *☞	L	Griffith Neck Rd (unmarked) at T; becomes Bestpitch Ferry Rd
55.2	L	Greenbriar Rd
57.6	L	Maple Dam Rd (unmarked) at SS
58.0	R	Key Wallace Dr
59.1	L	Wildlife Dr to enter Wildlife Refuge at Blackwater Refuge Office
59.4	BL	toward foot trails and observation tower
59.5	L	into foot trails parking lot

---

* 28 Mile Ride

13.3	S	Griffith Neck Rd at Henrys Cross Rd (Pick up cues in 10.2 miles at mile 55.2 on the 60 mile ride – * ☞)

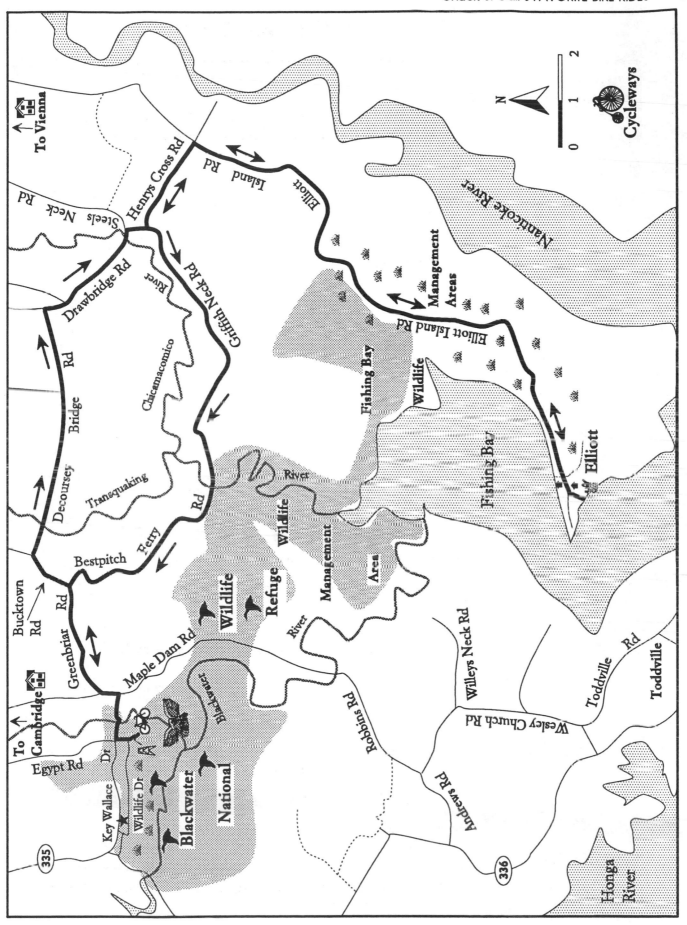

61. Saxis-of-Pearl

Distance:	**29** or 49 miles
Rating:	I; Paved roads
Start:	Arcadia High School in Oak Hall, Va. on Virginia's Eastern Shore

29 Mile Ride

0.0	L	702, Horsey Rd from rear of school with baseball diamond on your right
0.1	R	Rte 13, Lankford Hwy ⊗ (use shoulder)
0.2	L	694, Jerusalem Rd
2.3	R	695, Temperanceville Rd (Store)
2.5	S	695, Saxis Rd at Rte 13
4.3	L	793, Will Fisher Rd
4.8	S	693, Neal Fisher Rd; becomes Corbin St then Main St in **Hallwood**
6.9	R	692, Savannah Rd
8.3	R	692, Savannah Rd at 690, Whites Crossing Rd
10.2	L	692, Savannah Rd at Ross Rd
10.9	R	692/698, Savannah Rd/Marsh Market Rd at T
11.0	L	692, Belinda Rd
12.6	L	695, Saxis Rd at T in **Sanford**
15.8	L	Saxis Rd (unmarked) at Wayne Dr at T in **Saxis** at T; Store/Food at mile 16.0
16.8	L	817, Starling Creek Rd
16.9		Arrive at harbor and dock; Turn around
17.0	R	695, Saxis Rd at T; follow road thru and out of town
25.1	L	701, Jenkins Bridge Rd
25.7	R	702, Horsey Rd
28.9	L	into school parking lot

🖘 *

* 49 Mile Ride

26.3	L	703, Withams Rd at T
27.0	R	701, Bullbeggar Rd at T
29.6	R	709, Pitts Creek Rd at T
31.7	L	705, Holland Rd at T
32.5	BR	709 at SS at Y
33.3	R	709 at T (unmarked); becomes Depot St in **New Church**
35.0	L	709, Nelson Rd (Store)
35.1	R	709; becomes Horntown Rd at Rte 13 (Store)
39.1	R	679, Fleming Rd at T in **Horntown** (Store at Rte 175 in **Matthews** at mile 42.8)
44.3	R	679, Atlantic Rd at 798
45.7	R	703, Greta Rd in **Atlantic**
48.1	L	702, Knoxs Landing Rd at T
48.9	R	into school parking lot

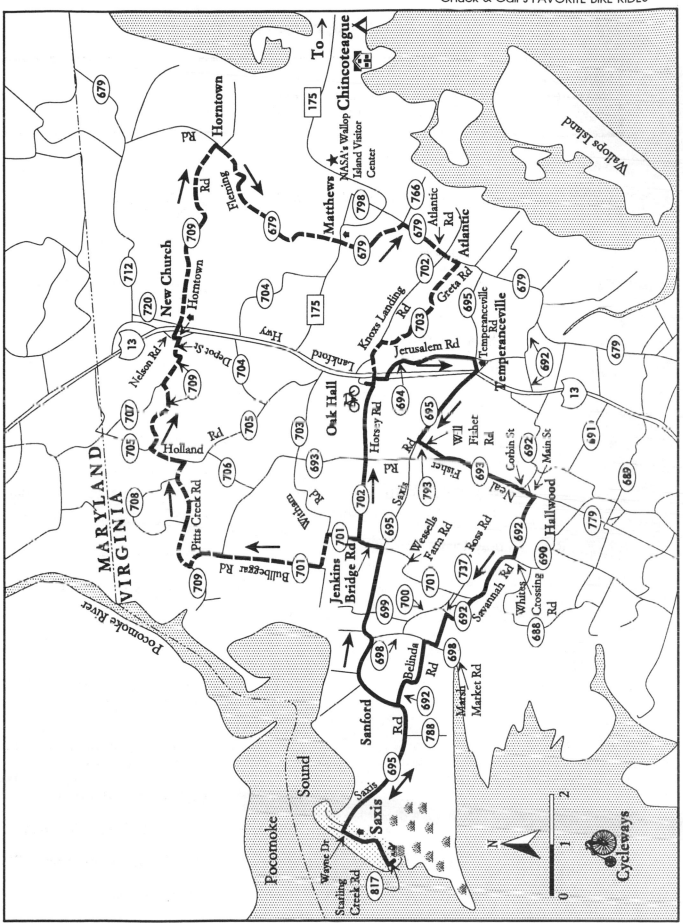

62. Land Across the Water

Distance:	10 or 12 miles
Rating:	I; Paved bike paths closed to cars before 3 pm and an optional paved road
Start:	Chincoteague Wildlife Refuge Visitor Center in Chincoteague, Va.

10 Mile Ride

0.0   L   Wildlife Drive from parking lot or bike path from town, following one way sign

0.5   R   Black Duck Trail

1.4   Cross Beach Drive toward Woodland Trail; Enter onto trail and follow it back to Beach Drive

3.5   S   Black Duck Trail

4.4   R   Wildlife Drive at T

5.0   S   Swan Cove Trail toward beach

6.4   Arrive at beach and Tom's Cove Visitor Center; Turn Around and follow the Swan Cove Trail back to Wildlife Drive

            * For 12 Mile Ride continue straight onto the paved road that follows the beach to its end; Turn around and return to the Swan Cove Trail

7.7   R   Wildlife Drive loop

9.4   R   toward exit

9.5   Arrive at Visitor Center or bike path to town

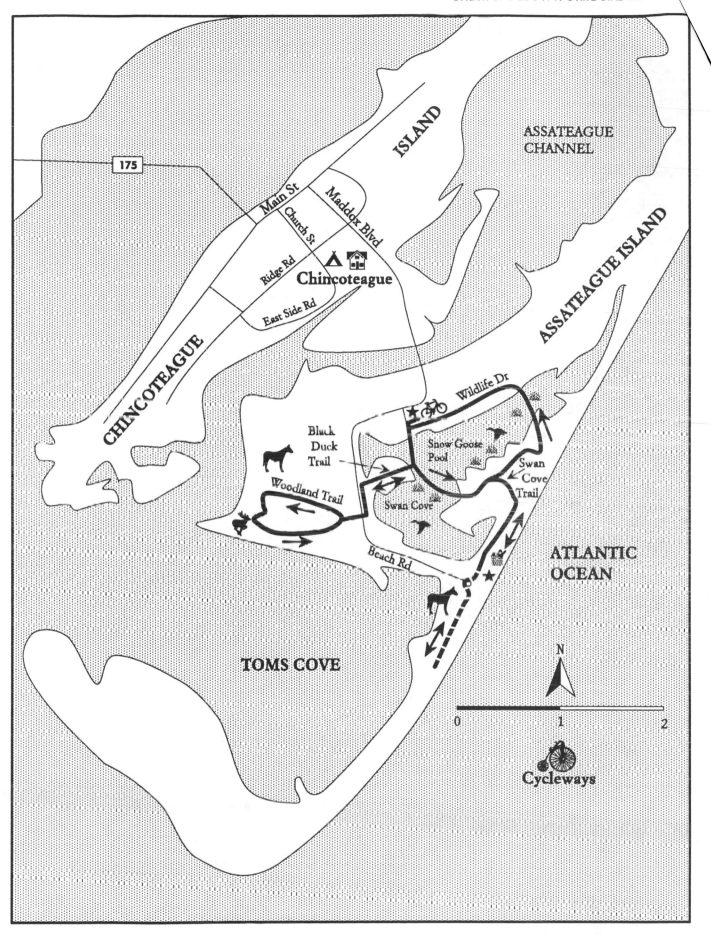

ASSATEAGUE
CHANNEL

ISLAND

ASSATEAGUE ISLAND

175

Main St

Maddox Blvd

Church St

Ridge Rd

Chincoteague

East Side Rd

CHINCOTEAGUE

Wildlife Dr

Black
Duck
Trail

Snow Goose
Pool

Swan
Cove
Trail

Woodland Trail

Swan Cove

Beach Rd

ATLANTIC
OCEAN

TOMS COVE

N

0   1   2

Cycleways

THE BIG VALLEY

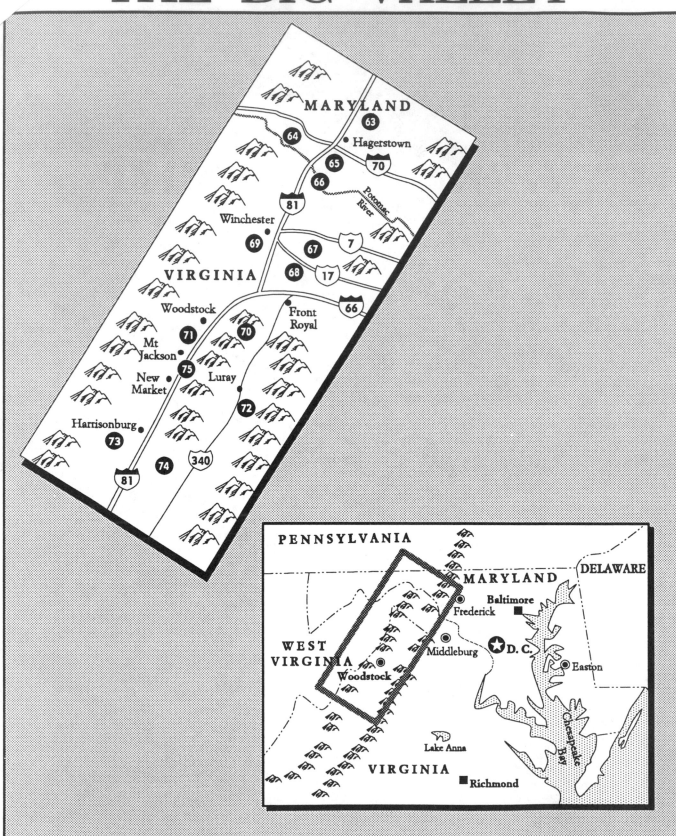

When we cross over Virginia's Blue Ridge Mountains to the west, the view always gives us pause. Before us lies an immense valley, a lush agricultural paradise. Small farms, charming towns and country roads abound, awaiting our exploration.

Cycling in the big valley is sheer joy. It has more miles of tranquil country lanes than any other area in the region. As you cycle along its peaceful roads, you pass verdant fields and prosperous farms. You cross stone bridges over lovely streams and enter quaint towns and villages. You look up to high forest-covered ridges and feel you have returned to an earlier, calmer century.

People call it the Shenandoah Valley in Virginia, the Great Valley in Maryland and the Cumberland Valley in Pennsylvania. Mountains define the valley – the Blue Ridge to the east and the main Appalachian ridges up to 20 miles to the west. It stretches southwest for over 180 miles in Virginia and northeast for 80 miles into West Virginia, Maryland and Pennsylvania.

This tranquil land hides a tumultuous past. In the early eighteenth century the valley was the American frontier, the far west. Settlers loaded their possessions into oxcarts and pushed down the Great Valley Trail in search of a new life. As the settlers established prosperous farms and new towns, more people followed and moved further west. The Great Valley Trail became the Valley Pike and today's Route 11.

The Civil War shattered the valley's peace and prosperity. The valley saw more battles than any other area in America. Winchester, Va. changed hands between the Union and the Confederacy more than 70 times. Stonewall Jackson conducted his brilliant Valley Campaign here in 1862, keeping two Union Armies at bay. Harpers Ferry, W.Va. saw John Brown's raid before the conflict and found itself on the border between two nations at war.

The Virginia part of the valley was known as the Breadbasket of the Confederacy. Confederate Armies used it to launch attacks on Maryland, Pennsylvania and even Washington, D.C. When Union General Phil Sheridan defeated General Jubal Early at the Battle of Cedar Creek in 1864, hostilities ended in the valley. However, as punishment for its support for the Confederacy, Sheridan sacked the Shenandoah Valley. Hardly a barn or a mill remained standing for more than 100 miles south of Winchester.

Today, the valley offers some of the best and the most rural cycling in the region. It has its own distinct personality. The cycling near Hagerstown, Maryland feels similar to that near Bridgewater, Virginia 130 miles to the south. However, do not come here expecting easy cycling terrain. The valley contains many steep hills, and the flanking ridges offer challenging climbs. Most of the rides in this chapter have ratings of III or IV. It is certainly more challenging than Chesapeake Bay country.

63. A Touch of Pennsylvania (25 or 40 miles; III)

Paved roads; starts at the Beaver Creek Park & Ride lot in Beaver Creek, Md.: Take I-270 to Frederick then I-70 West toward Hagerstown. From I-70, take exit 35, Route 66 North. Turn right at end of ramp. Go 0.2 miles and turn right into the parking lot.

Most of us city dwellers associate valley cycling with long drives. However, a mere hour's drive from Washington, D.C. or Baltimore, Md. brings you to the pleasant roads near Hagerstown, Md. Here, back roads and rustic farms abound. Ironically, you face the problem of having too many fine roads to ride.

The first part of both these rides takes you through this rustic farm country. In the last part you cycle through the fruit orchards at the base of South Mountain. The longer ride takes you across an 1863 stone bridge and into Pennsylvania. It then offers fine views of the valley and the local mountains. The shorter ride heads more directly toward the orchards that surround Smithsburg, Md. You find restaurants and stores in State Line, Pa. and in the center of Smithsburg. From Smithsburg you cycle south along the flank of South Mountain through more orchards. This offers a gentle downhill run to end the ride.

64. Fort Frederick (39 or 44 miles; III)

Paved roads; starts at the Salem Avenue Park & Ride lot in Hagerstown, Md.: Take I-270 to Frederick then I-70 to Hagerstown. Take exit 26, I-81 North. Follow for 4.1 miles to exit 7A, Route 58, Salem Avenue, towards Hagerstown. In 0.3 miles, turn right on Woodpoint Avenue, then right on Broadfording Road and right again into the parking lot.

Fort Frederick was the cornerstone of Maryland's frontier defense during the French and Indian War. The colony of Maryland built Fort Frederick in 1756 to protect settlers from attack along the Potomac River. Built of stone and reconstructed during the 1930s, it is the only original French and Indian War fort in the United States.

The fort is the ride's destination and is open year-round. During the weekends from May to October you may find military musters and persons in period dress. After strolling around the fort, enjoy a restful picnic under a big tree on the grounds or along the C&O Canal. Snack foods are available at the gift shop during the warmer months.

On your way to the fort you cycle west through the open valley to Clear Springs at the base of Fairview Mountain. From the fort you return to Hagerstown on a combination of delightfully rural roads and the shoulders of busier highways.

65. Relics of the Past (22 or 32 miles; III)

Paved roads; starts at the Antietam Battlefield Visitor Center in Sharpsburg, Md.: Take I-270 to Frederick and then I-70 to Hagerstown. Exit I-70 on Route 65 South to Sharpsburg. Go 9.7 miles and turn left into the battlefield at the sign for the battlefield. Proceed straight to the visitor center.

With the popularity of encampments and re-enactments, we never quite know what to expect when we cycle at Antietam Battlefield. Once a Confederate general parked next to us, and we watched four Confederate soldiers emerge from a pickup truck. On another ride we had to pull our bikes to the side of the road and let a group of Union soldiers march past.

One of the great battles of the Civil War occurred near Sharpsburg, Md. on the banks of Antietam Creek. There the Union army under General George McClellen fought Robert E. Lee's Confederate troops on September 17, 1862, the bloodiest day of the war. By nightfall the two armies had more than 22,000 casualties.

Several stone bridges dating from before the Civil War sit over streams just east of the battlefield. South of Sharpsburg is the house where John Brown plotted his 1859 attack on Harpers Ferry, W.Va. His attack inflamed the South and led to the Civil War.

On Antietam Creek sit the remains of the once flourishing Antietam Village. Looking at the few buildings that remain, it is hard to imagine the industrial center Antietam Village was in the 18th and 19th centuries. The heart of the village was the Antietam Iron Furnace which is marked by the lime kiln chimneys, about one-quarter mile to the right on Harpers Ferry Road. The furnace supplied cannons, cannon balls and muskets during

The farmhouse where John Brown plotted his raid on Harpers Ferry

the American Revolution. Most of the machinery for James Rumsey's steamboat was made here. At the village's height there were nine water wheels.

Just past Antietam Village, on Canal Road, you come to the C&O Canal. If you travel to the left along the canal towpath for 200 yards, you reach Antietam Aqueduct. This 140-foot structure is one of eleven stone aqueducts and one of the few completely standing.

66. The River Ramble (26 miles; III)

Paved roads, one rough gravel road and unpaved C&O Canal towpath; starts at C&O Canal National Historic Park Headquarters in Sharpsburg, Md.: Take I-270 to Frederick and then I-70 to Hagerstown. Exit I-70 on Route 65 South to Sharpsburg. Go 10.6 miles and turn right on Route 34. In 3.2 miles turn right into park headquarters, just before crossing the Potomac River into West Virginia. If the gate is closed, turn left on River Road at the entrance to the headquarters, go down the hill and park at the C&O Canal.

Built at the confluence of two rivers and dwarfed by a high ridge, Harpers Ferry, West Virginia sits in one of the loveliest locations around. You ride by historic buildings that date from the days when the town was a bustling mill town, including the building John Brown captured in his 1859 raid.

You begin your ride on the high bluffs overlooking the Potomac River. The large stone monument you see from the bridge entering Shepherdstown, West Virginia is dedicated to James Rumsey, who built and tested the first steamboat. Linger for a moment at the storefronts and historic buildings in West Virginia's oldest town. Upon leaving town you descend to the Potomac River and pass Boteler's Ford, one of the earliest known fords on the river.

You turn away from the river and ride through hilly terrain on paved roads before coming to a rough two-mile gravel road. Here, you follow the river and the old arsenal canal into Harpers Ferry. This section, covered with large gravel pieces, will challenge your

...nical skills if the bumpy ride doesn't get to you. To avoid this rough road, continue south on the paved road to Route 340, go east on 340's shoulder and then left into Bolivar Heights and Harpers Ferry.

The National Park Service manages Harpers Ferry as a National Historic Park. Take some time to explore the town's buildings and exhibits. Stop for a moment and contemplate the view at the confluence of the Potomac and Shenandoah Rivers. Thomas Jefferson proclaimed this view worth a journey across the Atlantic.

To leave Harpers Ferry you walk along the pedestrian walkway built on the railroad bridge over the Potomac River into Maryland. Once back in Maryland you cycle along the unpaved and flat C&O Canal Towpath. After 13 miles of enjoyable views of the Potomac River, you climb from the towpath to C&O Canal Headquarters.

67. Berry Nice (21 or 36 miles; II)

Paved roads; starts at Boyce Elementary School in Boyce, Va.: Take I-66 west to exit 23, Route 17 North toward Paris. Follow Route 17 for 8.1 miles. Turn left on Route 50/17 at the traffic light. In 4.6 miles turn right onto 723 toward Boyce and Millwood. Follow 723 for 4.4 miles, through Millwood to Boyce. After crossing Route 340, Main Street, in Boyce, go 0.3 miles and turn left into the school.

When you find gently rolling terrain in the valley, you savor it. You value it even more when it is combined with pretty towns and nice countryside. This area has long been a favorite with the local cyclists.

You cycle north from the village of Boyce to picturesque Berryville. On the longer ride you enter West Virginia and visit the hamlet of Summit Point. The shorter ride goes directly to Berryville. Berryville's wide variety of eateries offers choices to suit almost any taste. South of Berryville you encounter a few hills that are harder than those in the rest on this ride. This is the valley, after all.

68. Oh Shenandoah! (17, 28 or 35 miles; III)

Paved roads; starts at Boyce Elementary School in Boyce, Va.: see directions in Ride #67.

Over the years we keep returning to ride the roads in this area. These loops make an excellent introduction to the pastoral charms of the Shenandoah Valley and the Shenandoah River. Near the start of the ride you pass the restored Burwell Morgan Mill, open for tours. You then choose to ride either of the two loops or combine them into a longer ride.

The longer loop heads south past large estates through somewhat hilly terrain that offers wonderful views. You cross the Shenandoah River on a low water bridge. In high water and flood the bridge becomes impassable, and you have to stay on the west side of the river. After you cross the bridge, you return north on the east side of the Shenandoah River past several stores and one serene stretch of the river.

The shorter loop heads east, then north, before dropping to the Shenandoah River. On the long downhill on Route 621, before you reach the Shenandoah River and after crossing a small bridge, look to the stream on your right. There, tucked into the small chasm below you, sits a small but roaring waterfall. You then climb west away from the river and return to your start through open farm country. The return offers first-rate views of the wide valley and the distant ridges.

69. Apple Pie Country (21, 36 or 52 miles; III)

Paved roads; starts at Lord Fairfax Community College in Middletown, Va.: Take I-66 west into the Shenandoah Valley to I-81. Take I-81 north for 2 miles to Exit 302 and turn left onto Route 627 toward Middletown. At the T intersection turn right onto Route 11. Go 0.2 miles and turn right into the college.

In the springtime, apple blossoms from the many orchards west of Middletown and Winchester sweeten the air. Farmers have grown apples in this area since 1749. Hessian prisoners during the Revolutionary War camped north of Winchester and named one such area Apple Pie Ridge.

In the beginning of the ride you pass the Wayside Inn in Middletown. It was originally Wilkerson's Tavern and has taken in travelers since 1797. Middletown became a stagecoach stop 20 years later when the Valley Pike, now Route 11, was hacked out of the wilderness. At the front of the Community College sit historical markers explaining the Battle of Cedar Creek. This overwhelming Union victory on October 19, 1864 ended Civil War hostilities in the Shenandoah Valley.

The two longer rides wander up the west side of the valley to Winchester. In 1748 George Washington began to survey lands in the region; his survey office still sits in town. George Washington commanded the Virginia militia from Winchester during the French and Indian War. Winchester changed hands more than 70 times in the Civil War. You can modify the ride to begin at the James Wood High School at Amherst Street, Route 50, and Fox Drive in Winchester.

70. Passage Thru Mudhole Gap (12, 17 or 23 miles; IV or V)

Mostly unpaved forest and gravel roads, some rough; six stream crossings; advanced beginner mountain biking skills needed; starts opposite Elizabeth Furnace Campground in Fort Valley, Va.: Take I-66 west to exit 6, Route 340/522. Turn left at the end of the exit ramp toward Front Royal. Follow for 1.1 miles and turn right onto Route 55 after crossing the Shenandoah River. In 5.2 miles turn left onto 678, Fort Valley Road. Go 4.5 miles and turn right onto the gravel road opposite the campground. Park near the first gate.

With six stream crossings, you want to ride along Little Passage Creek in low water. However, when we laid out the ride, the Shenandoah Valley had received three days of steady rain. The stream was a swollen torrent, and the forest road to Strasburg Reservoir was more puddle and creek than road. We started the ride trying to stay dry, riding daintily around the puddles. We then gave up trying to stay dry and had fun. By the end of the ride, we rode straight through the deepest puddles as fast as we could, trying to get the other even wetter.

The ride begins on a gravel road and appears to climb forever before you finally begin a long downhill run. You then cycle on a beautiful, rough road through a narrow gap that is lined with hemlocks. This is the heart of the ride. You will need at least advanced-beginner mountain biking skills on the rockier sections.

You come to a gravel road and either turn left for the short ride or continue uphill along a rutted forest road to Strasburg Reservoir. The reservoir makes a good lunch spot and turn-around point. From the reservoir, prepare to enjoy a long descent, first on the forest road, then on a gravel road. You descend on another gravel road past the ruins of Boyer Furnace near the national forest boundary and return on a paved road through gorgeous Fort Valley.

...ngest ride climbs steeply up gravel roads to the top of the ridge and Woodstock ... Worthwhile views of the seven bends of the Shenandoah River reward your hard ... Then hold on for a screaming descent on the roads you have just climbed.

71. The Valley Sampler (20, 39 or 49 miles; III)

Paved roads; starts at Central High School in Woodstock, Va.: Take I-66 west into the Shenandoah Valley to I-81. Follow I-81 south for 17.4 miles and take Exit 279, Route 42, toward Woodstock. Go 0.4 miles and turn right onto Susan Avenue. In 0.2 miles turn left into the school.

In the heart of the breadbasket

In recent years Virginia has become a producer of notable wines. Shenandoah Vineyard is near the end of this ride. With only a few miles to go, you don't have far to carry a bottle or two of wine as a memento of your trip.

You sample the valley's charms on these loops: graceful towns, prosperous farms, splendid views of the local ridges, little-travelled roads and the winery. The longer two rides visit Mount Jackson and Edinburg, two sleepy towns. On the longer ride you pass near Shenandoah Caverns. A tour of the caverns costs $7.00 and takes about an hour. The coffee shop and picnic grounds at the caverns offer an inviting place for a stop. The caverns also have most souvenirs known to modern civilization.

72. Valley of the Hills (25 or 39 miles; III or IV)

Paved roads; starts at Luray Inn Lawn Park in Luray, Va.: Take I-66 west to exit 43A, Route 29 South in Gainesville. Take Route 29 for 11.5 miles and exit on business 29/15 to Warrenton/Winchester. Go 2.0 miles and turn right onto 211 West. Follow for 42.7 miles and exit onto Route 340 South toward Luray. In 1.0 mile turn left on Campbell Street, past

Main Street. In 0.1 mile turn right on Zerkel Street into the park. Park on the left side of street near the picnic tables.

The name refers more to the views from the ride than the hills on the ride itself, at least on the shorter ride. Hills and ridges surround you in the picturesque valley of the South Fork of the Shenandoah River. You ride south from Luray and explore the area around Stanley and Alma.

On the longer ride, however, the name refers to the noteworthy pitches you climb. On this loop you cycle south down the valley as it narrows. You descend to pastoral sections that travel next to the Shenandoah River and then climb away from the river. You repeat this several times. As a result, you experience rewarding views, fun descents and breathtaking climbs. The last climb, after the village of Newport, is particularly noteworthy.

73. The Breadbasket (20, **36** or 52 miles; III or IV)

Paved roads; starts at Bridgewater Fairgrounds in Bridgewater, Va.: Take I-66 west into the Shenandoah Valley to I-81. Follow I-81 south for 60.5 miles, past Harrisonburg, to Route 257, Mt Crawford/Bridgewater. Take 257 west for 0.8 miles into Mt Crawford. Turn right onto Route 11 North and then left onto Route 257. Follow 257 for 2.5 miles into Bridgewater. Turn right onto Route 42/257. In 0.1 miles turn left onto Green Street, then right onto N. Grove Street. Park on the left in 0.1 miles.

Mennonite buggies west of Harrisonburg, Va.

Cycling through this lush agricultural area, it is very easy to see why it was called the Breadbasket of the Confederacy. When we want to escape far away from cities, we come here, south and west of Harrisonburg. On our first ride in this area in the 1970s, we were startled to see a couple in a black horse-drawn buggy. We had associated Mennonites and Amish with Pennsylvania, not Virginia.

and west of Bridgewater lives a large, traditional Mennonite community that still se-drawn carriages as transportation. You are likely to see the Mennonites near ine and south of Mount Clinton on the two longer rides.

On the two shorter rides you cycle past Natural Chimneys Regional Park. The chimneys (admission fee) are large limestone towers that make an interesting backdrop for a picnic lunch. On the longest ride you visit George Washington National Forest. You climb up, up and up to Todd Lake where you can refresh yourself with a swim before the return ride.

74. Back Road Heaven (47 miles; IV)

Paved roads; starts at Bridgewater Fairgrounds in Bridgewater, Va.: see directions in Ride #73.

Grand Caverns has been open to the public longer than any other cave in the Shenandoah Valley. It held antebellum dances during the 19th century. Stonewall Jackson garrisoned men inside the caverns in the Civil War. Now a regional park, it still welcomes visitors. The park picnic grounds on the banks of the South River as well as the caverns make an attractive cycling destination. A tour of the caverns costs $7.00 per person.

South of Massanutten Mountain the valley widens. You ride east from Bridgewater through a line of hills toward the base of the distant Blue Ridge Mountains. Only signs mark the sites of the Battles of Cross Keys and Port Republic (part of Jackson's Valley Campaign) as you cycle toward Grottoes and Grand Caverns.

From the caverns you cycle back to Bridgewater on nice rural roads that reward you with more views of the mountains. The last section, from Fort Defiance to Bridgewater, challenges you with many long hills. You pass the only stores on the ride in Grottoes and Fort Defiance.

75. Shenandoah Valley Tour (170 miles; IV)

Paved roads with 0.2 miles unpaved; starts at Town Hall and Police Department parking lot in Front Royal, Va.: Take I-66 west to exit 13, Route 55, Linden/Front Royal. Turn left on Route 79 at the end of the ramp. Turn right on Route 55 and follow it for 5.3 miles into Front Royal where is becomes South Street. At the T turn right on Route 340, South Royal Avenue. In 0.5 miles turn left on 1st Street, after Main Street and the Town Hall. Immediately turn left on Union Street to go behind the Town Hall. Park on the right in the Town Hall parking lot. Notify the police department, on Main Street and visible from the parking lot, for overnight parking.

Does anyone tour anymore? We remember the mid-1970s and the glory days of touring. The Bikecentennial Trail was hot and every bike shop sold touring bikes. Touring's popularity has cooled to the point where you have to look around for a road bike suitable for touring. We offer this 170 mile tour in memory of the "old days" and for those who like to get away for several days.

This tour is not easy. It is certainly not one to try for your first tour. It features some of the most wonderfully rural roads and nicest scenery in the entire region. It visits small and large towns and travels in some sections far away from well-travelled areas. You ride through hilly terrain and over a 1.7 mile climb on the first day. Since restaurants and stores are few in some sections, carry extra food with you. You will ride through somewhat heavy town traffic in Front Royal, Harrisonburg and Woodstock.

We designed the tour around staying at inns, B&Bs and hotels/motels. For those who like to camp, we have listed area campgrounds at the end of the book. If you take four days for the tour, you ride 42 miles to Luray, 44 miles to Harrisonburg, 47 miles to Woodstock and 37 miles back to Front Royal. If you take three days, you ride 66 miles to a small B&B (Joanne's B&B) near Elkton, 58 miles to Mount Jackson and 50 miles back to Front Royal. If you are very strong, take two days: 86 miles to Harrisonburg and 84 on the second day.

The Front Royal Police have said that cyclists can park their cars for this tour behind the town hall. The town hall is on Route 340, Royal Street, in the center of Front Royal. The police ask that you let them know you are leaving your car there for several days. The telephone number for the Front Royal Police is (703) 535-2111.

On the first day you travel south through rustic Fort Valley. Flanked by the ridges of Massanutten Mountain, you cycle down the length of this narrow valley. You then climb over the mountain (remember, this is the easy way to do this climb) and arrive in Luray. You pass Luray Caverns and have your choice of B&Bs and motels in town.

From Luray you ride south, climbing tough hills near Alma and Shenandoah. We found a friendly restaurant, the Quincy Street Cafe, a half mile off the ride (see the cue sheet) in Shenandoah. You can change the second day of the tour by connecting it with ride #72. You cycle around the south end of Massanutten Mountain as the valley widens and ride into sprawling Harrisonburg. This section connects with ride #74 and can connect with ride #73.

From Harrisonburg, you ride along the base of the Allegheny Mountains on the west side of the valley. For most of the day you ride far away from the towns and settlements. This section has just one store, 11 miles north of Harrisonburg in Singers Glen. This store is closed Wednesdays and Sundays.

In Forestville you can join the tour with ride #71 to visit Shenandoah Caverns and Mount Jackson. The tour passes Shenandoah Vineyards near Woodstock.

From Woodstock you again ride along the west side of the valley on little-travelled roads. You turn east and ride through Middletown where you find stores and restaurants. You can join the tour with ride #69 to extend it north to Winchester. To end the tour you ride southeasterly around the north end of Massanutten Mountain and return to Front Royal.

Tour Stop at Kings Crossing, Va.

63. A Touch of Pennsylvania

```
Distance:   25 or 40 miles
Rating:     III; Paved roads
Start:      Beaver Creek Park & Ride lot in Beaver Creek, Md.
```

40 Mile Ride

0.0	L	Rte 66 from parking lot		24.1	R	Rte 316 at T
1.3	R	Beaver Creek Pike		24.2	L	Lyons Rd after bridge
1.6	R	Beaver Creek Church Rd		25.5	R	Goods Dam Rd
3.1	R	White Hall Rd at T		26.3	R	Anthony Hwy, PA 997 at T
6.5	BL	White Hall Rd (unmarked) at Chewsville Rd at SS		26.8	L	Barkdoll Rd in Md.
7.1	L	Main St at T in **Chewsville**		27.2	L	Cemetery Lane Rd; becomes Hess Rd
7.2	S	62 at Y		28.7	R	Welty Church Rd at T
7.5	R	62 at T at Trovinger Mill Rd		29.2	L	Edgemont Rd
☜*				*☞		
8.8	L	Old Forge Rd (Stone bridge at mile 9.9)		30.1	L	Greensberg Rd at T
10.4	R	Herman Myers Rd		30.1	R	Greensberg Rd (unmarked)
11.8	L	Rte 60 (unmarked) at T (⊗ - use shoulder)		31.1	L	66 (unmarked) at T; becomes Pennsylvania Ave
11.9	R	Miller Church Rd		31.8	R	E Water St at T in **Smithsburg**
12.9	L	Lehmans Mill Rd		32.0	L	Maple Ave (Store 0.2 mile to left on Main St, Food); becomes Crystal Falls Dr
14.9	S	Reid Rd at Marsh Pike				
16.9	R	Oak Rd (unmarked) at T; becomes Reid Rd as road swings left		37.8	R	Black Rock Rd (sign hidden)
				38.6	R	Black Rock Rd at T at Ridenour Rd
17.4	R	East Ave at T in **State Line, Pa.** (Store, Food 0.2 mile to left at Rte 11)		38.8	R	Black Rock Rd at T at Stottlemeyer Rd
20.4	R	Leitersburg Rd at T		39.7	R	Rte 66 (unmarked) at SS
20.7	L	Marsh Rd after creek		40.1	R	into Park & Ride lot
21.4	R	Iron Bridge Rd				

---

* 25 Mile Ride

8.8	R	Old Forge Beards Church Rd		14.0	R	Edgemont Rd (Pick up cues in 0.9 miles at mile 30.1 on the 40 mile ride — *☞)
10.9	BR	Rowe Rd at Unger Rd				
13.1	R	Welty Church Rd at SS; continue Straight at Greensburg Rd				

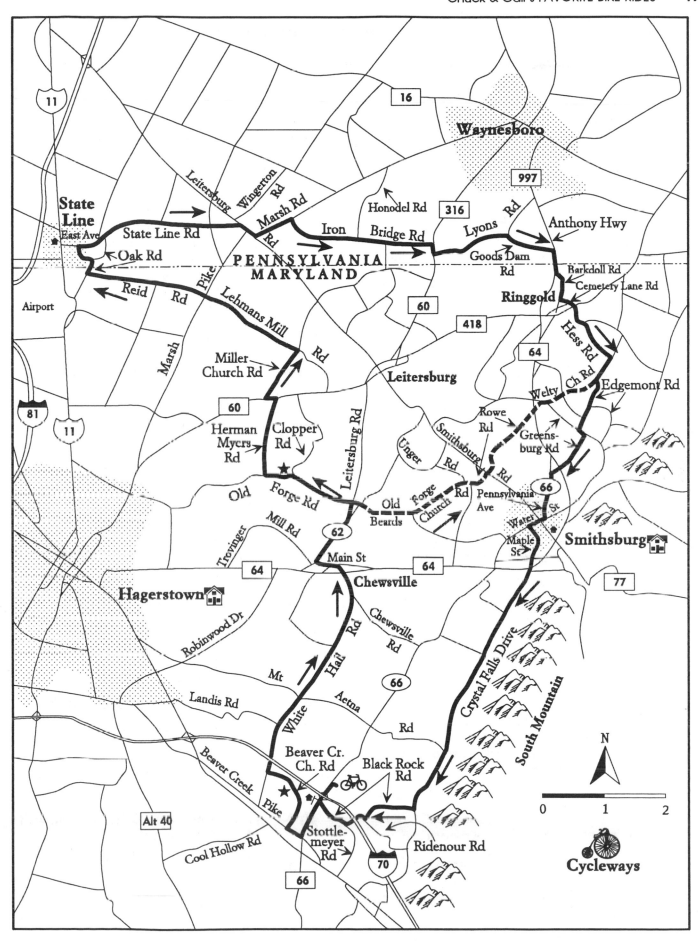

64. Fort Frederick

Distance:	39 or **44** miles
Rating:	III; Paved roads
Start:	Salem Ave Park & Ride lot in Hagerstown, Md.

44 Mile Ride

0.0	L	Rte 58, Salem Ave toward I-81 from Woodpoint Ave, with parking lot on your left
0.4	L	Broadfording Rd, after I-81
0.7	R	Broadfording Rd (unmarked) at T
5.6	BR	Gossard Mill Rd
6.9	S	494, Fairview Rd (unmarked) at Rockdale Rd
7.4	BL	to stay on 494, Fairview Rd
9.8	BL	Dry Run Rd
10.5	L	Mercersburg Rd
14.1	L	Blairs Valley Rd at T
14.5	R	Broadfording Rd at T
15.6	R	Rte 40 (unmarked) at SS at high school (Food, Store 0.3 miles to left)
15.7	L	Boyd Rd
18.4	R	Big Pool Rd (unmarked) at T

* For the **39 Mile Ride**, turn left at this point onto Big Pool Rd (Pick up cues in 1.7 miles at mile 25.9 on the 44 mile ride – *☞)

20.7	L	into Fort Frederick State Park; continue straight at first Y, following signs to the fort
21.3		Arrive at Fort Frederick (Food, Water, Restroom in season); Turn Around
21.9	R	Big Pool Rd (unmarked) at T to leave park

*☞

25.9	BR	56 at Big Springs Rd (Store at mile 28.2)
28.7	R	68 at T (⊗ - use shoulder) (Store at mile 30.1)
30.3	L	Pinesburg Rd
30.9	R	Kemp Mill Rd at T
31.8	R	Kemp Mill Rd at T after bridge
33.2	R	at SS at T
33.7	L	at dead end sign
33.8	S	Wright Rd at Rte 63 at SS
33.9	R	Wright Rd at Elliott Rd
34.5	L	Hopewell Rd
38.0	L	Rte 144 (unmarked) at T
38.2	R	McDade Rd
39.5	R	Broadfording Rd (unmarked) at T
40.7	L	Broadfording Rd at dead end sign
41.0	R	Rte 58 (unmarked) at T
44.4	R	Woodpoint Ave and into parking lot

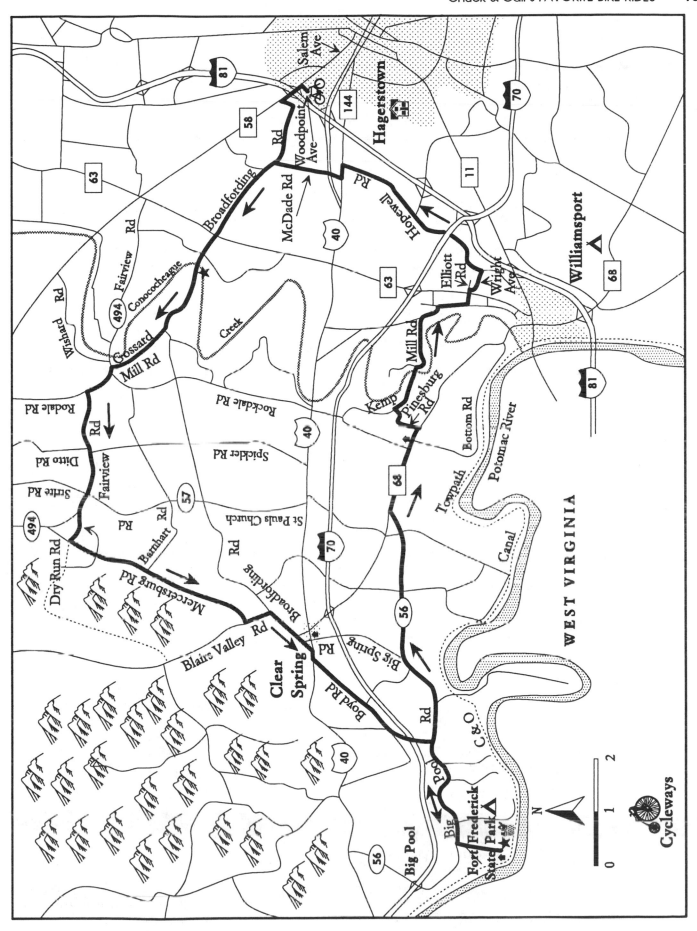

65. Relics of the Past

Distance:	**22** or 32 miles
Rating:	III; Paved roads
Start:	Antietam Battlefield Visitor Center in Sharpsburg, Md.

22 Mile Ride

0.0	R	thru parking lot with flagpole at your back
0.1	R	at yield sign onto Dunker Church Rd (unmarked)
0.2	R	Smoketown Rd
0.8	R	Mansfield Rd (unmarked) at Mansfield Monument
2.7	R	Keedysville Rd at T - cross stone bridge; becomes Main St in **Keedysville** at Rte 34
3.8	R	Dog St Rd (Store 0.3 mile ahead on Main St)
4.4	L	Dog St Rd (unmarked) at Red Hill Rd
4.7 *☞	R	Mt Briar Rd
7.6	R	Chestnut Grove Rd (Store at mile 10.0) (Kennedy Farm on right at mile 12.2, after Mt Lockhill Rd)
12.8	R	Harpers Ferry Rd at T
13.9	L	Limekiln Rd on the long downhill after Dargan Rd (easy to miss)
16.4	S	Harpers Ferry Rd at SS in Antietam Village, crossing stone bridge
16.6	L	Canal Rd (Antietam Aqueduct at C&O canal)
18.1	R	Millers Saw Mill Rd
19.8	L	Harpers Ferry Rd at T
20.6	R	E Main St, Rte 34 in **Sharpsburg** (Store)
20.8	L	N Church St, Rte 65
21.7	R	Dunker Church Rd into Antietam Battlefield
21.9	S	into Visitor Center

* 32 Mile Ride

0.0	R	from parking lot with flagpole at your back
0.1	R	at yield sign onto Dunker Church Rd (unmarked)
1.0	L/R	at SS to leave battlefield and go North on Rte 65
2.0	L	Taylors Landing Rd
2.4	R	Fairplay Rd
4.9	BR	Rte 63 at SS in **Fairplay**
5.3	S	Manor Church Rd at Rte 65
8.7	L	Wheeler Rd at T
8.8	BR	Monroe Rd at Y
10.6	L	Rte 34 at T (unmarked) (⊗ - use shoulder)
11.1	R	King Rd (Food ahead in **Boonsboro**)
12.5	R	Nicodemus Mill Rd - **Dangerous bridge surface at mile 13.4 – Walk bike!**
13.5	R	Dog St Rd at T - Felfoot Stone Bridge at mile 14.2
14.4	L	Mt Briar Rd (Pick up cues in 2.9 miles at mile 7.6 on the 22 Mile Ride – *☞)

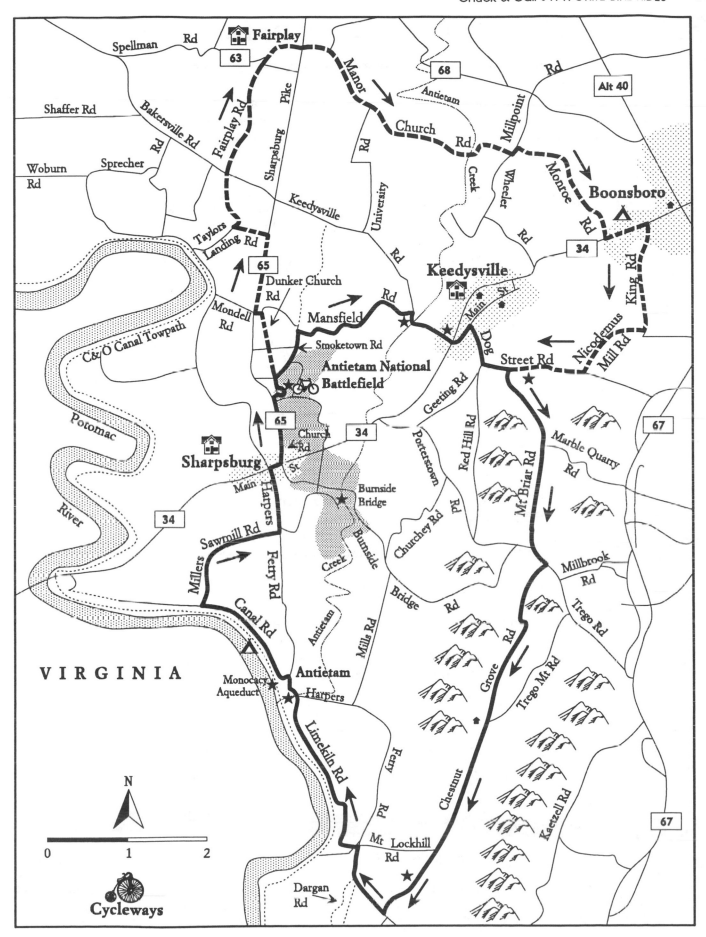

66. The River Ramble

Distance:	**26** miles
Rating:	III; Paved roads, one rough gravel road and unpaved C&O Canal towpath
Start:	C&O Canal National Historic Park Headquarters, Sharpsburg, Md.

26 Mile Ride

0.0	R	paved Rte 34 from entrance of C&O headquarters crossing Potomac River; becomes Duke St in **Shepardstown**, West Virginia
0.8	L	W German St, Rte 230 at SS; continue on road straight out of town as it descends to the river (Do not follow Rte 230) (Boteler Ford at mile 2.6)
6.5	R	unmarked road at T at SS
6.7	L	1st unmarked paved road at Bethesda Methodist Church
11.8	S	downhill at SS as main road goes right under the railroad bridge; becomes unpaved; follow road through private campground along Potomac River; some sections of road are rough with large pieces of gravel
13.4		cross train tracks into **Harpers Ferry**; becomes paved Potomac St (Food)
13.7		Dismount at Shenandoah St at T (Water, restrooms to right). Walk your bike straight ahead up the gravel path and then left onto the pedestrian walkway to cross the Potomac River
13.9	L	unpaved C&O towpath at end of bridge
22.7		cross Monocacy Aqueduct
26.1	R	cross canal at Lock 38 before crossing under the highway bridge, ride through the parking lot and then climb paved Canal Rd up to Rte 34
26.4	S	into C&O headquarters at the SS

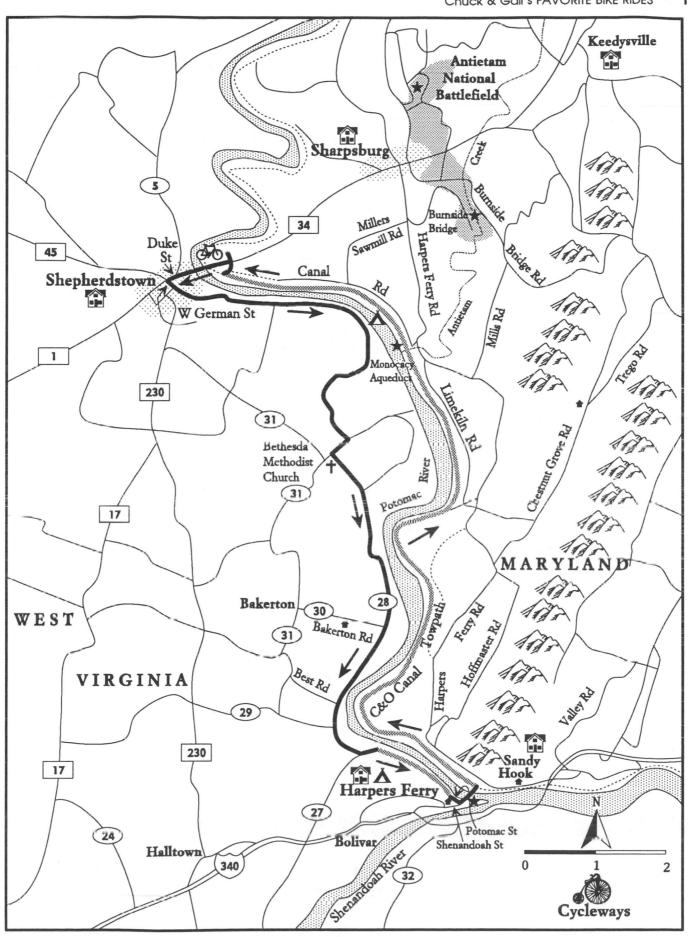

67. Berry Nice

Distance:	**21** or **36** miles
Rating:	II; Paved roads
Start:	Boyce Elementary School in Boyce, Va.

21 Mile Ride

0.0	L	723 from school parking lot
2.1	R	655; becomes 634
5.1	R	657 at T
☜*		
9.0	L	636
10.5	R	Business 7 east at T; becomes Main St in **Berryville** (Food, Stores)
*☞		
12.2	R	613, Springsbury Rd
15.7	R	618 at T
16.8	R	617 at T; becomes Old Chapel Ave in **Boyce**
20.4	R	723, Main St at T (Store 0.1 mile to left)
20.8	L	into school parking lot

* 36 Mile Ride

6.4	L	632
13.0	R	761 at T; becomes 2, Hardesty Rd in **West Virginia**
15.3	R	13, Summit Point Pike (unmarked) at T
16.5	R	Hawthorne Ave at stone building in **Summit Point** (Food, Store); becomes 1, Leetown Rd (unmarked); becomes 611 in Virginia
21.5	R	654
23.1	L	653 at T
24.6	L	Rte 7 at T ⊗ (Store)
24.7	BR	Business 7 east into **Berryville** (Town Traffic) (Food, Stores in town) (Pick up cues in 2.4 miles at mile 12.2 on the 21 mile ride – *☞)

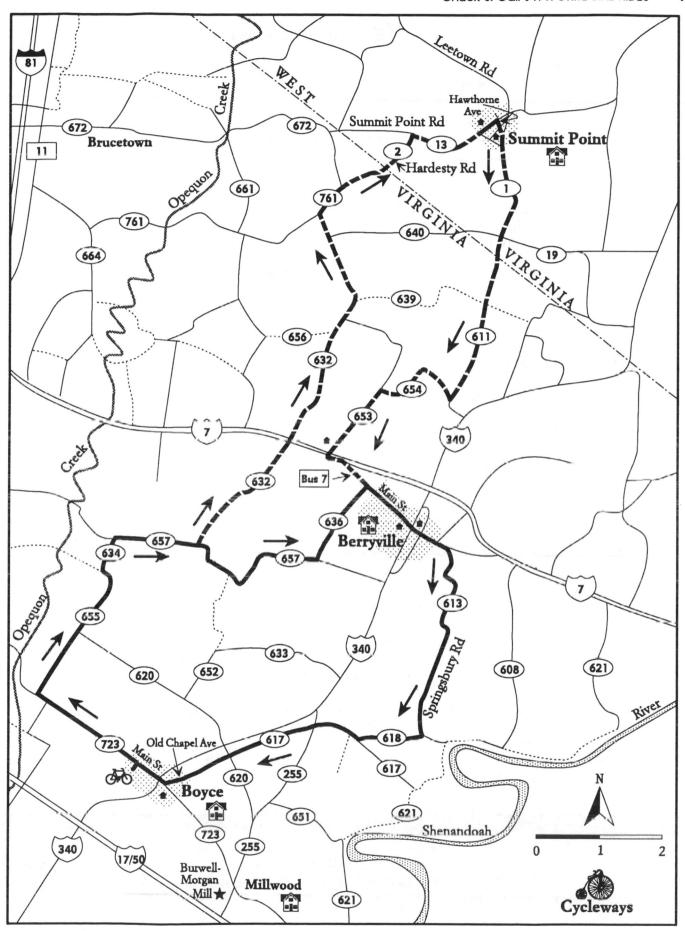

68. Oh Shenandoah!

Distance:	17, **28** or 35 miles
Rating:	III; Paved roads
Start:	Boyce Elementary School in Boyce, Va.

28 Mile Ride (Southern Loop)

0.0	R	723 from school (Store at mile 0.4 in **Boyce** & mile 2.4 in **Millwood** - closed Sundays)	22.2	L	Rte 17/50 at T (⊗ ; use shoulder)
			23.0	R	723
2.5	R	255	25.2	S	255/723, pass Burwell-Morgan Mill in **Millwood** (Store - closed Sundays)
3.1	S	624 at Rte 50/17			
3.8	L	624 at 626 at T; becomes Milldale Rd; becomes Morgan Ford Rd	25.4	S	723
			27.7	L	into school parking lot
12.4	L	643, Howellsville Rd, after low water bridge; becomes 603; becomes 638 in **Howellsville** (Store) (Store at mile 18.9)			

(At mile 23.0: 🔁**)

---

* 17 Mile Ride (Northern Loop)

0.0	R	723 from school (Store at mile 0.4 in **Boyce** & at mile 2.4 in **Millwood**- closed Sundays)	8.2	L	255 at T
			8.7	R	620
2.5	L	723, past mill	10.1	S	620 at 340
4.6	L	621 (waterfall on right at mile 6.1, just past bridge on long downhill)	13.2	L	655 at T
			14.4	L	723 at T
**🖝			16.6	R	into school parking lot
6.8	BL	651 at Shenandoah River			

** 35 Mile Ride (Begin on Southern Loop, finish on Northern Loop)

23.1	R	621 (waterfall on right at mile 24.6, just past bridge on long downhill) (Pick up cues in 2.2 miles at mile 6.8 on the 17 mile ride – **🖝)

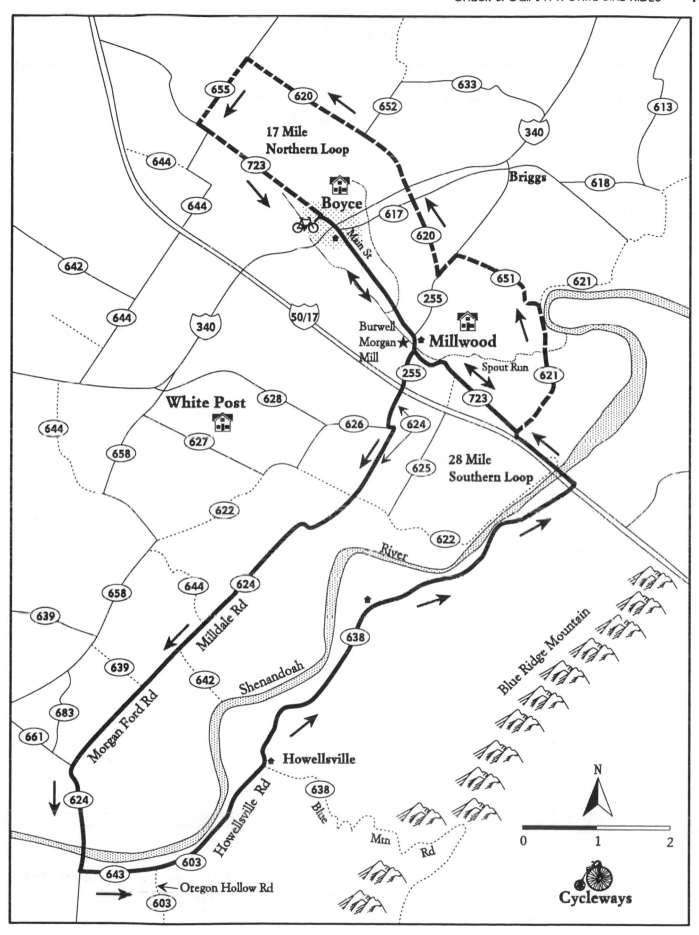

69. Apple Pie Country

Distance:	21, 36 or **52** miles
Rating:	III; Paved roads
Start:	Lord Fairfax Community College in Middletown, Va.

52 Mile Ride

0.0	L	Rte 11, Main St, from left side of parking lot
0.6	R	627 at blinking light; rough RR tracks ahead
4.9	R	622 near bottom of long downhill
5.4	R	628/622 at T
5.6 🔁*	L	622
12.8	L	620 at T in **Opequon**
16.4	R	803 at T (Store in **Round Hill**)
16.9 🔁**	L	654 before RR tracks (Stores to right at Rte 50)
19.1	R	679 at T
19.4	L	654 on the downhill
19.7	R	654 at 630 (Stores at mile 21.4 in **Nain** at Rte 522 and at mile 23.2 in **Cedar Grove** at Rte 677)
26.2	R	671 at T (Store at mile 26.8)
27.8	R	739 (Store)
34.1	L	Rte 522 at TL ⊗
34.5	R	739 at TL after Rte 37 overpass; becomes Fox Dr in **Winchester**
35.8	R	Amherst St, Rte 50
36.2 **☞	L	621, Merrimans Lane at the First Christian Church
40.9 *☞	R	628 at T (Store at mile 43.8)
46.0	L	631
46.9	R	625 at top of hill
50.5	L	627 at T; rough RR tracks entering **Middletown**
51.6	L	Main St, Rte 11
52.2	R	into college parking lot

* 21 Mile Ride

10.2	R	732
12.0	R	628 at T (Pick up cues in 2.4 miles at mile 46.0 on the 52 mile ride – *☞)

** 36 Mile Ride

16.9	S	803 at 654 in **Round Hill**
19.3	R	Rte 50 ⊗ (Food)
20.2	R	621, Merrimans Lane at the First Christian Church (Pick up cues in 4.7 miles at mile 40.9 on the 52 mile ride – **☞)

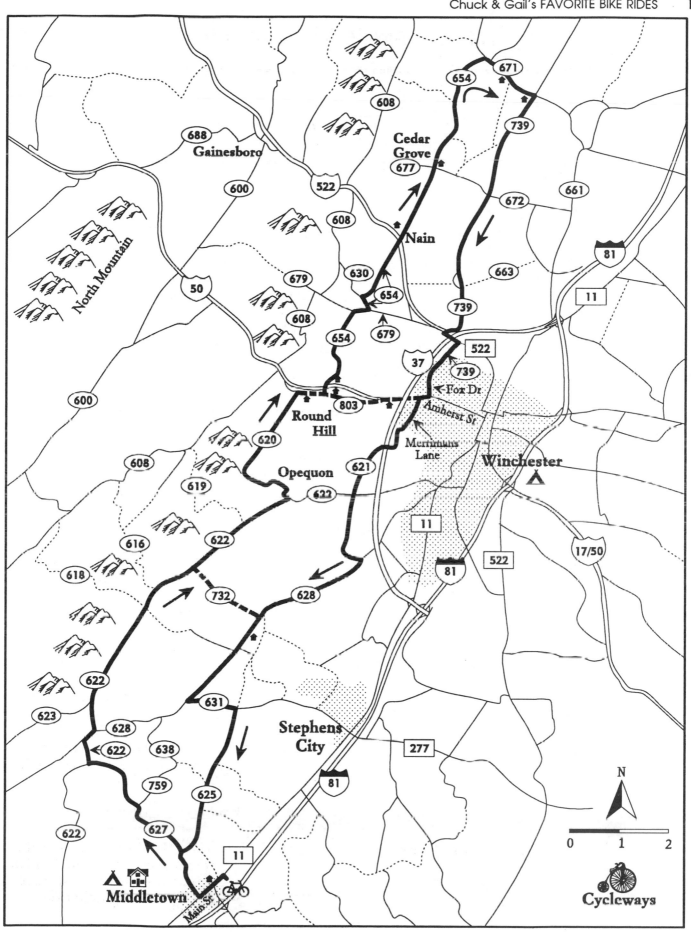

70. Passage Thru Mudhole Gap

Distance:	12, **17** or 23 miles	
Rating:	IV or V; Mostly unpaved forest and gravel roads, some rough; 6 stream crossings; advanced beginner mountain biking skills needed	
Start:	Elizabeth Furnace Campground in Fort Valley, Va.	

17 Mile Ride (IV)

0.0	L	past barrier on gravel road, bearing right uphill, with the car at your back
0.2	S	continue uphill past second gate on gravel road
3.3	S	downhill on narrow path as the gravel road ends in a small clearing
3.4	R	unmarked rough forest road at T at bottom of hill before stream; follow the road upstream thru 5 stream crossings and past a barrier
4.3	R	unmarked gravel road at T
	*	**For the 12 mile ride**, turn Left at this point onto the unmarked gravel road (Pick up cues in 2.3 miles at mile 11.1 on the 17 mile ride – *☞)
4.4	S	past barrier onto an unmaintained dirt road
6.3	S	uphill on the dirt road as the blazed trail goes left toward Signal Knob
6.5		Arrive at reservoir; Turn Around and descend the dirt road you came up
8.7 ☜**☜***	S	at barrier onto well-maintained gravel road
11.1	L	unmarked gravel road at T; becomes 771 (Boyer Furnace ruins on left)
12.7	L	paved 678 at T
16.9	L	gravel road opposite Elizabeth Furnace Campground and arrive at car

** 23 Mile Ride (V)

11.1	R	unmarked gravel road at T; begin climbing
13.4	BR	unmarked gravel road at T at SS, toward Woodstock Tower; keep climbing
14.1		Arrive at top of hill; tower is 0.2 miles down path to left; Turn Around
14.8	L	first gravel road toward Powell's Fort at the big hairpin turn
18.7	L	paved 678 at T
22.9	L	gravel road opposite Elizabeth Furnace Campground and arrive at car

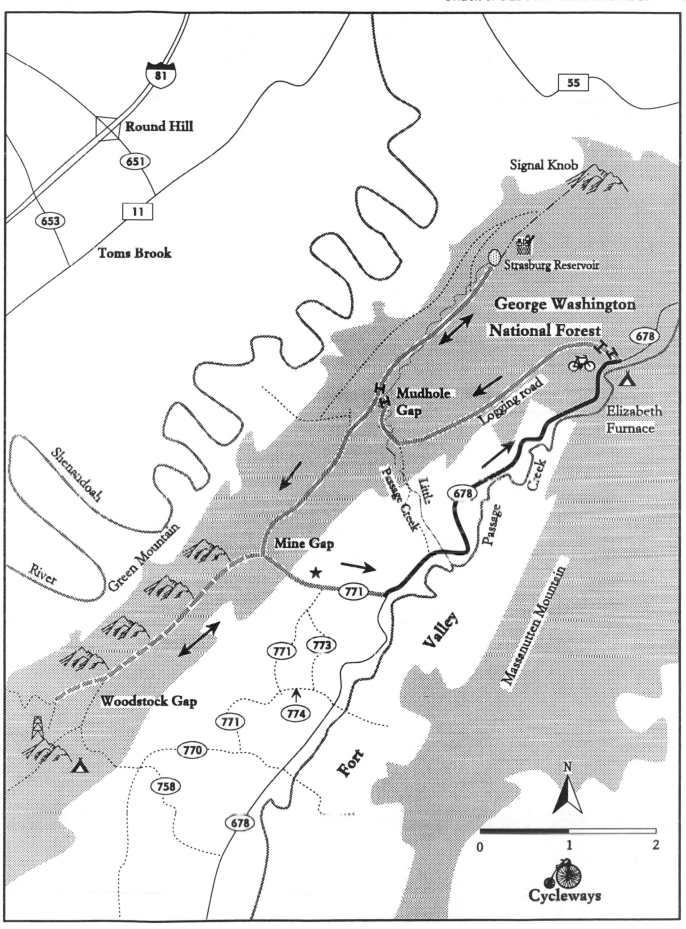

81

Round Hill

651

653

11

Toms Brook

Signal Knob

Strasburg Reservoir

55

George Washington

National Forest

678

Mudhole Gap

Logging road

Elizabeth Furnace

Shenandoah

Green Mountain

River

Mine Gap

Little Passage Creek

Passage Creek

678

678

771

773

771

Valley

Massanutten Mountain

Woodstock Gap

771

774

771

770

758

678

Fort

N

0   1   2

Cycleways

71. The Valley Sampler

Distance:	20, 39 or **49** miles
Rating:	III; Paved roads
Start:	Central High School in Woodstock, Va.

49 Mile Ride

0.0	R	Susan Ave from parking lot	27.3	L	730
0.3	L	Fairground Rd at T	28.8	BR	731 at Y
0.4	R	Ox Rd at SS; becomes Massanutten Hgts	29.7	L	698 at T (Food at Shenandoah Caverns 0.2 mile to right at mile 30.4 at 730); becomes Orchard Dr
1.3	L	Commerce St after RR tracks			
1.3	R	W Spring St	33.1 **☞	R	263, Bryce Blvd at T
1.4	L	Muhlenburg St	33.3	L	Rte 11, Main St at T in **Mt Jackson**
1.9	L	W North St at T			
3.0	L	676 at T	33.5	R	698, Daniel Gray Dr (Store 0.2 mile ahead on Rte 11)
3.2	BR	676 at 816 at Y	42.5	R	Rte 11 at T
5.6	L	623 at T (Store at mile 7.3)	43.0	L	185/675, Stoney Creek Blvd in **Edinburg** (Store at mile 43.2)
10.4	BR	623 at SS at signs for Rte 42			
10.6	S	675 at bottom of hill	44.0	R	686 (Shenandoah Vineyard at mile 45.6)
10.7	R	Rte 42 at T in **Columbia Furnace**	*☞ 47.4	R	605 at T
10.8 ☜*	L	675 (Store)	47.5	L	605; becomes Ox Rd
15.2	R	686	48.2	R	Reservoir Rd, Rte 42
17.1 ☜**	R	614 at T	48.3	R	Susan Ave
26.7	L	767 at Rte 42	48.6	L	into parking lot

* 20 Mile Ride

15.3	L	686 (Shenandoah Vineyard at mile 16.9) (Pick up cues in 3.4 miles at mile 47.4 on the 49 mile ride – *☞)

** 39 Mile Ride

22.5	L	Rte 263 (Pick up cues in 2.1 miles at mile 33.3 on the 49 mile ride – **☞)

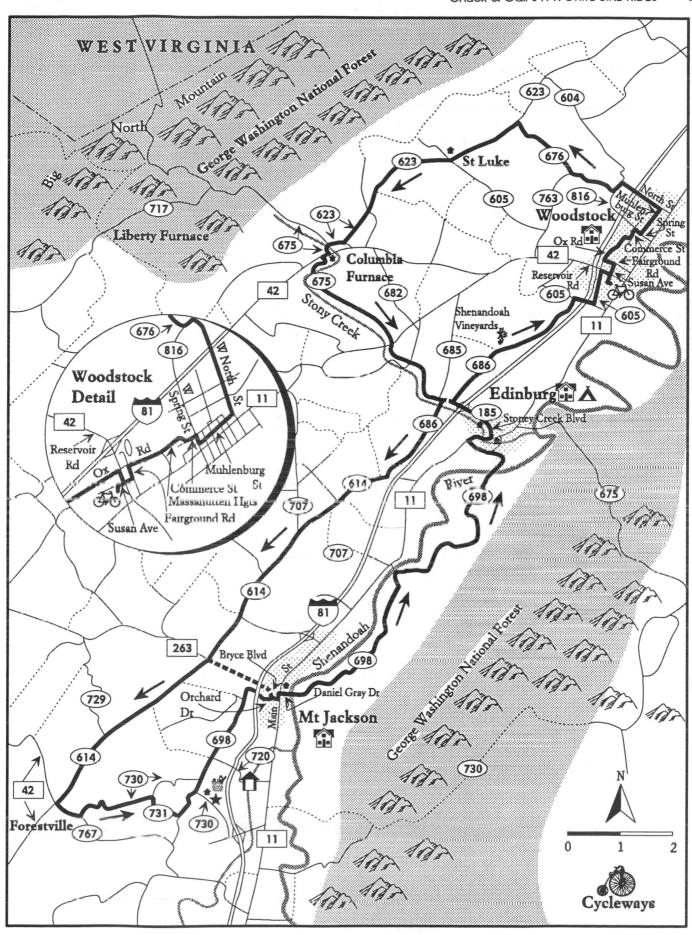

72. Valley of the Hills

Distance:	**25** or **39** miles
Rating:	III or IV; Paved roads
Start:	Luray Inn Lawn Park in Luray, Va.

25 Mile Ride (III)

0.0	R	Zerkel St with Library at your back
0.1	L	Unmarked road at Senior Center
0.1	R	Jamison Rd
0.2	R	Big Spring St
0.3	R	Linden Ave
0.5	L	Virginia Ave, Rte 340 at T
0.8	L	642, becomes 689
9.2	R	689 at T (611 to left)
11.0	L	Main St, Rte 340 in **Stanley**
11.5	L	638, Honeyville Ave (Food; Store 0.2 mile ahead on Main St)
11.9	R	638 at 622

11.9	L	638, Honeyville Ave (Store at mile 12.7)
		☞*
15.2	R	650 at T
15.9	S	636 at Rte 340 (Store)
		*☞
16.3	L	616 at T
22.3	R	639
23.0	L	638 at T; becomes Court St
23.6	R	Court St Ext (unmarked) at SS at bottom of hill
24.0	L	Virginia Ave, Rte 340 at T
24.1	R	Linden Ave
24.3	L	Big Spring St
24.4	L	Jamison Rd
24.5	L	Inn Circle
24.6		Arrive at park

* 39 Mile Ride (IV)

15.2	L	650 at T
21.1	R	Rte 340 at T
21.4	R	613
24.3	L	Rte 340 at T
24.4	R	685

25.7	R	685 at T
28.0	L	Rte 340 at T (Store)
28.7	R	615; steep hill
30.2	R	Rte 340 at SS
30.4	L	636 (Store) (Pick up cues in 0.4 miles at mile 16.3 on the 25 mile ride — *☞)

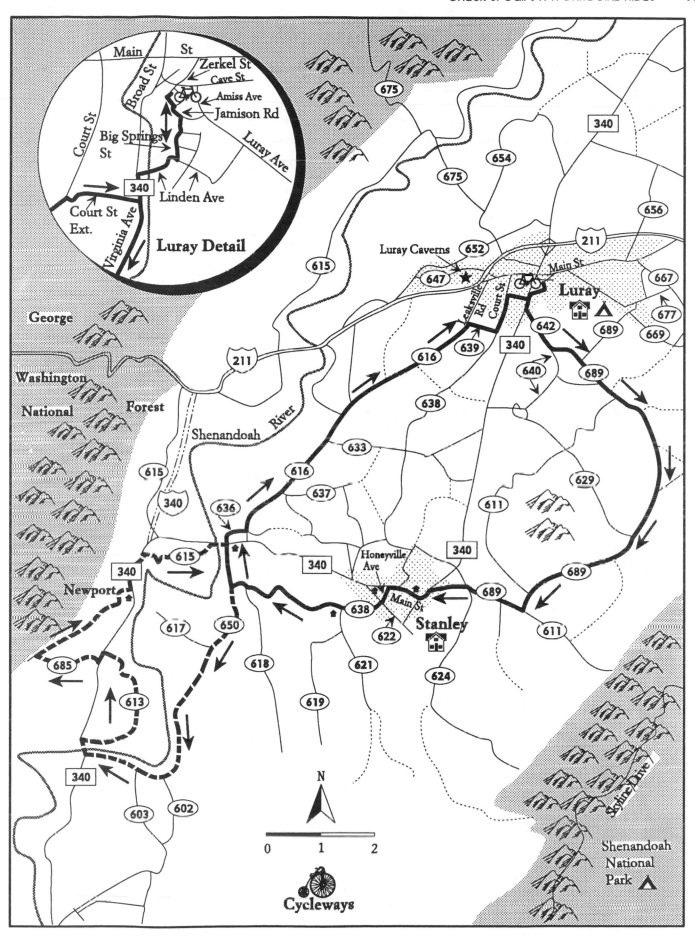

Luray Detail

Main St
Zerkel St
Cave St
Broad St
Court St
Amiss Ave
Jamison Rd
Big Springs St
Luray Ave
340
Linden Ave
Court St Ext.
Virginia Ave

675
340
654
675
656
211
615
Luray Caverns
652
647
Main St
667
Luray
211
Leaksville Rd
Court St
642
689
677
616
639
340
640
689
669
638
633
629
616
611
637
636
615
340
340
Shenandoah River
Honeyville Ave
340
Newport
617
650
638
Main St
689
685
618
622
Stanley
611
613
621
624
340
619
602
603

Washington
George
National   Forest

N

0   1   2

Cycleways

Shenandoah
National
Park

Skyline Drive

73. The Breadbasket

Distance:	20, **36** or 52 miles
Rating:	III or IV; Paved roads
Start:	Bridgewater Fairgrounds in Bridgewater, Va.

36 Mile Ride (III)

0.0	R	N Grove St from parking lot	17.2	L	731
0.1	L	Green St	18.8	R	742
0.2	R	Main St, Rte 42 at T ⊗	20.3	L	613 at 257 (Store) (Store at mile 22.1)
1.4	L	699			
4.2	R	646 at T	25.8	R	726
6.0	R	Rte 42 at T	27.0	R	752 in **Mt Clinton**
6.4	L	809; becomes 747	28.7	R	Rte 33 at T ⊗
7.4	L	747 at 613	28.8	L	752 in **Hinton** (Store-closed Sunday)
☞*					
			31.7	R	752 at 737
9.8	R	731 in **Mt Solon**; Natural Chimneys Regional Park on right at mile 10.5 (Admission charge) (Store)	32.3	L	738 (unmarked) at unpaved 752
			34.1	L	257 at T
10.9	R	730 at T (Store) (Store at mile 13.2); becomes 731	34.3	R	738; becomes Dry River Rd in **Bridgewater**
☞**			35.8	L	N River St at T
*☞			35.9	R	N Grove St
17.0	S	257 (Store)	36.1		Arrive at parking lot

---

* 51 Mile Ride (IV)

13.2	S	730	19.1		Arrive at Todd Lake (Fee during season) (Water, restrooms); Turn around and retrace route
14.5	S	718 at 730 (Store to right)			
15.5	L	at sign toward Todd Lake			
18.6	R	523 at sign for Todd Lake			
			23.7	L	730 (Store) (Store at mile 27.0); becomes 731 (Pick up cues in 9.7 miles at mile 17.0 on the 36 mile ride – *☞)

** 20 Mile Ride (III)

13.2	R	727 in **Sangerville** (Store)	19.6	L	Green St in **Bridgewater**
15.7	R	727 at 613	19.7	R	N Grove St
19.1	L	Rte 42 at T ⊗	19.8		Arrive at parking lot

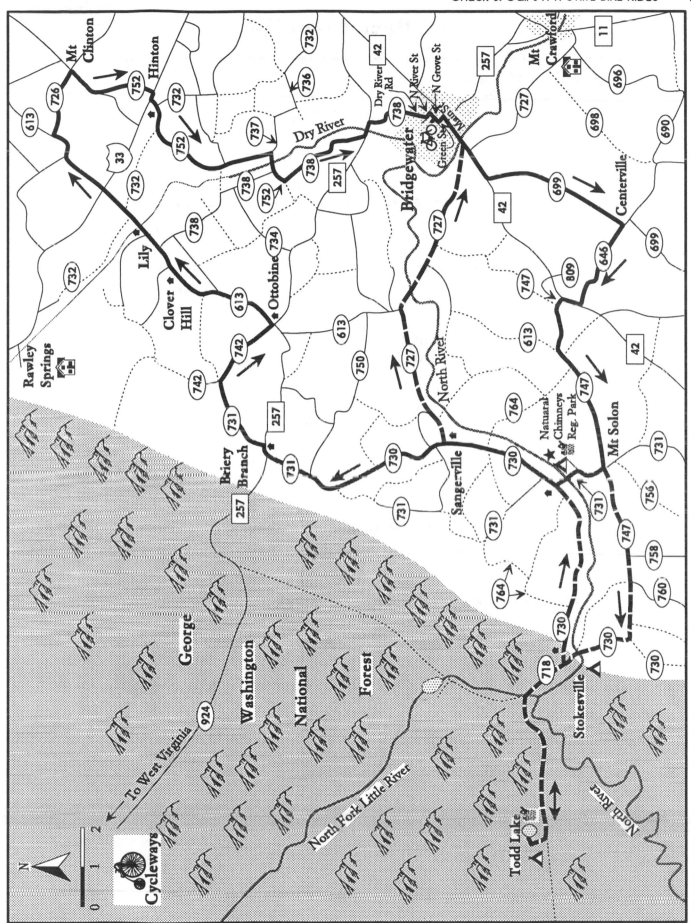

74. Back Road Heaven

Distance:	47 miles
Rating:	IV; Paved roads
Start:	Bridgewater Fairgrounds in Bridgewater, Va.

47 Mile Ride

0.0	R	N Grove St from parking lot
0.1	L	Green St
0.2	R	Main St, Rte 42 ⊗
0.8	L	727
3.9	L	Main St, Rte 11 at T in **Mount Crawford**
4.2	R	867, N River Rd
6.1	R	682 at T
8.7	L	680
10.2	R	679 at SS
11.2	L	Rte 276 at T in **Cross Keys**
11.4	R	679
12.7	R	Rte 659 at T
13.1	L	757
13.3	L	676 at T
13.7	R	708 at SS
16.4	R	655 at T
18.7	L	659 at T
19.4	R	825; becomes Dogwood Ave in **Grottoes** (Store, Food); Grand Caverns Regional Park on right at mile 22.0 (Water, restrooms) Admission to Caverns
24.9	R	778 at T
28.8	L	608 at T
28.9	R	778
31.2	L	777
33.9	R	616 at T (Store at mile 34.3 at Rte 11 in **Fort Defiance**)
35.4	R	616 at 744
36.6	S	804
38.7	R	732 at T
39.3	S	646 at SS
42.4	R	699 in **Centerville**
45.2	R	Rte 42 at T ⊗
46.4	L	Green St in **Bridgewater**
46.5	R	N Grove St
46.6		Arrive at parking lot

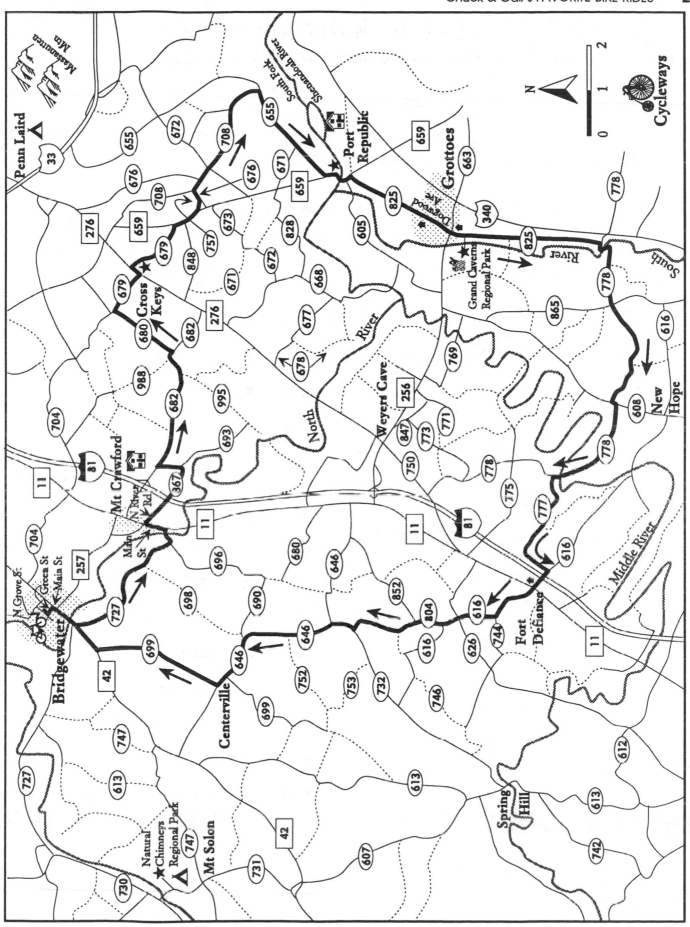

75. Shenandoah Valley Tour
Day 1: Front Royal to Luray

Distance:	**170** miles: Day 1 - **42** miles
Rating:	IV; Paved roads
Start:	Town Hall and Police Dept. parking lot in Front Royal, Va.

0.0	R	S Royal Ave, Rte 340 from the front of the town hall (South)
1.6	R	619, Rivermont Drive (Stores at miles 3.4, 4.2, 5.6); becomes Mountain Rd
10.2	L	678, Fort Valley Rd at T (Water & restrooms at Elizabeth Furnace at mile 12.9); Fort Valley Museum (open Sat/Sun afternoons May to Sept) at mile 20.1 at 770 (Store at mile 21.6 in **Fort Valley**)
28.7	BL	675 at **Kings Crossing** (Store)
32.0	BL	675 and begin climb over Massanutten Mountain
36.5	L	675 at 615 at T on the descent
36.9	R	675 at 684; cross Shenandoah River (Store to right at mile 37.2)
39.2	R	652, following sign toward airport
40.6	L	647 toward Luray Caverns; becomes Northcott Drive in **Luray**; Luray Caverns on right at mile 41.5
41.8	R	Main St at T; Motels/B&B lodging, Food/Stores to left

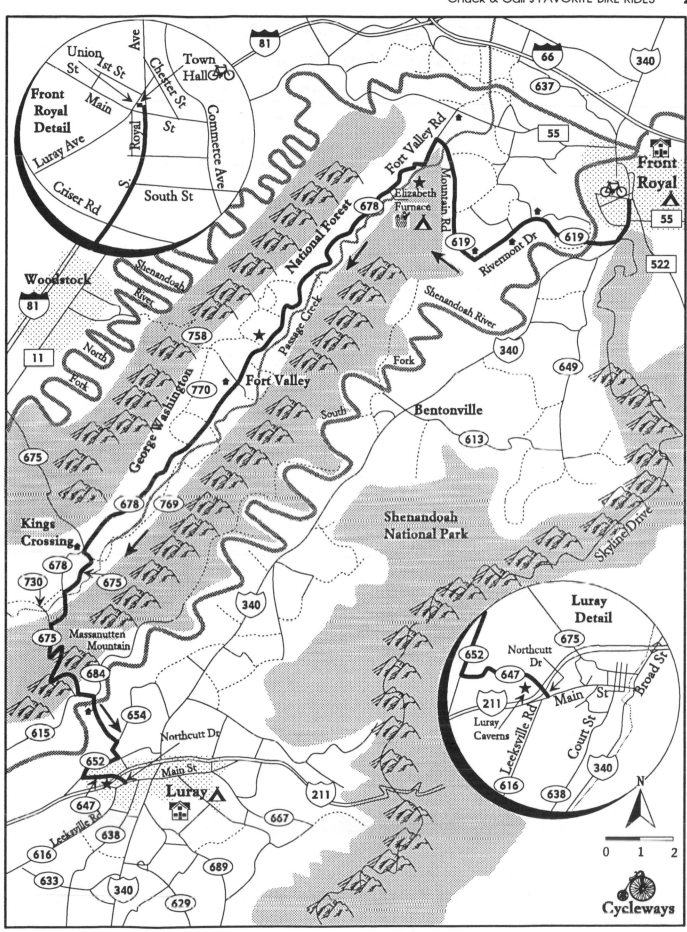

Front Royal Detail

Union St
1st St
Ave
Chester St
Town Hall
Main
Royal
St
Commerce Ave
Luray Ave
Criser Rd
South St

81
66
340
637
55
Front Royal
55
522
Woodstock
81
Fort Valley Rd
Elizabeth Furnace
678
Mountain Rd
619
619
Rivermont Dr
Shenandoah River
Shenandoah River
North Fork
11
758
National Forest
Passage Creek
340
649
770
Fort Valley
Fork
George Washington
South
Bentonville
613
675
678
769
Shenandoah National Park
Kings Crossing
678
730
675
Skyline Drive
675
Massanutten Mountain
340
684
615
654
Luray Detail
652
652
647
647
Northcutt Dr
211
Northcutt Dr
Main St
Main St
Luray Caverns
Leeksville Rd
Court St
Broad St
Luray
211
340
647
667
616
638
Leeksville Rd
638
616
633
689
340
629

N

0   1   2

Cycleways

75. Shenandoah Valley Tour
Day 2: Luray to Harrisonburg

Distance:	**170** miles: Day 2 - **44** miles
Rating:	IV; Paved roads, 0.2 miles unpaved road
Start:	Intersection of Main St. and Northcott Dr. in Luray, Va.

41.8	R	Main St from Northcott Drive (West)
41.9	L	Leeksville Rd, 616
48.6	R	636, just before T in **Alma**
49.0	S	650 at Rte 340 (Store)
54.6	L	603
56.2	BR	602 at SS; becomes Maryland Ave in **Shenandoah**
59.0		Cross Rte 340 at TL continuing on 602; (Stores/Food to left); Food at Quincy St Cafe (left 0.5 miles on 340 then right Quincy St just past IGA) (Store at mile 62.6)
65.4	R/L	644 at unpaved 646 (Joanne's B&B 0.6 mile up 646)
68.7	R	paved 646, past Massanutten Village (Shenandoah Valley Farm & Inn on left at mile 69.5)
70.5	R	996 at T (0.2 mile of gravel between Rte 33 and 996) (Store)
73.3	L	672 in **Montevideo**
76.5	R	708
76.8	R	676
79.4	R	276 at T (⊗ - use shoulder)
80.7	S	620 at TL at Rte 33
82.2	L	925, Keezletown Rd in **Keezletown**
84.9	R	Country Club Rd at SS in **Harrisonburg**
86.0	L	Carlton St
86.2		Cross Rte 33; Motels along Rte 33; B&Bs in town (see listing)

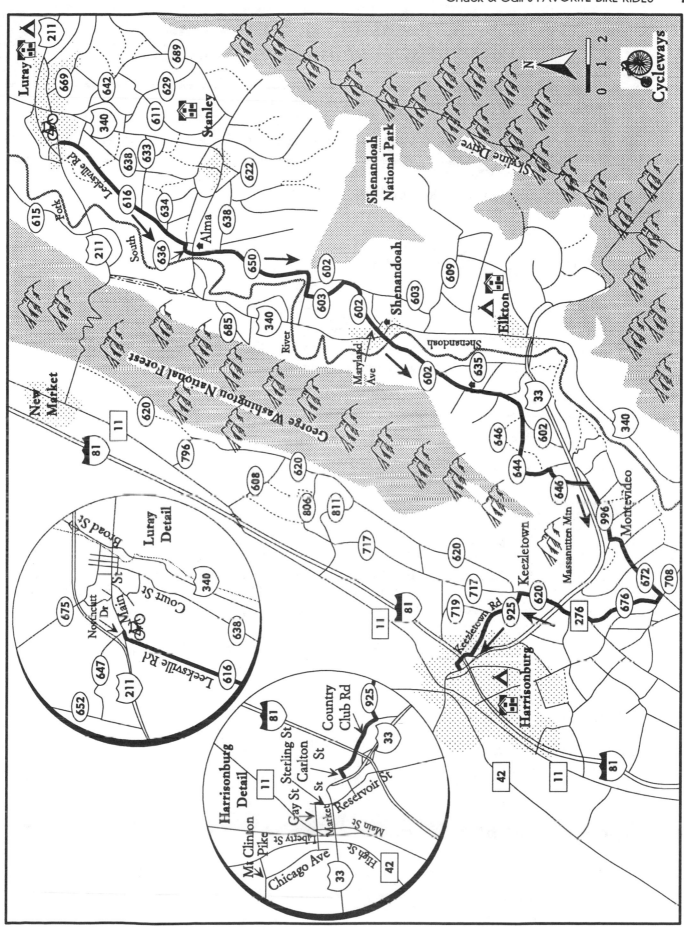

75. Shenandoah Valley Tour
Day 3: Harrisonburg to Woodstock

Distance:	**170** miles: Day 3 - **47** miles	
Rating:	IV; Paved roads	
Start:	Intersection of Route 33 and Carlton St. in Harrisonburg, Va.	

86.2	S	Carlton St at Rte 33 (West)
86.4	R	Reservoir St (Food)
86.7	S	Sterling St at Market St
87.0	L	Gay St
87.8	R	Chicago Ave (Store at mile 88.1)
88.9	L	Mt Clinton Pike; becomes 763
94.2	S	613
97.7	L	613 in **Singers Glen** (Store-closed Sun/Wed)
104.9	L	259 at T
105.1	R	613
114.1	R	Rte 42 at T
117.6	L	614 in **Forestville** (To visit Shenandoah Caverns (Food) continue straight picking up cues at mile 27.3 to 33.1 on The Valley Sampler. At mile 33.1 turn left on Rte 263 then right on 614 to get back onto tour.)
127.2	L	686 at I-81 (Store 0.6 mile ahead on 614 at Rte 11)
129.1	R	675 at T
129.3	L	686 (Shenandoah Vineyards at mile 130.9)
132.8	R	605 at T
133.4	L	Rte 11; becomes Main St in **Woodstock**; Motels/B&B's along Main St & Rte 42; Inn at Narrow Passage to the right on Rte 11
135.6	L	604, North St in **Woodstock**

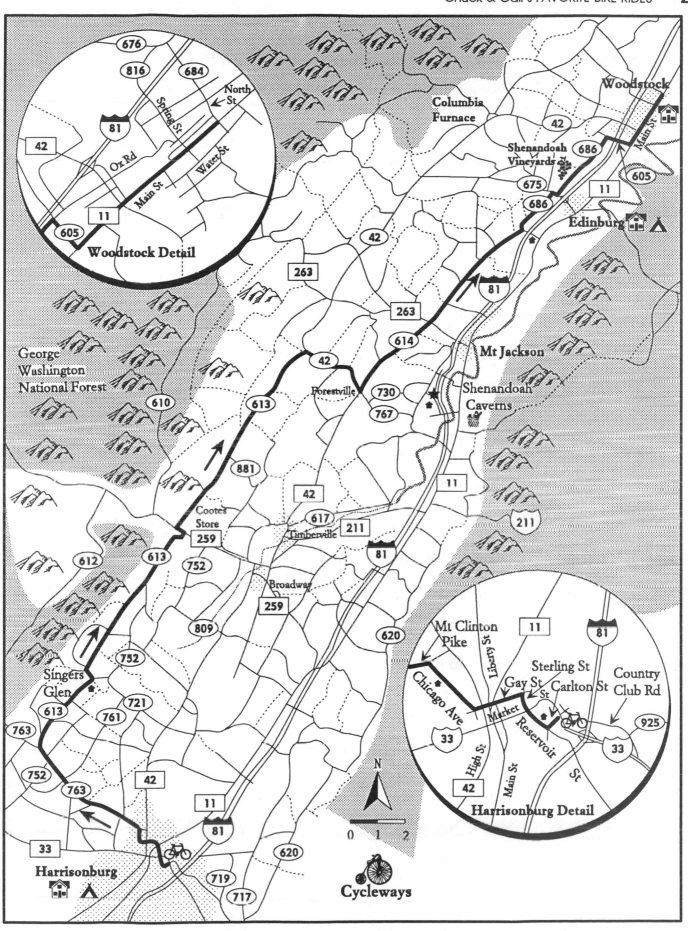

Woodstock Detail

Harrisonburg Detail

George Washington National Forest

Columbia Furnace

Shenandoah Vineyards

Woodstock

Edinburg

Mt Jackson

Shenandoah Caverns

Forestville

Cootes Store

Timberville

Broadway

Singers Glen

Harrisonburg

Cycleways

N

0 1 2

Mt Clinton Pike

Chicago Ave

Sterling St
Gay St
Carlton St
Country Club Rd

Liberty St

Market

High St

Main St

Reservoir St

75. Shenandoah Valley Tour
Day 4: Woodstock to Front Royal

Distance:	**170** miles: Day 4 - **37** miles
Rating:	IV; Paved roads
Start:	Intersection of Route 11 (Main St.) and Route 604 (North St.) in Woodstock, Va.

135.6   L   604, North St from Main St, Rte 11 in **Woodstock** toward Fairview (West)

135.9   R   N Lee St past RR tracks; becomes 642

139.1   L   600 at SS

139.8   R/L 600 at 652

140.8   R   623 (Store at mile 145.5 in **Mt Olive** - closed Sunday)

150.6   L   Rte 55 at T

152.0   BR   paved 628 at **Lebanon Church** (Store)

155.1   R   622

155.6   L   627 at T

159.9   L   Rte 11, Main St in **Middletown** at TL (Food & Lodging at Wayside Inn)

160.3   R   627, Chapel Rd (Store/ Food)

162.8   R   637, North River Rd

163.8   L   637, Guard Hill Rd

168.1   R   Rte 522/340 at T (⊗); Cross Shenandoah River into **Front Royal** (Stores/ Food)

169.3   L   Rte 340; becomes Royal Ave

170.4   BR   Union St at 1st St and Right into the Town Hall parking lot

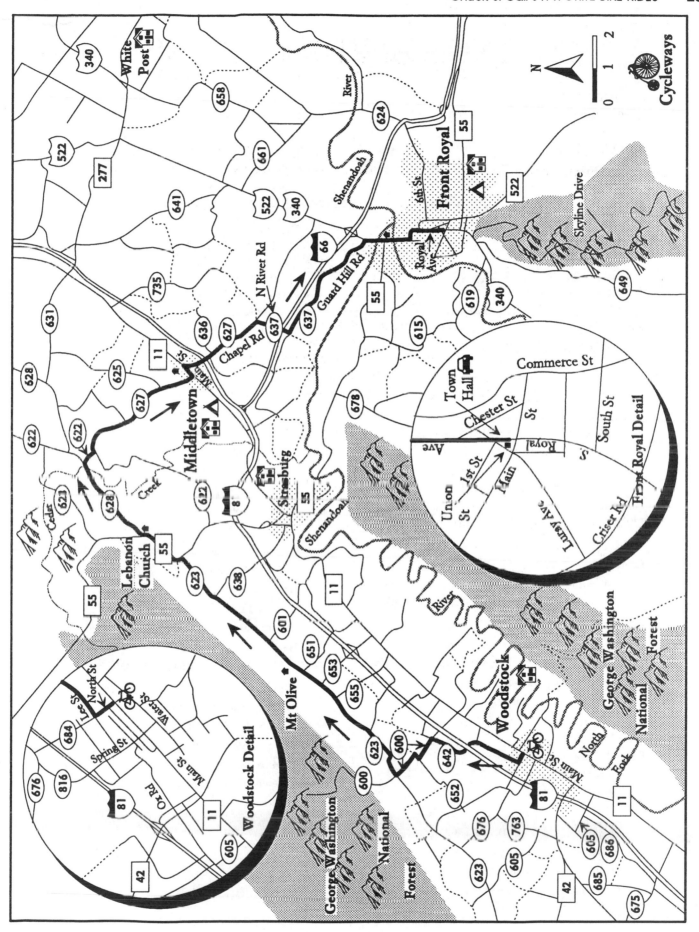

INNS AND EATERIES

Bicycling is only one activity we cyclists enjoy. We also like to escape the city for a weekend retreat in a country inn or bed and breakfast (B&B). And, of course, we like to eat.

The countryside in the Mid-Atlantic states has many country inns, B&Bs and campgrounds. We have compiled our listing from many sources. We have listed inns and B&Bs that are either on or near the rides in this guidebook. Most of the inns and B&Bs are small and require reservations. For those who like to camp, we list area campgrounds.

We suspect that many cyclists ride to eat. A good meal often adds the finishing touch to a ride. To compile the list of "cyclist's recommended" eateries, we asked area cyclists for their favorite places. We thank the following contributors: Christa Borras, Bob & Kathy Dollar, Bob & Willa Friedman, Janet & Dick Hays, Jack Marney, Paul Oberg, Bob Piper, Ed Reardon, George Schneider, Ballard Troy and Steven Walker.

We have not had the opportunity to personally check each listing. These lists are by no means complete. More importantly, the lists are **not** recommendations as to the quality of service provided.

COUNTRY INNS AND BED & BREAKFASTS

MARYLAND INNS AND B&B'S

Betterton
The Lantern Inn (410) 348-5809
Buckeystown
The Inn at Buckeystown (301) 874-5755
Catoctin Inn (301) 875-5555
Cascade
Inwood Guest House B&B (301) 241-3467
Bluebird on the Mountain (301) 241-4161
Cambridge
Sarke Plantation (410) 228-7020
Lodgecliffe on the Choptank (410) 228-1760
Glasgow Inn (410) 228-0575 or (800) 225-0575
Oakley House (410) 228-6623
Commodore's Cottage & The Carriage House (410) 228-6938
Chestertown
Imperial Hotel (410) 778-5000
Widow's Walk Inn (410) 778-6455
White Swan Tavern (410) 778-2300
Brampton B&B (410) 778-1860
Radcliffe Cross (410) 778-5540
Hill's Inn (410) 778-1926
Cole House (410) 928-5287

Deale
Makai Pierside (301) 867-0998
Easton
Bishop's House (410) 820-7290
Tidewater Inn (410) 822-1300
Hynson's Tourist Home (410) 822-2777
John S. McDaniel House (410) 822-1300
Weaver's Inn (410) 820-7669
Emmitsburg
Silver Fancy B&B (301) 447-6627
Stonehurst Inn B&B (301) 447-2880
Fairplay
Candlelight Inn (301) 582-4852
Frederick
Spring Bank (301) 694-0440
The Tyler-Spite House (301) 831-4455
Tran Crossing (301) 663-8449
Hagerstown
Beaver Creek House B&B (301) 797-4764
Lewrene Farm (301) 582-1735
Huntington
Ches'bayvu (301) 535-0123

Keedysville

Kings' Sunny Acres (301) 432-6125

Knoxville

Harpers Ferry AYH Hostel (301) 834-7652

Middletown

Fountaindale Inn (301) 371-9449

The Mendall Inn (301) 371-4214

Marameade (301) 371-4214

New Market

National Pike Inn (301) 865-5055

Strawberry Inn (301) 865-3318

North Beach

Westlawn Inn (410) 855-8410

Olney

Thorough B&B (301) 774-7649

Tranquil Forest (301) 774-6052

Oxford

1876 House (410) 226-54996

Robert Morris Inn (410) 226-5111

Oxford Inn (410) 226-5220

Sharpsburg

The Inn at Antietam (301) 432-6601

Piper House (301) 797-1862 or (301) 432-5466

Smithsburg

Blue Bear B&B (301) 824-2292

Still Pond

Still Pond Inn and B&B (410) 3428-2234

St. Michaels

Fox Run Farm (410) 745-2381

Hambleton Inn (410) 745-3350

Inn at Perry Cabin (800) 722-2949 or (410) 745-5178

Kemp House Inn (410) 745-2243

The Parsonage Inn (410) 745-5519

St. Michaels Inn (410) 745- 3303

Two Swan Inn (410) 745-2929

Victoriana Inn (410) 745-3368

Palmer House (410) 745-3319

The Getaway B&B (410) 745-2094

Wades Point Inn on the Bay (410) 745-2500

Royal Oak

The Pasadena Inn & Conference Center (410) 745-5053

Taneytown

Antrim 1844 (410) 756-6812

Glenburn (410) 751-1187

Thurmont

Ole Mink Farm Cabins (301) 271-2204

Uniontown

The Newel Post (410) 775-2655

Urbana

Turning Point Inn (301) 831-8232 or 874-2421

Vienna

The Governor's Ordinary (410) 376-3530

Nanticoke Manor House (410) 376-3530

Tavern House (410) 376-3347

Westminster

Westminster Inn (410) 857-4445; 876-2893

Avondale (410) 876-8815.

Judge Thomas House (410) 876-6686

The Winchester Country Inn (410) 876-7373

Woodsboro

Rosebud Inn (301) 845-2221

VIRGINIA INNS AND B&B'S

Aldie

Little River Inn (703) 327-6742

The Castle (703) 327-4113

Alexandria

Princely B&B Service (703) 683-2159

The Little House (703) 548-9654 or 548-8675

Amissville

Bunree (703) 937-4133

Four & Twenty Blackbirds B&B (703) 937-5885

Banco

Olive Mills B&B (703) 923-4664

Berryville

Battletown Inn (703) 955- 4100

Blue Ridge B&B Reservation Service (703) 955-1246

Maple Lane Farm B&B (703) 955-4800

Bluemont

Bears Den Youth Hostel (703) 554-8708

Boston

Meadowood (703) 547- 3851

Boyce

The River House B&B (703) 837-1476

Broadway

Shenandoah Valley B&B Reservations (703) 896-9702

Chincoteague

Channel Bass Inn (804) 336-6148

Main Street House (804) 336-6030

Miss Molly's Inn (804) 336-6686

Victorian Inn (804) 336-1161

Year of the Horse Inn (804) 336-3221

Birch's Guest (804) 336-6365

Churchville

Buckhorn Inn (703) 337-6900

Culpeper

Fountain Hall (703) 825-8200

Stuartfield Hearth B&B (703) 825-8132

Edinburg

Mary's Country Inn (703) 984-8286

Elkton

Joanne's B&B (703) 298-9723

Etlan

Dulaney Hollow Guesthouse (703) 923-4470

Front Royal

Constant Spring Inn (703) 635-7010

Chester House Inn B&B (703) 635-3937

Flint Hill

Caledonia Farm B&B (703) 675-3693

The Schoolhouse Inn & Restaurant (703) 675-3030

Hamilton

Stonegate (703) 338-9519

Harrisonburg

Kingsway B&B (703) 867-9696

The Joshua Wilton House (703) 434-4464

Haywood

Shenandoah Springs Inn (703) 923-4300

Hillsboro

The Inn Between the Hill (703) 668-6162

Ridgefields (703) 668-6500

Leesburg

Colonial Inn of Leesburg (703) 777-5000

Norris House Inn (703) 777-1806

Laurel Brigade Inn (703) 777-1010

Fleetwood Farm (703) 327-4325

Lincoln

Oakland Green B&B (703) 338-7628

Springdale Country Inn (703) 338-1832

Luray

Boxwood Hill (703) 743-3550 or 743-9484

Boxwood Place (703) 743-4748

Spring Farm (703) 743-4701

The Ruffner House (703) 743-7855

Grey House Inn (703) 743-3200

Shenandoah River Roost (703) 743-3467

Shenandoah Countryside (703) 743-6434

McGaheysville

Shenandoah Valley Farm & Inn (703) 289-5402

Middleburg

Luck House (703) 687-5387

Middleburg Inn Guest Suites (703) 687-3115

Middleburg Country Inn (703) 687-6082

Stray Fox Inn (703) 687-6301

Red Fox Inn (800) 223-1728 or (703) 687-6301

Welbourne Country Inn (703) 687-3201

Windsor House Country Inn (703) 687-6800

Middletown

Wayside Inn (703) 869-1797

Millwood

Brookside B&B (703) 837-1780

Mt Crawford

The Pumpkin House Inn (703) 434-6963

Mt Jackson

The Widow Kip's Country Inn B&B (703) 477-2400

Nethers

Nethers Mill (703) 987-8625

New Market

A Touch of Country B&B (703) 740-8030

Red Shutter Farmhouse B&B (703) 740-4281

Orlean

Hilltop Manor (703) 364-3292

Paeonian Springs

Cornerstone (703) 882-3722

Paris

Ashby Inn (703) 592-3900

Port Republic

Busy Bee (703) 289-5480

Purcellville

The Cottage (703) 338-3225

Rawley Springs

Boxwood (703) 867-5772

Round Hill

Round Hill Hall (703) 338-9221

Sperryville

Conyers House (703) 987-8025

Spotsylvania

Spotswood Country Inn (703) 582-5382

Standardsville

Edgewood Farm B&B (804) 985-3782

Stanley

Jordan Hollow Farm Inn (703) 778-2285/2209

Milton House (703) 778-3451

Strasburg

Hotel Strasburg (703) 465-9191

Tumbling Run B&B (703) 465-4403

Swope

Lambsgate B&B (703) 885-8798

Syria

Graves Mountain Lodge (703) 923-4231

Upperville

1763 Inn (703) 592-3848 or (800) 669-1763

Gibson Hall Inn (703) 592-3514

Warrenton

Rosemont Farm Inn (703) 347-5422

Washington

The Inn at Little Washington (703) 675-3800

Foster-Harris House (703) 675-3757

Heritage House (703) 675-3207

Sycamore Hill House (703) 675-3046

Waterford

The Pink House (703) 882-3453

The Waterford Inn (703) 882-3465

James Moore House (703) 882-3342

White Post

Dearmont Hall (703) 837-1397

L'auberge Provencale (703) 837-1375

Woodstock

The Inn at Narrow Passage (703) 459-8000

The Country Fare (703) 459-4828

The Azaela House (703) 459-3500

PENNSYLVANIA INNS AND B&B'S

Cashtown

The Cashtown Inn (717) 334-9722

Gettysburg

Abraham Spangler Inn (717) 337-3997

The Brafferton Inn (717) 337-3423

Brierfield B&B (717) 334-8725

Bishop's Rocking Horse Inn (717) 334-9530

Farnsworth House Inn (717) 334-8838

Doubleday Inn (717) 334-9119

Keystone Inn (717) 334-3888

Tiber House (717) 334-0493

Gettystown Inn (717) 334-2100

Old Appleford Inn (717) 337-1711

Twin Elms (717) 334-4520

Gettysburg International Hostel (717) 334-1020

Orrtanna

Hickory Bridge Farm (717) 642-5261

WEST VIRGINIA INNS AND B&B'S

Harpers Ferry

Between the Rivers B&B (304) 535-2768

The View (304) 535-2688

Middleway

The Gilbert House B&B (304) 725-0637

Shepherdstown

Thomas Shepherd Inn (304) 876-3715 or (304) 754-7646

Little Inn Above The Yellow Brick Bank (304) 876-2208

Mecklenburg Inn (304) 876-2126

Shang-Ra-La Retreat (304) 876-2391

Stonebrake Cottage (304) 876-6607

Summit Point

The Countryside (304) 725-2614

CAMPGROUNDS

MARYLAND CAMPGROUNDS

Boonsboro

Greenbier State Park (301) 791-4767

Big Pool

Fort Frederick State Park (301) 842-2155

Indian Springs Campground (301) 842-3336

Brandywine

Cedarville State Forest (301) 888-1622

Brunswick

Brunswick Municipal Camp Site (301) 834-8050

Chestertown

Duck Neck Campground (301) 778-3070

C & O Canal

C&O Canal National Historical Park (301) 739-4200

Clarksburg

Little Bennett Regional Park Campground (301) 972-9222

Frederick

Gambrill State Park (301) 473-8360

Gapland

Maple Tree Camp, Ltd (301) 432-5585

Jefferson

Gathland State Park (301) 293-2420

Knoxville

Canal Campground (800) 852-CAMP or (301) 834-9240

Madison (Dorchester Co.)

Madison Bay Campground (301) 228-4111

Middletown

Washington Monument State Park (301) 432-8065

Newburg (Charles Co.)

Aqua-Land Campground (301) 259-2575

Port Tobacco

Port Tobacco Campground (410) 934-9707

Prince Frederick

Patuxent Campsites (410) 586-9880

Smithsburg

Mountain Farm Campground (301) 824-2481

Taylors Island

Tideland Park Waterfront Campground (410) 397-3473

Taylors Island Family Campground (410) 397-3275

Thurmont

Crow's Nest Lodge Campground (301) 271-7632

Ole Mink Farm Campground (301) 271-7012

Owens Creek Campground (301) 663-9388

Cunningham Falls State Park (301) 271-7574

Welcome (Charles Co.)

Goose Bay Campground (301) 934-3812

Williamsport

Snug Harbor KOA Campground (800) 457-3096

Safari Campground (301) 223-7117

VIRGINIA CAMPGROUNDS

Bridgewater

Todd Lake (703) 828-2591

Burke Lake

Burke Lake Campground (703) 323-6601

Chincoteague

Camper's Ranch (804) 336-6371

Maddox Campground (804) 336-3111

Pine Grove Campground (804) 336-5200

Tom's Cove Campground (804) 336-6498

Culpeper

Rolling Acres Campground (703) 547-3374

Edinburg

Creekside Campground (703) 984-9915 or 984-8618

Elkton

Swift Run Campground (703) 298-8086

Front Royal

Front Royal KOA (703) 635-2741

Fishnet Campground (703) 636-2961

Massanutten Camp Forest (703) 636-6061

George Washington National Forest

Camp Roosevelt (703) 984-4101

Elizabeth Furnace Campground (703) 984-4101

Twin Lakes (703) 933-6633

Harrisonburg

Harrisonburg-New Market KOA Campground (703) 896-8929 or (800) 336-5461

Haymarket

Silver Lake Campground (703) 754-7565

Luray

Skyline Drive - Shenadoah National Park (703) 999-2282 Campgrounds at Lewis Mountain, Loft Mountain, Big Meadows, and Mathews Arm

Yogi Bear's Jellystone Park Camp-Resort (703) 743-4002

Madison

Bud Lea Campground (703) 948-4186

Middletown

Battle of Cedar Creek Campground (703) 869-1888 or (800) 343-1562

Mt Solon

Stokesville Park (703) 350-2343

Natural Chimneys Regional Park (703) 350-2510

New Market

Harrisonburg/New Market KOA (703)896-8929 or (800) 336-5461

Endless Caverns Campground (703) 740-3993 or 896-CAVE

Rancho Campground (703) 740-8313

Paris

Sky Meadows State Park (703) 592-3556 or (804) 786-1712

Penn Laird

Gerundo Family Campgound (703) 289-5351

Prince William Forest Park

Oak Ridge Campground (703) 221-7181

Winchester

Candy Hill Campground (703) 662-8010

PENNSYLVANIA CAMPGROUNDS

Gettysburg

Artillery Ridge Campground (717) 334-1288

Drummer Boy Camping Resort (717) 334-3277

Gettysburg KOA Campground (717) 642-5713

Round Top Campground (717) 334-9565

Welcome Traveller Campsite (717) 334-8226

WEST VIRGINIA CAMPGROUNDS

Harpers Ferry

Harpers Ferry Resort Campground (304) 535-6895

CYCLIST RECOMMENDED EATERIES

✳ Indicates a dressier establishment that may be reluctant to accept biking attire, especially cleats. We list these as places for a meal after a day in the saddle.

D.C. EATERIES

Georgetown

Furin's, 2805 M St, N,W,

The Booeymonger, 3265 Prospect St, N,W,

MARYLAND EATERIES

Adamstown

The Bank, Mountville Rd

Annapolis

Cantler's Riverside Inn, Forest Beach Rd

Beallsville

Staub's Country Inn, 19800 Darnestown Rd

Broomes Island

Stoney's Seafood House, Oyster House Rd

Charlotte Hall

Saint Mary's Landing, Rte 5 ✳

Chesapeake Beach

Rod N' Reel, Shore Dr

Chestertown

Old Wharf Inn, Cannon St ✳

Clear Spring

Windy Hill Restuarant, Rte 68

Deale

Happy Harbor, Rte 256

Suzy's, Rte 256

Fishing Creek

Old Salty's, Rte 335

Frederick

Health Express Food Market, West Point Plaza, 1450 W Patrick St/US 40

Il Forno Pizzeria, Westridge Square, 1035 W Patrick St/US 40 ✳

Galesville

Pirates Cove, Riverside Dr

Steamboat Landing, Riverside Dr

Hagerstown

Airport Inn, US 11 North at airport ✳

Hyattstown

Comus Inn, 23900 Old Hundred Rd

Jefferson

Ingram's Diner, Mountville Rd

Keedsyville

Red Byrd Restaurant, Rte 34

Kennedyville

Vonnies, Rte 213

Mechanicsville

Hill's Halfway House, Rte 5/235 ✳

Middletown

Main's Ice Cream, Main St

Mitchellville

Rip's Country Inn, Crain Hwy, Rte 301

Mt Pleasant

Avalon, Main St, Rte 26

New Windsor

Kozy Corner, Rte 31

Olney

Olney Ale House, Rte 108

Popes Creek

Robertson's Crab House, Popes Creek Rd

Captian Billy's, Popes Creek Rd

Port Tobacco

Barbeque rib place at Rte 6 & Chapel Point Rd

Potomac

Cafe Royal, located in shopping center at Falls & River Rd

St Micheals

The Crab Claw Restuarant, Navy Point

Silver Spring

The Parkway Deli, 8317 Grubb Rd (about 1/2 mile from Rock Creek Bike Trail)

Taneytown

Country Kitchen Restuarant, 112 E Baltimore St (Rte 140)

Thurmont

The Cozy Restaurant, 103 Frederick St

Bollinger's Restaurant, Thurmont Plaza, Church St

Safari Ice Cream, 12917 Catoctin Furnace Rd/MD 806

Westminster

Baugher's Restaurant, 289 West Main St

Williamsport

Jeannie's Restaurant, Potomac St/US 11 & Conococheague St/MD 68

Hickory Corner (Deli), Rte 11

Woodsboro

Towne Restaurant, 200 North Second St

VIRGINIA EATERIES

Alexandria

The Fish Market, Union St

Deli-on-the-Strand, Union St

The Bread & Chocolate, 600 King St

Bayse

Bryce Resort Dining Room ✳

Chincoteague

Bill's Seafood Restaurant, 303 S Main Street

Don's Seafood Restaurant, S Main Street

Culpeper

Gayheart's Drug Store, Davis & Main St

Culpeper Pharmacy, Locust & Main St

Culpeper Culinar, Davis St

Davis Street Ordinary, Davis & East St ✳

Edinburg

Edinburg Mill, 214 S Main St, Rte 11

Front Royal

The Royal Dairy Restaurant, Chester St

Harrisonburg

Ole Virginia Ham Cafe, 85 W Market St

Herdon (W&OD mile 20)

Ice House Cafe, 760 Eldon St

Great Harvest Bread Company, 785 Station St

Anita's, Eldon St

Leesburg (W&OD mile 34)

Knossos, 341 E Market St

Tuscarora Mill, Market Station off the W&OD Trail

Payne's Old Towne Pub, 5 N King St

Leesburg Restaurant, 9 King St

Luray

Intown Restaurant, 410 W Main St

Middleburg

The Upper Crust Bakery, 2 Pendleton St

The Magpie Cafe, 112 W Washington St

Mosby's Tavern, Marshall St

Scruffy's Ice Cream Parlor, 6 W Washington St

Middletown

Wayside Inn, Rte 11, Main St

Mt Jackson

Coffee Shop at Shenandoah Caverns

New Market

Southern Kitchen, US 11

Purcellville (end of the W&OD Trail)

21st Street Cafe, 144 N 21st St

Purcellville Country Store & Deli, 120 N 21st St

Purcellville Inn, Main St

George's Plaza Restaurant, 110 W Main St

Reston (W&OD mile 18)

Reston Town Center-- L&N Seafood Grill, Clydes, Pizzeria Unos, Allegro Deli & Bake Shop, Lees Ice Cream, Everything Yogurt

Shenandoah

Quincy Street Cafe & Pizza, 211 Quince St

Shirlington

The Subway, Shirlington Mall

Strasburg

Hotel Strasburg, 201 Holliday St

Syria

Graves' Mountain Lodge, Rte 670

The Plains

The Rail Stop, Main St

Vienna

Anita's, Maple St

Woodstock

Spring House Restaurant, S Main St, Rte 11

PENNSYLVANIA EATERIES

Biglerville

Glenn's Family Restaurant, 5 S Main St

Fairfield

Village Book & Table Restaurant, 29 W Main St/PA 116

Gettysburg

Avenue Restaurant, 21 Steinwehr Ave

Blue Parrot Bistro, 35 Chambersburg St ✳

Gingerbread Man, 217 Steinwehr Ave ✳

Lincoln Diner, 32 Carlisle St

Sunny Ray Family Restaurant, 90 Buford Ave/US 30

Dobbin House Tavern, 89 Steinwehr Ave

Mason Dixon Dairy, Mason Dixon Rd (ice cream only)

State Line

Lantern House Restaurant, Rte 11

WEST VIRGINIA EATERIES

Harpers Ferry

Hill Top House, Ridge St

Shepherdstown

Bavarian Inn, Rte 34

Summit Point

Grannary Restaurant & Carry-Out

APPENDIX

Connecting Rides

Sometimes you feel like riding a short ride, sometimes a longer ride. The table lists which rides connect. With this information you can join rides together for longer distances or different loops.

#	Connects With	#	Connects With	#	Connects With
1	6, 13, 14, 18, 19, 20, 64, 65, 66	24	21, 23, 25	57	58
2	5, 38, 39	25	24, 26	58	57
3	4, 5	26	25	59	60
4	3, 6	32	33	60	59
5	2, 3	33	32, 43	64	1
6	1, 4, 7	34	35	65	1, 66
7	6	35	34, 36, 38, 40, 41	66	1, 65
13	1, 18	36	35, 38	67	68
14	1, 15, 16	37	38, 40	68	67
15	14, 16	38	2, 35, 36, 37, 39	69	75
16	14, 15, 17, 19	39	2, 18, 20, 38	70	75
17	16, 19	40	35, 37, 41	71	75
18	1, 13, 19, 20, 39	41	35, 40	72	75
19	1, 16, 17, 18, 20	43	33, 44	73	74, 75
20	1, 18, 19, 39	44	43	74	73, 75
21	23. 24	50	51	75	69, 70, 71, 72, 73, 74
23	21, 24	51	50		

Combinations for Longer Rides or Tours

Touring by bicycle is a delightful way to both get away and explore the region. There are several other tour possibilities in addition to the one tour we have fully mapped. You can design your own tour by tying together connecting rides into a longer loop. On these tours you ride to an inn or campground for one or several nights and then return to your start.

Super Bike Trail Treks You can connect several of the Washington, D.C. bike trails for either a long trek or to get through the city with a minimum of traffic. The two Rock

Creek rides, Rides 6 and 7, connect. The C&O Canal, Ride 1, connects with the Rock Creek Trail. You can connect the Rock Creek Trail with the Mount Vernon Trail, Ride 3 via Memorial Bridge. You can use Ride 5 to connect the Mount Vernon Trail with Ride 2, the W&OD Trail.

W&OD Trail and C&O Canal Loop For a 70 mile ride, you can follow Ride 2, the W&OD Trail, from Washington, D.C. to Leesburg, Virginia. Turn right on King Street, Business 15 in Leesburg and follow it north through town to Route 15. Ride north on busy Route 15 on the unpaved shoulder (this road is too dangerous to safely ride the pavement) to Route 655. Turn right and follow the road to the Potomac River. Cross on Whites Ferry and join the unpaved C&O Canal (Ride 1) on the Maryland side of the river. Follow the C&O towpath back to Washington.

For a longer tour, continue on the W&OD to either Paeonian Springs or Purcellville in Virginia. Take Ride 39 north and then Ride 20. Ride 20 will take you to either Brunswick or Point Rocks in Maryland, where you join the C&O. Ride the towpath east, back to Washington. If you go west on the canal, you will come to Harpers Ferry, West Virginia.

Washington, D.C. to the Shenandoah Valley Take the W&OD Trail west from Washington to Purcellville, Virginia. Follow Ride 38 to Middleburg and Ride 35 to Marshall. Take Ride 41 to Markham and continue west on Route 55 to Linden. Turn right on Route 647, Dismal Hollow Road at the Apple House and follow it to Route 624 at the T. If you turn right, you will join Ride 68, Oh Shenandoah! If you turn left you enter Front Royal where the road becomes 6th Street. Turn left on South Royal Avenue and you join Ride 75, *Shenandoah Valley Tour*.

Skyline Drive and Shenandoah Valley Tour Options These options add more challenges to the first day of Ride 75, *Shenandoah Valley Tour*. They are for stronger, more experienced cyclists only. Turn left into Shenandoah National Park (admission fee) off Route 340 and ride Skyline Drive south. You can ride Skyline Drive 32 miles to Panorama (food) and then descend off the ridge on Route 211 (high-speed traffic) west toward Luray. Turn left on Business 211 into Luray and pick up the second day of the tour.

From Luray you can ride north using the first day of the *Shenandoah Valley Tour*. This option gives an approximately 70 mile loop from Front Royal and involves a climb over Massanutten Mountain, one of the toughest climbs in the area.

A harder option is to continue south on Skyline Drive to Route 33 at Swift Run Gap, mile 66. You can find lodging and food at Skyland and camping, lodging and food at Big Meadows. Descend the mountain on Route 33 (high-speed traffic) west to Elkton (food). From Elkton take Route 637 west to Route 602 where you join the Valley Tour.

A yet harder option is to ride the entire 105 mile length of Skyline Drive to Rockfish Gap. Food and camping is available at Loft Mountain. Descend the mountain on Route 250 west to Waynesboro (food, lodging). From Waynesboro take Route 865 north to Ride 74, *Back Road Heaven*. This ride connects with the *Shenandoah Valley Tour*.

Virginia Foothills Tour You can combine Rides 32, 33, 43, and 44 to tour the rolling countryside between Nokesville and Culpeper, Virginia. This allows you to start at Nokesville or Calverton and ride through Remington and Brandy Station to Culpeper and back.

ou can then join Ride 44 with Ride 45 by taking Route 614 west from Rapidan. At
e 15 you take Route 634 north. This brings you onto Ride 45. This allows you to ride
yria at the base of the Blue Ridge Mountains from Nokesville or Culpeper..

Longer Horse Country Rides You can combine any of Rides 34, 35, 36, 37, 38, 39,
40, 41 and 1 to a circuit of your liking. Possible starts are Purcellville, Middleburg,
Marshall or The Plains in Virginia. You can take the W&OD Trail west to Purcellville and
then do a loop or tour.

Lengthening the Blue Ridger If *The Blue Ridger* in Virginia doesn't give you enough
hills, begin on Ride 40 and finish with Ride 41. You can extend the ride to two days by
staying at the Ashby Inn in Paris, Virginia.

Seneca, Maryland to Frederick, Maryland To ride north to Frederick, Maryland
through the Poolesville area, combine Rides 14, 16 and 19. You can ride New Design Road
into Frederick.

Frederick, Maryland to Gettysburg, Pennsylvania To ride north to Gettysburg,
Pennsylvania from Frederick, combine the finish of Ride 21 with Rides 23, 24 and 25. For
a shorter distance, begin your ride in Thurmont, Maryland.

Connecting Horse Country with The Heartland Rides 20 and 39 allow you to
connect together these two popular riding areas. This allows you to ride from Gettysburg,
Pa. to the Shenandoah Valley. You could ride from Washington, D.C. to Gettysburg via
Horse Country rides and the W&OD Trail, returning via *The Heartland* rides through
Seneca, Maryland and the C&O Canal to Washington.

Areas for Weekends Away

It is always gratifying to escape the daily routine by getting away for a weekend of
country cycling. Listed here are suggestions for towns where you can find at least two days
of nearby riding.

The Heartland
Frederick/Thurmont Area, Maryland: Rides 19, 20 23, 24, 21 and 22.
Gettysburg, Pennsylvania: Rides 25, 26 and 24.

Horse Country
Middleburg/Purcellville Area, Virginia: Rides 34 through 41
Culpeper, Virginia: Rides 43, 44 and 33

Chesapeake Treasures
Easton, Oxford or St. Michaels, Maryland: Rides 57 and 58
Cambridge or Vienna, Maryland: Rides 59 and 60
Chincoteague, Virginia: Rides 61 and 62

The Big Valley
    Hagerstown/Sharpsburg Area, Maryland: Rides 63, 64, 65 and 66
    Winchester, Middletown/Berryville Area, Virginia: Rides 67, 68 and 69
    Luray or Woodstock, Virginia: Rides 71 and 72 (car transfer between the rides)
    Harrisonburg Area, Virginia: Rides 73 and 74.

Honorable Mention Rides

When this book was put together, we had more rides than we had room. The following are rides that we seriously considered but did not include in the final cut.

National Arboretum, Washington, D.C. The arboretum (entrance from New York Avenue, N.E.) contains about nine miles of paved roads that you can connect into a loop of about 4 miles. In the arboretum are very pretty grounds and gardens. The columns from the Capitol Building are alone almost worth the trip. The roads through the gardens become clogged with car traffic during spring weekends when the azaleas are in full bloom.

Fredericksburg National Battlefield, Fredericksburg, Virginia. The battlefield (south of Business Route 1) contains one quiet, five mile road that travels the length of the park. Some sections are very pretty and others butt against nearby subdivisions.

Northwest Branch Bike Path, Adelphi, Maryland. You start this 4.5 mile paved bike trail at Adelphi Mill off Riggs Road. The northern section travels through a steep, wooded canyon and feels far removed from the city. The southern section opens into grassy and treed parklands.

Route 1 Bike Lanes, Ocean City, Maryland to Rehobeth, Delaware. The bike lanes are the paved shoulders of busy Route 1. This flat ride is popular with beach cyclists and travels between two beach communities, passing through Bethany, Delaware. The northern section between Rehobeth and Bethany is prettier and less built-up. While the bike lanes are traffic-free, much traffic will speed by on the parallel road.

Skyline Drive, between Front Royal and Waynesboro in Virginia. Skyline Drive in Shenandoah National Park (admission fee) offers the most challenging riding in the area. Skyline Drive climbs from Front Royal onto the Blue Ridge and then follows the spine of the ridge south for 105 miles to Rockfish Gap. From Rockfish Gap the Blue Ridge Parkway continues south along the ridge into North Carolina. Car traffic becomes heavy during the spring wildflower season and fall foliage.
    Many local cyclists start in Front Royal and ride part or all of the 32 miles to Panorama in Thornton Gap at Route 211. You can eat at the restaurant and then ride back north to your start. In season you can buy food at the store at Mathews Arm Campground.
    Another popular tough ride is to begin at the Panorama parking lot in Thornton Gap (mile 32) and ride south to either Big Meadows at mile 51 or Swift Run Gap at mile 66. You can find food, camping and lodging in season at Skyland and Big Meadows.
    The southern section of Skyline Drive is more remote and less cycled. The only food and camping in this section is at Loft Mountain.

Mason Neck Wildlife Refuge and State Park, Lorton, Virginia. Mason Neck is a large peninsula that juts into the Potomac River. The state park has a three mile road that easy, shaded cycling. You begin the ride at the visitor center in the state park or ston Hall, home of George Mason. If you start at Gunston Hall, turn left onto Route om the entrance and then right on High Point Road to enter the park. The one-way ce between Gunston Hall and the visitor center is 4.3 miles. You reach Gunston Hall the state park by taking Route 242 south from Route One. Route 242 becomes Route 600.

Calvert Cliffs State Park, Lusby, Maryland off Route 4. This remote park offers one unpaved service road open to cyclists. You can ride the length of the road for two miles to the beach and then return by the same road. At the beach you can enjoy the views of the cliffs and the bay and search for fossils that wash ashore.

Liberty Reservoir, just north of the Baltimore, Maryland Beltway. At publication time, it was unclear whether this popular mountain biking area would remain open. The reservoir watershed contains many unmarked dirt service roads suitable for mountain biking. Check with Baltimore bike shops or Baltimore bike clubs before venturing into this area.

Frederick Watershed, north of Frederick, Maryland. The Watershed contains some of the best mountain biking around. It contains many unmarked dirt logging roads and steep terrain. The area suitable for mountain biking is generally found between the gravel roads we have mapped in Ride 22, *Up the Creek* and south of Delauter Road. Obtain topographical maps and check with Frederick bike shops before venturing off the gravel roads.

Map Resources

The following are the five map resources we find the most useful in planning our bike rides.

Maryland county road maps (1" = 1.6 miles) Order for $1.25 plus postage from the State Highway Administration, Map Distribution Section, 2323 W. Joppa Road, Brooklandville, Md. 21022; (410) 321-3518. The maps do not distinguish the type of road surface.

Virginia county road maps (1" = 2 miles) Order for 25 cents each from Virginia Department of Highways and Transportation, 1401 East Broad Street, Richmond, Va. 23219; (804) 786-2838. The maps are updated every two years and distinguish the type of road surface.

Alexandria Drafting Company county map booklets ADC, 6440 General Green Way, Alexandria, Va. 22312. $8.95 per county booklet from bookstores. The series covers most area counties. The maps do not distinguish the type of road surface.

Washington, D.C. 50 Mile Radius Map ADC, 6440 General Green Way, Alexandria, Va. 22312. The map shows much of the area covered in the book. The map shows most, but not all, country roads, and does not distinguish the type of road surface.

ADC's Washington Area Bike Map; 1988; Metropolitan Washington Council of Governments, 1875 Eye Street, NW, Washington, D.C. 20006 or ADC, 6440 General Green Way, Alexandria, Va. 22312. A large, detailed map with bike trails and bike routes on urban and suburban streets.

A leisurely spin along the C&O Canal towpath

ABOUT THE AUTHORS

It is hard to find two people more passionate about bicycling than Chuck and Gail Helfer of Takoma Park, Maryland. Whether it is on their single road bikes, their mountain bikes or tandems, chances are you'll find them on weekends and in the evenings riding the region's country roads and parklands. They have toured locally and in Europe and enjoy cycling with a small but growing group of tandemists. When they are not on their bikes, they are either running, hiking or skiing.

Chuck and Gail have probably mapped out more bicycle rides in the Mid-Atlantic region than anyone else, publishing their first guidebook in 1984. This is their ninth bicycling guidebook. They have assisted several local charities with preparing routes for bike trek fund raisers.

Chuck rediscovered cycling in 1971 when he was a Peace Corps teacher in West Africa and rode a three speed Raleigh with balloon tires. Prior to this, he was an active mountaineer and rock climber, and has climbed throughout the West. Bicycling in the region since 1975, Chuck is a past chairman of the nation's largest bicycle club, the Potomac Pedalers Touring Club. He is a regular contributor to the local cycling press.

Gail has been a competitive athlete in skiing, rowing and cycling. A member of four national rowing teams, her rowing is highlighted by a national sprint championship and a bronze medal at the 1976 Olympic Games. Gail has worked for a bicycle touring company and has completed two major bike tours — a Pacific Coast trip in 1977 and a cross country trek in 1980.